HAIRY MEN IN
CAVES

TRUE STORIES OF AMERICA'S MOST COLORFUL HERMITS

MARLIN BRESSI

SUNBURY
PRESS

Mechanicsburg, PA USA

Published by Sunbury Press, Inc.
50 West Main Street
Mechanicsburg, Pennsylvania 17055

SUNBURY
PRESS

www.sunburypress.com

For information about special discounts for bulk purchases, please contact Sunbury Press Orders Dept. at (855) 338-8359 or orders@sunburypress.com.

To request one of our authors for speaking engagements or book signings, please contact Sunbury Press Publicity Dept. at publicity@sunburypress.com.

ISBN: 978-1-62006-630-0 (Trade Paperback)
ISBN: 978-1-62006-631-7 (Mobipocket)

Library of Congress Control Number: 2015951593

FIRST SUNBURY PRESS EDITION: September 2015

Product of the United States of America
0 1 1 2 3 5 8 13 21 34 55

Set in Bookman Old Style
Designed by Crystal Devine
Cover by Lawrence Knorr
Edited by Janice Rhayem

Continue the Enlightenment!

CONTENTS

FOREWORD

For thousands of years, the reclusive lifestyle of the hermit has fascinated and captured the imaginations of people around the world. The very image of the hermit conjures many different visions in the minds of different people. To some, hermits are romantic figures; many men and women have turned away from society after the sudden death of a beloved, or after a rejection by the objects of their affection. The man who chooses to spend the remaining days of his life inside a cold, dark cave after the tragic death of his lover, facing each bitter winter and sweltering summer with only the most primitive of possessions, cannot help but arouse the hearts of those who intimately understand the hermit's private world of heartache and despair. To others, hermits are figures of wisdom, viewed as snowy-bearded gurus who embrace solitude and asceticism in order to attain some sort of spiritual enlightenment or some higher understanding of themselves and the universe in which they reside. Others may regard hermits as misanthropes, bitter and tormented souls removed from society because society refused to accept them. Still, others may regard hermits as peaceful, nature-loving eccentrics or maniacal, cave-dwelling savages.

The fact of the matter is that the world of hermitry is populated by those who fit all of the above depictions. Hermits come in all shapes, sizes, genders, colors, and can be found in any given geographical area. They come from all ethnic, religious, and socio-economic backgrounds and can be found in rural and urban environments alike.

Disciples of the hermitic lifestyle can be found in castles as well as rustic cabins, in booming metropolises and small villages. If hermitry were a vocation, it could be argued that it is perhaps the world's only true "equal opportunity employer," gathering into its fold men, women, and children from every walk of life without the slightest bit of discrimination.

Since people tend to view hermits in many different ways, perhaps it may be that the light in which we see hermits is the same light in which we see ourselves. Like a Rorschach ink blot test, an impression pops into our brains when we think of hermits, so it very well may be that if you are a person with strong spiritual ties, your vision of the hermit is that of a wise, old sage, while those who are sentimentalists may conjure up the image of a romantic hermit, and those who are embittered may immediately envision a hermit as a misanthropic recluse. Maybe we are fascinated by hermits because they are, in many ways, mirrors in which we see our own reflections.

We may also be captivated by hermits because they seem to have a dual nature; a hermit is both an eccentric and an Everyman at the same time. Though they may be the ultimate nonconformists, we can all commiserate with them. After all, who among us, after a devastating loss or tragedy, hasn't thought about running away and inhabiting a simple shack in the wilderness? Who among us hasn't felt the urge to crawl into a hole and hide after experiencing a great embarrassment? In the throes of grief or depression many of us react by silencing our phones and retreating to a darkened bedroom, where we seek solitary sanctuary beneath our blankets and comforters. In such self-imposed seclusion we often find a small, yet substantial, measure of comfort and safety, if only for a little while. The dual nature of hermits makes them both simple and complex. In their abject poverty, they may still be the richest of the rich. They are the objects of our pity as well as our envy, and, even though we may fear them, a part of us cannot help but admire their fearless way of single-handedly confronting the wild and untamed universe on their own terms. The hermit is, in many ways, unevolved, yet highly evolved at the same time, having surpassed man's basic need for companionship and the primitive herd mentality, which mandates that members of the same species congregate together and form families and communities. We are fascinated with hermits because they are, quite simply, walking contradictions.

THE THREE CATEGORIES OF HERMITS

In his 2005 novel *Velocity*, author Dean Koontz writes: *A fine line separates the weary recluse from the fearful hermit. Finer still is the line between hermit and bitter misanthrope.* To most of us, that line is so fine that it is virtually impossible to see. We often use these words—hermit, recluse, and misanthrope—interchangeably when referring to a human being who prefers solitude to society. While I disagree with Koontz's assertion that hermits are fearful and recluses are weary, I believe the esteemed author has managed to accurately categorize the three varieties of hermits that exist among us: true hermits, recluses, and misanthropes.

Prior to researching the lives of the eighty American hermits described in the pages of this book, I was guilty of not understanding the subtle differences between the three aforementioned classes. However, I soon discovered that a fine, but definite, line does indeed separate the hermit classes, and by examining the fears, beliefs, and motivations of the individuals depicted in *Hairy Men in Caves: True Stories of America's Most Colorful Hermits*, the differences between true hermits, recluses, and misanthropes become clear and unmistakable.

"The True Hermit"

He is as harmless as a gentle breeze, yet more misunderstood than quantum physics; he is the "true" hermit. Though his exterior may be gruff and grizzled, inside his chest beats the heart of a hopeless romantic and inside his skull churns a poet's brain, filling his thoughts with whimsical daydreams. Unlike the other two categories of hermits, the true hermit's hallmark is sensitivity and emotion. True hermits don't shun society, nor are they fearful of it; they simply prefer peace and solitude because it allows them to deepen their relationship with the universe in which they are a small and insignificant part. While the typical human being yearns for a slab of granite at the end of his life to mark his place in the world, a true hermit cares not about marble monuments or panegyrical poems immortalizing his name.

True hermits are often poets, writers, scholars, and artists. If you should happen to encounter them while strolling through the wilderness, they are more likely to want to discuss philosophy with you than to chase you through the underbrush while howling unintelligently (but if they do chase you through the underbrush howling unintelligibly, they're probably doing it for their own amusement). True hermits vary greatly in personality; they range from the free-spirited lovers of nature to the sullen survivors of heartbreak. Yet, at their core, they are all creatures who view and experience the world more deeply and fully than the rest of us. The true hermit is what some new age psychologists and metaphysical experts would refer to as an "empath," or one who feels things to the extreme.

The romantic hermit falls into this category, whether driven to the life of self-imposed isolation by unrequited love or devastating loss. Those who turn to hermitry after the entire world has been turned upside down following the unexpected death of a lover are hermits in the truest sense, since they can hardly be labeled as misanthropes or outcasts. Their lonely journey is one which they have willfully undertaken, sometimes amid the protest of friends and family. If these individuals should ever decide to return to civilization, they do so on their own terms and conditions. No one has forced them into exile, and no one can lure them out of it.

Others, like Henry David Thoreau and John Muir, embrace solitude because they love peacefulness and find contentment in the simple life. These hermits, like those who have been hurt by love, were not sentenced to seclusion by mainstream society. True hermits, such as romantic hermits and naturalist hermits, volunteered for the position; it was never thrust upon them. Thoreau, who once stated that he never found a companion that was as companionable as solitude, is the poster child of true hermits everywhere, from the windswept shores of Maine to the twinkling lights of Hollywood. This hermit spirit influenced, and continues to influence, generations of men and women who find pleasure in primitive living and contentment in the great outdoors, such as legendary naturalist and author John Muir. Muir, who once remarked that the clearest way into the universe is through a forest wilderness, lived much of his later years among friends and family, but the true hermit spirit never left the depths of his soul. In 1878, while in middle age, he returned to Oakland and married the socialite daughter of a prominent physician and, for several years, operated a fruit farm. While he was an excellent husband and father, his wife recognized Muir's frequent need for seclusion, and often encouraged him to go off into the mountains for extended periods of time in order to appease the hermit spirit within.

The final sub-category of the true hermit includes the men and women known as anchorites and anchoresses. An anchorite is one who voluntarily takes up the hermit life for religious reasons. These are the monks who dwell in drafty monasteries and the religious zealots who make their homes in caves. The anchoritic lifestyle is most commonly associated with the Middle Ages, but anchorites can be found throughout the world even today. While some may argue that anchorites are not hermits by definition, since their solitary cells often reside in monasteries and convents occupied by like-minded individuals, they may be considered true hermits because they have willfully chosen their path of seclusion and exile, just like romantic hermits and naturalist hermits.

"The Recluse"

The recluse is, more often than not, a victim of circumstance. Recluses had no intention of embarking on the lonesome journey of hermitry but, for one reason or another, they have found themselves in a position of isolation, usually as the result of their own deeds or misdeeds. While most true hermits are at peace with the universe, the recluse is at odds with it; the recluse's head is often filled with paranoid thoughts, and the heart is often leaden with guilt. Recluses are fearful creatures that utilize seclusion as a means of self-preservation rather than enjoyment. They shun conversation and prefer to keep their life story a mystery, and they erect emotional barriers in order to hermetically seal themselves from mainstream society because mainstream society presents some type of threat to their livelihood and well-being.

While a true hermit, penniless and destitute, attaches no weight to material possessions or societal titles, the recluse is often defined by them. Greta Garbo, Howard Hughes, and J. D. Salinger have all been labeled as recluses, yet it is hard to imagine them as true hermits, since it is highly unlikely that Ms. Garbo ever contemplated removing herself to a cave and dining on nuts and berries. Likewise, it is absurd to imagine Salinger penning *The Catcher in the Rye* while clad in dingy rags and sporting a tangled and filthy beard. While they share many qualities with the true hermit, recluses are defined more by apathy than empathy. They are oblivious or unfeeling to the march of progress or the ticking of time; they live in an impenetrable bubble.

The recluse lives a sheltered and mysterious life in urban environments, as well as in small towns and suburbs and from behind the iron gates of mansions. But recluses can also be found in the remote depths of the uncharted wilderness, in crude shacks and abandoned cabins just like their true hermit cousins. In many cases, these wilderness recluses have been driven to the hermit lifestyle as a consequence of their own actions, or even as a consequence of fame, wealth, or notoriety. Such was the case of university professor John Holden, one of the hermits featured in this book, who fled to America because he believed he had murdered one of his pupils in a fit of rage. Holden lived a long life, but most of his existence was spent in a perpetual state of fear and anxiety. He lived, and died, tormented by his own inner demons, fearing that justice was waiting just around the bend.

Fear and mistrust are what separates the recluse from the true hermit, whether it's fear of retribution, fear of intimacy, or mistrust of society. While Dean Koontz correctly identified the three categories of hermits, he should have written of the fine line that separates the weary hermit from the fearful recluse, rather than the line that divides the weary recluse from the fearful hermit, since true hermits are not the least bit fearful. Not even the bitter misanthrope, the final category of hermit, is fearful.

"The Misanthrope"

The last of the three varieties of hermit is the ornery misanthrope, who feels no kinship with his or her fellow man. They can be harmless curmudgeons at odds with the technological or social progress of mankind, or they can be dangerous miscreants motivated by hatred and vengeance. Misanthropes shun conversation and loathe intercourse with other humans, because they consider the human race to be the enemy. They live in a state of constant belief that they have had something very dear and important unfairly taken away from them, such as a lover, a spouse, a child, a business, or wealth. Misanthropes blame others for their own predicaments, and refuse to acknowledge any wrongdoing. They are proud, they are stubborn, and they make lousy dinner companions.

Guilt is the primary difference between the true hermit and the bitter misanthrope. If a young bride should perish on her way to the church on her wedding day, the true hermit, in tortured introspection, continually asks himself: "What have *I* done that the heavens should deem it necessary to snatch away my one true love? What sin have *I* committed to justify such horrid retribution?" Conversely, the misanthrope would not ask what *he* had done to suffer such a fate; instead, he would blame the universe at large and live out the remainder of his days bearing a grudge toward whatever unseen force had interceded in his life and reduced his dreams to ashes. Simply put, the true hermit feels guilt for a crime that he had never committed, while the misanthrope views himself as the victim of a crime which had never been committed.

Yet, there is a more dangerous and sinister sub-category of misanthrope. Members of this group include those who believe that they are on the side of righteousness, even when their actions prove otherwise. These "self-righteous misanthropes" tend to capture the collective imagination of society the most, and often become fodder for newscasts, non-fiction novels, and made-for-television movies. One sterling example of this type of misanthrope is Ted Kaczynski, the infamous "Unabomber." Kaczynski was labeled a child prodigy when he enrolled at Harvard at the age of sixteen, and he later became an assistant professor at UC Berkeley at the age of twenty-five. In 1971 he moved into a rustic cabin in Montana and became a recluse. As time progressed, he gradually made the transition from recluse to dangerous misanthrope. He harbored a deep resentment toward modern technology and culture and was viewed by many as an anarcho-primitivist, or one who advocates a return to primitive ways of life based on political reasons. Like many anarcho-primitivists, Kaczynski believed that the natural evolution of the human race, from the days of the hunter-gatherer to the era of industrialization, was responsible for social stratification, class warfare, and government dependence. Although Kaczynski's reign of terror (through the use of home-made bombs mailed to his targets) injured dozens and claimed three lives, Kaczynski truly believed that his actions would ultimately benefit the human race as a whole.

As the story of Ted Kaczynski illustrates, it is not uncommon for one individual to evolve from one variety of hermit to another. Many hermits have started out as angry misanthropes, only to discover the peace and comfort afforded by solitude, which they had, unbeknownst to themselves, been seeking their entire lives. Their hostility fades and they become true hermits in every sense of the word. The recluse, after years of isolation, may even come to terms with his or her irrational fears and rejoin society.

While hermits have figured prominently in fiction and folklore for centuries, perhaps no other author has possessed a greater understanding of the inner nature of the hermit than nineteenth century English novelist Mary Wollstonecraft Shelley. Shelley's *Frankenstein*, first published in 1818, tells the story of a young scientist named Victor Frankenstein who succeeds in his goal of reanimating a corpse. The nameless monster, abandoned by his horrified creator, follows Frankenstein throughout Europe (hiding in caves and seeking shelter in shacks along the way) while murdering Dr. Frankenstein's loved ones until the scientist agrees to build the monster a female companion to ease his loneliness. Throughout the novel, Frankenstein's nameless creature is referred to as a "demon," "fiend," and "monster," but Dr. Frankenstein's creature may very well have been labeled a hermit, recluse, and misanthrope. Shelley, perhaps unwittingly, weaves into her novel a sub-plot, which extraordinarily describes the evolution from gentle hermit to savage misanthrope. In the chapter in which Victor Frankenstein listens to his monster's story from inside an abandoned cabin high in the Alps, the creature describes his initial wonderment with things such as rain, snow, fire, sunsets, flowers, and the changing colors of the seasons. Frankenstein's monster, strangely enough, begins life as a naturalist hermit, possessing many of the same traits and emotions as Thoreau or Muir. One day, the nature-loving creature saves a small child from drowning in a wilderness stream, and is "rewarded" for his efforts by being shot at and chased through the woods by frightened villagers. This experience transforms the gentle hermit into a fearful recluse; the creature finds shelter inside a dilapidated shack adjoining a house occupied by a family whose manners he studies through a slit in the wall. He yearns for companionship, but when the fearful recluse attempts to establish a friendship with the family he has been observing, they react with horror and violence toward the ugly, deformed creature. This marks a turning point for Frankenstein's monster, who no longer blames himself for his misfortunes and loneliness but, instead, blames his creator. The creature becomes a bitter misanthrope whose desires can only be satiated by the blood of Dr.

Frankenstein's friends and family. Shelley succeeded in creating not only the world's most enduring monster story, but also in creating the novel that best describes the blurry lines that separate the hermit, recluse, and misanthrope.

This book contains its fair share of true hermits, fearful recluses, and bitter misanthropes alike. It is, to the best of my knowledge, the largest compendium of real-life hermits ever assembled on paper. The men and women depicted in this book were chosen not so much because of the bizarre twists and turns of their lives, but because their stories, like parables and fables, have a great deal to teach about the human condition.

PART I
HERMITS OF THE NORTHEAST

NEW YORK

1. Old Shep

George William Shepherd, otherwise known as "The Hermit of Leydecker Road," was a man so colorful that his life could have provided writers with enough material for a long-running television series. When the grizzled old-timer first arrived in West Seneca in the early 1900s, not much was known about "Old Shep," who built a shack along the banks of Cazenovia Creek and earned a living by sharpening knives and scissors. When Old Shep decided to put wheels on his shack in an attempt to cheat the taxman, folks around West Seneca began to suspect that the ornery hermit may have had a rather interesting past. Their suspicions would prove to be correct.

Shepherd was born in 1830 in Missouri and, as a boy, developed a taste for adventure. At the age of fifteen he enlisted in the army and fought under General Albert Sidney Johnston during the conflict known as the Utah War, a year-long armed confrontation between Mormon settlers and the government of the United States. During the Civil War, Shepherd fought for the Confederacy and participated in The Battle of Wilson's Creek in Missouri and The Battle of Pea Ridge in Arkansas.

The border between Missouri and Arkansas was a dangerous place during the war; citizens who desired to remain neutral took up arms against both the Confederacy and the Union, with neighbors taking up arms against other neighbors. These conditions led a guerrilla fighter from Missouri by the name of William Clarke Quantrill to form a band of rangers and drive Union sympathizers out of the state. These men, the famed Quantrill's Raiders, perfected military ambush tactics and specialized in attacking Union convoys. As a result of their efforts, Quantrill and his band of raiders were mustered into the Confederate Army in 1862. It could be argued that Quantrill's Raiders were the first "special forces" in America, and fellow Missourian George William Shepherd soon joined their ranks, along with two young men named Frank and Jesse James.

Shepherd rode with Quantrill's Raiders into Kentucky in the spring of 1865, where the guerillas were ambushed and captured by Union forces outside of Taylorsville. Quantrill was mortally wounded during the ambush, thus bringing an end to Quantrill's Raiders. Several of these raiders later applied the tactics they had learned under Quantrill to robbing trains and banks. The James-Younger gang, comprised of several ex-raiders, was formed, and George William Shepherd and his cousin, Oliver, were among the members.

The Shepherds were involved in the gang's bank robbery in Russellville, Kentucky, in March of 1868. George was caught and served two years in prison, but was granted an early release for helping the authorities track down members of the James-Younger gang. According to some accounts, Oliver escaped to Missouri but was hunted down and died in a hail of gunfire, receiving twenty gunshot wounds in his body. Shepherd believed that he and his cousin had been framed by Jesse James, and Old Shep was determined to get his revenge. Tensions between Shepherd and James had been growing long before the bank robbery, however.

In 1866 Jesse James and Jim Anderson (brother of famed anti-Union guerrilla "Bloody Bill" Anderson) learned that Shepherd's nephew, Ike Flannery, had inherited a large sum of money. The men befriended the young man and offered to let him join the gang. They invited Flannery to go shooting with them, but it was a trap; they murdered young Ike Flannery and stole the large sum of money, which he had been told to bring along. Old Shep tracked Jim Anderson to Austin and slit his throat on the lawn of the state capitol building in revenge.

It was around this time, a few years before the Nimrod & Co. Bank robbery in Kentucky, Shepherd married Martha Sanders Maddox, the famous Confederate spy who was known as "Matt Sanders." During the war she was married to Richard Maddox. Martha, dressed as a man, would often ride with her husband and participate in secret missions. Although Richard Maddox was killed shortly before the end of the war, Matt Sanders continued to spy for the rebels until the end. While Shepherd was in prison for bank robbery, Martha abandoned him and married a wealthy landowner by the name of McMakin. Once Shepherd got out of prison he charged Martha with bigamy, but Martha was awarded a pardon by the governor, and the charges against her were dropped.

Old Shep spent several years helping the authorities track down Jesse James. In 1878 he arranged a secret meeting with the notorious outlaw near Joplin, Missouri, and begged James to allow him back into the gang. After James agreed, Shepherd informed the authorities. The plan was to have Shepherd ride along with the gang members the following morning on the way to their next robbery while the lawmen hid in bushes along the trail. However, when the outlaws arrived at the predetermined location on the trail and no lawmen appeared, Old Shep grew outraged and decided that he would take matters into his own hands. He slowed his horse and fell back in line. This aroused the suspicions of some of the outlaws, but George explained that something was caught in his horse's hoof and that he would catch up with the rest of the group. He fell back in line until he was riding alongside Jesse James. "This is for killing Ike Flannery!" he shouted, as he drew his gun and fired. When he saw Jesse James fall from his horse, George was certain that he had killed the famous outlaw. He was also certain that the rest of the gang would riddle his body with hot lead unless he made a quick escape. While Shepherd made his getaway, one of the members of the James gang fired a shot that struck him in the leg.

Around ten o'clock on the morning of November 2, a doctor named Burns was driving his buggy through Shoal Creek, a few miles south of Joplin, when the Sunday morning silence was shattered by gunshots. A few moments later Burns encountered a bewildered man on horseback. He was brandishing two revolvers and bleeding profusely from a wound in one of his legs. Doc Burns asked the rider about the exchange of gunshots he had heard. "I've just shot a man back there!" the wounded man shouted before galloping away at lightning speed. A few seconds later Burns came across two more men on

George W. Shepherd, "The Hermit of Leydecker Road."
Courtesy of the West Seneca Historical Society.

horseback. They accosted the doctor and told him that there was an injured man down the road who needed medical attention. George Shepherd made his way to Galena, Kansas, and checked into a hotel, where he told anyone who would listen that he had just killed Jesse James. The notorious outlaw survived, however; Shepherd's shot had only grazed him behind the ear.

James kept a low profile while he recuperated from his injury, leading many newspapers to proclaim that the famed outlaw was dead. Old Shep fancied himself a national hero but, much to his amazement, he found that his opinion of himself was unshared by others. George found that most folks could be divided into one of two categories: those who thought of Jesse James as a folk hero and were angered by the rumors of the outlaw's death, and those who thought Old Shep was full of malarkey. Shepherd remarked that he received more criticism for shooting Jesse James than the entire James gang received for all of their misdeeds.

Shepherd spent the following decades living the life of a tumbleweed, bouncing around from town to town and state to state. By the time his wanderings led him to West Seneca, he was over the age of eighty, but he made his home in a cave and a series of shacks, the last of which stood by the old covered bridge on Leydecker Road over Cazenovia Creek. Even in old age the ornery hermit lived a colorful life. Old Shep had many run-ins with the locals, but one event, which took place in 1913, is still remembered by residents of West Seneca. A man named Henry P. Heck was hunting on property along Leydecker Road, which had been in his family's possession for generations. Henry strayed a little too close to the hermit's shack, and Old Shep was so infuriated that he came out and demanded that Mr. Heck leave immediately. The hunter turned and headed back in the direction from which he had come, but it must have been too slow for the cantankerous hermit's liking, because Old Shep grabbed an axe and threw it at Henry. Fortunately for the hunter, the octogenarian's aim was a little off, and the head of the axe lodged in the trunk of a tree. Henry retrieved the axe and quickly left the area. The axe, now a treasured family heirloom, has been handed down to Mr. Heck's grandchildren, who still have it to this day.

Old Shep spent most of his West Seneca life in a wooden shack erected near the creek on the edge of farmland owned by the Kloiber family. He hunted and fished for food and would only venture into town on rare occasions. Though he seldom conversed with anyone, it was said that he had a soft spot for children and would entertain them with stories about the Wild West, the Civil War, and his days of riding with Jesse James and his gang. When the government decided that Shep should pay property taxes, the wily, old hermit remedied the situation by attaching wagon wheels to his home so that it could no longer be classified as a permanent structure.

Old Shep lived to the ripe old age of 103, but his death wasn't due to the ravages of time. Shepherd died on March 31, 1933, after his shack caught on fire. Since he had died penniless and had no next of kin, he would have been laid to rest in a pauper's grave if not for the generosity of the Lang family, who provided the eccentric hermit with a proper burial and a grave marker at Saint Matthew's Cemetery in West Seneca.

2. The Prodigal Father

In the 1880s there was a prosperous hop farmer named Henry Smith who lived in the town of Ogden in Monroe County in upstate New York. The first fifty-eight years of his life had been very productive and adventurous, and Henry was regarded as a pillar of the community and a man of unusual intelligence. He had a love for the sporting life and had hunted and fished in virtually every state of the union. Henry's love for adventure had taken him from the sapphire waters of the West Indies to the smoking volcanoes of the Sandwich Islands to the icebergs of Cape Horn. Although he had been shipwrecked twice during these expeditions, he never lost his hunger for adventure. Henry's most prized possession was his fishing rod, which accompanied him on his many travels. According to Henry, his trusty rod had traveled more than fifty thousand miles, and it was this beloved bamboo fishing rod that Henry kept in his possession until the days of his explorations had come to an end.

There came a time in the life of the prosperous farmer when his good fortunes deserted him, however. His business affairs had gotten into bad shape, and he became financially embarrassed. Not only did his fortune vanish, but Henry's usual fortitude and courage vanished as well, leaving him dependent upon others for the first time in his life. This cruel and unforeseen twist of fortune was a humbling experience for Henry; so humbling, in fact, that he disappeared from his home and family. He left no trace behind, and the search party that was formed in light of his absence failed to turn up any clues that might indicate where the once-successful hop farmer had gone. The years passed by. The wife in her rural country home grew old, and the sorrow that had come upon her had aged still faster her lonesome, weary heart. Growing old long before her time, she died at the age of thirty-eight. Henry's son grew to manhood, never knowing whether his father was alive or dead.

One day, years later, a peculiar man arrived in Ceres, the tiny hamlet near the Pennsylvania border. Who he was or whence he came he refused to divulge. Quiet, harmless, but mysterious, the stranger aroused great curiosity among the disquisitive citizens of Ceres, and they soon troubled him with questions, which the man refused to answer. He pleaded with them to be left alone and, after much begging, was finally permitted to dwell in peace.

For several years he toiled as a common farmhand for various farmers in the vicinity until he grew tired of the work and retired to a shanty, which he had built in the forested hills north of the village. Thereafter, he lived the life of a hermit, returning to the village only at rare intervals for supplies and provisions. While in town, the hermit shunned conversation, preferring his self-imposed vow of silence to the catty chatting of the villagers. One day he became gravely ill; his age and the exposure to which he had been subjected had turned the once-robust stranger into a frail and sickly old man who was left clinging to life. Finally, realizing that he had not long to live, he summoned the villagers and spilled his secrets, revealing on his sickbed that he was the long-missing hop farmer from Ogden named Henry Smith. Henry's surviving family members were notified, and the son arrived in Ceres to be reunited with his father. The meeting was quite affecting.

Henry continued to cling to life, though he was feeble and gravely ill. Seventy-three hard years had passed over his head, leaving him bent and gnarled and turning his long hair and beard the color of snow. As summer gave way to autumn, he gave to his son his prized bamboo fishing rod, along with a few other possessions. When the weather grew mild, the son took his father home to Ogden, where the remaining days of his life were spent. On December 31, 1894, Henry Smith passed away. Henry's life had come full circle; after a lifetime of traveling the world, the prodigal farmer considered himself lucky to draw his last breath in the town of his birth and be reunited, if only for a brief time, with the son he had left behind.

3. The Hermit of West 16th Street

Hermits exist not only in remote wilderness landscapes, but also in the most bustling of urban environments. In fact, there may be more hermits in places like New York and Chicago than there are in the Appalachians or Rockies, owing to the fact that large cities present more opportunities for individuals to be scorned by lovers or cheated out of fortunes. Wherever a heart can be broken, wherever wealth can be won or lost, and wherever mankind faces tragedy or grapples with adversity, you may find a hermit—even on West 16th Street in the largest city in America.

For more than eleven years a man was buried alive in the heart of the Big Apple, living in a cave of his own design. William Galvin was his name, and when he was discovered in 1902, he had been living as a hermit on the waterfront for over a decade. Galvin didn't have a single friend in the world and had no desire to communicate with others, except for his angry grunts and curses projected toward anyone who attempted to help him. Through blizzards and downpours and sweltering summer days he chose to live his life in the manner of the most abject pauper, even though numerous passersby with charitable hearts offered their aid.

The home of William Galvin was perhaps one of the strangest in the world. From the outside, the pile of rocks situated between 15th and 16th Streets appeared unsuitable for human habitation. Galvin's home was composed of paving stones, which the city had rejected as defective, and therefore it is perhaps fitting that these castaway stones should serve as a home to a man who had also been rejected by society and deemed defective. The rock pile, 12 feet high and 150 feet long, was topped by a thin sheet of discarded tin. If you were to walk upon it, it would give under your foot with a hollow crackle. You would also hear an angry voice cursing you from the depths below; for you would be treading on the roof of William Galvin's mansion.

Ornery might be the best word to describe the hermit's demeanor. He passionately disliked the daylight, and laughter grated on his ears. He avoided these things by burrowing fifteen feet under the ground, existing in a man-made tomb, which sunlight could not penetrate. Surrounded by rats and the stench of foul air may be some people's vision of hell, but it was home sweet home for the grumpy hermit of West 16th Street.

Galvin solved the problem of sustenance by emerging from his rock pile every two or three days at the break of dawn, poking his shaggy head with its matted gray beard up through the rocks and surveying the surroundings like a cautious groundhog. If the city streets were quiet enough, he would emerge from his cavern and descend the pile of rocks, clad in rags and busted, shapeless things on his feet that once upon a time resembled shoes. With his head bent down and eyes glued to the ground, he would shuffle along 16th Street until reaching the horse trough on the corner of Eighth Avenue. Out of this trough he would take a drink. On Fifth Avenue he would stop at a barrel opposite a large brownstone mansion, knowing from experience that it often contained scraps of bread and ends of meat. These he would gather up and return to his cave.

The man-made cave consisted of one room with a dirt floor. In one corner of this room, which served as Galvin's kitchen, living room, and bedroom, was a small piece of matting upon which he rested his head when tired. Around 1900, a severe blizzard blanketed the city and several policemen visited the hermit's home, expecting to find him frozen to death. To their surprise, Galvin was alive and well, even though he refused to light a fire. No one ever saw smoke coming from the hermit's den, not even on the coldest nights. Meanwhile, citizens of the city, bundled up in sable shawls and mink overcoats, would scurry along the avenue, dreading frostbite and cursing the cold.

One day Galvin was arrested and taken to jail, presumably for his own safety, but after much argument was released. He never asked for charity, and grew quite offended whenever it was offered. This intrusion so offended the hermit that he grew more bitter than ever. From that point in time forward, the police never bothered him again; for what William Galvin lacked in money he made up for in pride, and what he lacked in material wealth he compensated with rugged self-sufficiency.

On the southern edge of the stone pile lot was a little restaurant, and the proprietor knew the "stone hermit" perhaps as well as anyone. "That man has lived there some years now," he told newspapers in 1902. "I have spoken to him only once. He came in here about four years ago and, putting five cents down on the counter, asked for a cup of coffee. I gave it to him. He drank it up and went out, never speaking a word, only to ask for the coffee." The hermit was also known to William Fagan, the city employee who worked as watchman at the stone dump. Fagan was never able to fathom the hermit but had learned, through various sources, a little bit about Galvin's background.

Twenty years earlier, Galvin and his younger brother had been merchants. The business partnership existed until the day Galvin fell ill and was taken to the hospital. After he was released, he discovered that his brother had deserted him. Worst of all, when Galvin's younger brother ran off, he had taken Galvin's wife with him. In the life of every hermit there comes a day when his future fate as a recluse is sealed—the point of no return, as some may say. For William Galvin, that was the day. Galvin didn't even go through the trouble of closing up the store; he left it unlocked, and it was eventually looted, much to the bitter hermit's indifference.

For three years Galvin slept in an old boiler in the yard of a machine shop facing the river, between 19th and 20th Streets. When the boiler was sold as scrap, he was forced to seek shelter elsewhere, and his wanderings soon led him to the pile of rejected paving stones. There, he burrowed a hole eight feet in diameter, covering the opening with a sheet of tin that he had found. Back then William Galvin had friends, and after about a year of living in the stone pile these friends came to visit. Galvin wasn't as cranky then; they liked him, and he found their company enjoyable. These friends, impressed by Galvin, went out and told their other friends, and soon a great number of visitors arrived at the stone pile. Galvin enjoyed their company so much that these friends never left. Like Galvin, they had found a new home beneath the paving stones. These friends, of course, were the enormous wharf rats famous in that part of the city for their sharp, razor-like teeth. These rats never harmed a hair on Galvin's craggy head. If anything, the rats adored the hermit and his long, gray beard, since he would keep his friends warm in the winter by tucking them under his facial hair and snuggling with them. In the summer, Galvin and his roommates would dine together. They picked clean the bones that he dropped on the floor and would take crumbs from his hands like obedient dogs.

Occasionally, Galvin would discover that no scraps of food had been left in the barrel on Fifth Avenue. On days like these he would wander the streets, foraging in other trash bins, until he had gathered enough food to get by for another day. His pantry consisted of everything from melon rinds to half-emptied cans of decayed tomatoes, from chicken bones to chunks of stale bread. He cared not whether the meat was rancid or if the vegetables were moldy. In the darkness of his cave he couldn't see what he was eating anyway.

Dozens had attempted, in vain, to ply the old recluse for details about his life. Numerous reporters have climbed the rock pile in order to interview the hermit of West 16th Street. All of these folks returned home disappointed, some returning worse for the wear, since Galvin was known to throw rocks at those who offended him. Someone once offered him a dollar if only he would emerge from his hovel and answer a few questions, but Galvin stoutly declined the offer.

Historical records do not describe the ultimate fate of this peculiar tramp, but it is doubtless he died as he had lived—shunning society, abhorring charity, and preferring the company of wharf rats to his fellow man. The rock pile on West 16th Street is long gone (the site is now home to super-chic, million-dollar, lower-Chelsea condominiums) and with it, every trace of William Galvin's mysterious life.

4. The Hermit of Broadway

When it opened in 1870 the Broadway Central Hotel was hailed as the largest hotel in America. Located between Amity and Bleecker Streets, this impressive structure was a New York landmark for over a century, until its collapse in 1973. So large was the hotel that it contained over seven acres of carpeting and had the capacity to house over 1,200 guests. Eight stories in height (which, at the time, was a marvel of engineering), the hotel was surmounted by three gothic towers, which overlooked the bustling thoroughfare of Broadway.

Many notable guests stayed at the Broadway Central Hotel during its century of existence; foreign dignitaries, robber barons, and movie stars alike rented its luxurious rooms. The hotel is perhaps best remembered as the scene of the 1872 murder of wealthy financier James "Diamond Jim" Fisk. Less famous is a guest who lodged at the hotel for three decades, an eccentric Spaniard named Manuel Martinez, who, in the early 1900s, became known throughout the city as the "Hermit of Broadway."

When Martinez first arrived at the hotel, the neighborhood had not yet developed into the bustling center of commerce that it would later become. Cloaking himself in self-created solitude, the Spaniard paid little attention to the human activity beyond the door to his hotel room, uninterested in the millions of people who scurried along the busy sidewalk outside of his urban cave during his thirty-year residence at 673 Broadway. The hermit's room bore the resemblance of a library more so than a luxurious hotel suite. Martinez slept little, rarely ate, but read and studied his books incessantly, like a student preparing for a final exam. He had chosen the apartment deliberately, with the goal of being able to shut himself off from the world. High up and to the rear of the building, it was a room chosen for its spectacular view of concrete and cement, without the unsightliness of crowds and automobiles and greenery. Not even the clang of the trolley crossed his threshold; for thirty years, all he heard were the screeches from the whistles of factories located behind the hotel. Martinez had only entertained three visitors during his entire stay at the Broadway Central. One visit was from a nephew, one visit from a building inspector, and one visit was from a newspaper reporter who, in 1911, interviewed the hermit and shared his story with the world.

Manuel Martinez was eighty-eight years old when his story was told. Clad in a linen dressing gown and reclining on a big, comfortable chair, the hermit revealed his reasons for becoming a recluse in one of the busiest neighborhoods in one of the world's busiest cities. As he told his story in broken English, he emphasized each word with feeble, yet graceful, gestures of his old, delicate hands. What it all boiled down to, explained Martinez, was religion.

"Before I drew away from the world I had traveled much," explained the Spaniard. "As a minor, a little fellow of sixteen, I left my home in Granada and began my travels." He paused to point to a picture of a majestic, Moorish mansion on the wall. It was the home of his family. "And I was but a little boy, but already I knew the writings of Voltaire, Rousseau, Plato, Aristotle. And I would see the world!

"I went to Austria, to Germany, France, Russia, England, and to Rome. And everywhere I found the people ruled and oppressed by religion. I visited the Holy Land of the New and Old Testament. I grew no more friendly toward religion. I became an atheist. And I tried to escape from the religious atmosphere in America, in Mexico, Canada, Cuba. It was all the same. I became disgusted with the childishness of the faith and beliefs and superstitions I found in men.

"I came to New York thirty-five years ago, assuming a banking business left by a brother. But after five years, my disgust against religion had increased rather than waned. I decided that I would withdraw as nearly as possible from all contact with men. I filled my room with the precious books of truth and philosophy and have had them for my only companions, augmenting my library from time to time as I learned of new works through the literary reviews.

"I have resisted learning English. The better to keep my solitude. Of course, I have maintained my courtesy toward them whom it was absolutely necessary for me to meet from time to time. But, save for the attendants who come silently daily to my room, I have passed months at a time in the solitude of my chamber. And I am not embittered. I have been content."

Though the hermit never left his room, his bills were always paid with businesslike regularity. The hotel clerk, a man by the name of Moubray, admitted that the Spaniard had never uttered a word to him. How he was able to manage his affairs in silence became an enigma; it was speculated that one of his fellow countrymen had been tasked with handling Manuel's finances.

The hermit admitted that he had never been to a doctor. "It would be useless," he explained to the newspaper reporter. "I am about to die. I am very old. I am worn out. It is natural that now I should be dying. I am not afraid." Perhaps Martinez granted an interview because he realized that his days were drawing to a close and simply wanted his story to be told. Even those who do not believe in the hereafter have a desire to leave behind some legacy, some evidence that they had been born, lived, and died; a testament that their time on Earth had not been in vain. Two months after Martinez told his story to the newspaper reporter, he passed away.

Religion has always been a popular motivation for those who choose to embark on a lifelong journey of hermitry. From the cave-dwelling ancient sect known as the Essenes to the medieval monks who dwelt in drafty monasteries, religion has always been, and continues to be, one of the most powerful motivators of the human spirit. In the case of Manuel Martinez, even contempt of religion can lead a wealthy, young man to a life of self-imposed exile, even in the heart of the world's most bustling city.

PENNSYLVANIA

5. Amos Wilson

Many real-life hermits have become fixtures of folklore, but few hermits have attained the fame of William "Amos" Wilson, whose life and times have inspired countless storytellers and authors for nearly two centuries. The story of Amos Wilson is one of unspeakable heartbreak and sorrow, and old Willy Shakespeare himself would've been hard pressed to weave a more soul-wrenching tale of tragedy.

The story of the man who would come to be known as "The Pennsylvania Hermit" begins in 1764 on a farm in Chester County. Amos was the first-born child to John and Elizabeth Wilson, who maintained a small but modest farm not far from the hustle and bustle of Philadelphia. Two years later a daughter was born and named after her mother, Elizabeth. Although the Wilsons had a fine reputation, John, like many early settlers who immigrated to America from England, made the unfortunate decision to side with the British during the Revolutionary War. As a result, most of the family property was confiscated by the government. Making matters worse, Amos and Elizabeth's mother died while the children were still young.

John Wilson soon remarried, but his second wife did not care for young Amos and Elizabeth. She insisted upon sending them away as soon as they were old enough to care for themselves. When Amos reached the age of sixteen he was sent fifty miles away to Lancaster County to apprentice as a stone carver under a man named Fahnestock. Elizabeth, who had grown up to become magnificently beautiful, was sent to Philadelphia, where she eventually found employment as a barmaid at the Indian Queen Tavern. In early 1784, Elizabeth was seduced by a smooth-talking traveler, whom she had met at the Indian Queen. Although he had promised to marry her, he disappeared like a thief in the night when he learned that Elizabeth was pregnant. This created quite a scandal around the tavern, whose owner decided that it was too much of an embarrassment to keep an unwed pregnant girl as a barmaid, so Elizabeth was forced to leave the Indian Queen. Disgraced, she returned to the family farm and gave birth to twin sons.

As soon as Elizabeth was well enough to travel, she returned to the Indian Queen Tavern in the hopes of meeting the man who had promised to marry her. Her lover, whose name has been recorded as Joseph Deshong, the sheriff of Sussex County in New Jersey, feigned happiness at seeing Elizabeth and once again assured her that he planned to take her as a bride. Brimming with happiness, she returned to the family farm in order to make arrangements for the wedding. In October she set out for Newtown Square, near Philadelphia, to meet her future husband.

Elizabeth was not seen by anyone for a week, and when she returned to Chester County she was disheveled and incoherent, and her newborn children were nowhere to be found. A few days later, a hunter found the bodies of the twin baby boys in the woods alongside the road to Newtown Square. According to court records of the time, Elizabeth was charged with "the murder of her Two Bastard Male Children" and imprisoned at the Fourth Street Jail in the city of Chester.

The trial of Elizabeth Wilson began in June of 1785 and was presided over by William Augustus Atlee, a justice of the Pennsylvania Supreme Court. Elizabeth not only refused to enter a plea, she also refused to speak a single word during the entire trial. Not sure how to proceed, Judge Atlee decided to postpone the trial until the fall court session. Her trial resumed in October and, even though Judge Atlee later remarked that he believed Elizabeth to be innocent, the jury convicted her of murder in the first degree, based on evidence that was wholly circumstantial. Elizabeth Wilson was sentenced to death by hanging and the date of execution was set for the seventh of December.

Amos Wilson was still working as a stone carver in Lancaster County when he heard the news about his sister, and he immediately left his employer and arrived at the Chester jail on the third of December. Elizabeth provided her brother with a detailed account of what happened to her infant children. Although Deshong had agreed to meet her in Newtown Square, he was waiting for her in a heavily wooded area a few miles outside of town. He confronted the young woman and demanded to examine the children to see if they bore any resemblance to him. When he saw that they were indeed his children, he ordered Elizabeth to kill them. When she refused, he threw the young boys on the ground and trampled them to death. He then pointed a pistol at Elizabeth and made her swear that she would never reveal what he had done.

Amos immediately left the jail and gathered several reputable witnesses, as well as Judge Atlee, and urged his sister to repeat the story. After the witnesses signed Elizabeth's confession, Amos presented the document to Benjamin Franklin, who was president of the Supreme Executive Council. The council ordered that the execution be postponed until the third of January, in order to allow them more time to reconsider Elizabeth's case.

In the meantime, Amos went in search of his sister's seducer and found him in New Jersey. Deshong, who was already married, denied having any knowledge of Elizabeth Wilson. Amos then went to Philadelphia and assembled a list of witnesses who had seen Deshong at the Indian Queen Tavern, but he became ill around Christmas and was forced to spend several days recuperating, drifting in and out of consciousness. He lost track of time, and when he recovered he was horrified to learn that it was the third of January, the day his sister was scheduled to hang. Amos raced to the home of Benjamin Franklin to request another postponement, but Franklin informed the young man that only Charles Biddle, the vice president of the Supreme Executive Council, had the authority to grant Amos's request. Amos located Biddle, who wrote an order, which read, "Do not execute Wilson until you hear further from Council." Armed with Elizabeth's pardon, Amos mounted his horse and raced to Chester, fifteen miles away.

Unfortunately, when Amos reached the Schuylkill River he discovered that the ferry was out of operation, as heavy rain had choked the swollen river with ice and debris. Amos pleaded with the ferry operator, but he refused to take Amos across, insisting that it would be too dangerous. In the throes of desperation, the young man spurred his horse and drove the bewildered beast into the

Amos Wilson,
"The Pennsylvania Hermit."

icy water. The horse, strug-gling for its life, had made it more than halfway across the river when it was struck on the head and killed by a large chunk of debris. Amos swam the rest of the way, but when he reached the opposite shore he found that the strong current had carried him more than two miles downstream. Amos stole the first horse he saw and raced like the devil toward the town square, where preparations were being made for Elizabeth's execution.

William Gibbons, the sheriff of Chester County, had stationed several flag men at intervals along Fourth Street in case a last-minute pardon was on its way. Gibbons, who also believed in Elizabeth's innocence, delayed the execution for as long as possible, but when noon came and went he could wait no longer; he was duty-bound to uphold the law, as the young woman had been tried and found guilty by a jury of her peers. Reluctantly, Sheriff Gibbons gave the order and the cart was pulled from beneath Elizabeth's feet. Suddenly, a terrific commotion broke out as a young man furiously spurred his horse down Fourth Street, screaming, "A pardon! A pardon!" The shouting of the crowd frightened the horse and Amos was thrown to the ground, landing headfirst into a puddle of mud beneath the gallows. The sheriff, meanwhile, frantically cut the rope and attempted to revive Elizabeth Wilson, but it was too late. According to legend, when Amos rose from the mud beneath the gallows, his hair had turned white from shock, and his speech was reduced to gibberish.

Amos attempted to return to work, but couldn't keep his tortured mind on his job. He had lost all interest in society and took up a life of wandering, making his home in wilderness caves throughout southeastern Pennsylvania. In 1802 he arrived at the cave along Swatara Creek, near Hummelstown, that would be his home for the remaining nineteen years of his life. The cave, which is known today as Indian Echo Caverns, had provided shelter for the Lenape and Susquehannock for hundreds of years, but was abandoned when Amos arrived. Amos used a ledge in the cave's main chamber as a bed and devoted most of his time to writing religious manuscripts, some of which survive to this day. His possessions, which were few, included a Bible, a straw mattress, and a few various cooking utensils.

Though he shunned society, Amos became acquainted with a farmer who lived across the creek and would occasionally make grindstones for the farmer in exchange for food and other supplies. On the morning of October 13, 1821, the farmer went to check on the hermit and discovered that he was dead. Sadly, Amos Wilson, "The Pennsylvania Hermit," was buried in an unmarked grave, its location lost to history.

6. "She Was Too Cruel"

In May of 1886, a farmer from Allegheny County decided to explore his many acres of forested property in the hopes of discovering natural gas. It had been nearly twenty-seven years since Edwin Drake drilled his now-famous well in Titusville, not far away, and the oil boom that followed had excited most of the folks of Western Pennsylvania because of the immense wealth that could be obtained beneath their very feet. After the oil rush, prospectors from all over the country turned their attention away from gold and silver to natural gas and other natural resources waiting to be discovered in Pennsylvania.

This farmer from Allegheny County was no exception. He plunged into the deep forest and vigorously explored the hollow near the corner of his property. He found a small stream and decided to follow the water to its source and was quite surprised to find, about two hundred yards upstream, a large opening flanked by moss-covered rocks. Even more surprising to the farmer was the discovery that the cave was occupied by a wild man.

The hermit told the farmer that his name was Edward Gaber, but refused to offer any further explanation about his living conditions. Based on the recluse's appearance, the farmer estimated that the hermit hadn't been occupying the cave for more than a few weeks; he lacked the long, flowing beard, the matted hair, and the tattered rags that result from a long life of hermitry. The hermit refused to answer the farmer's questions but assured him that he would do no harm, as long as he was permitted to live in peaceful solitude inside the cave. The farmer had no objection to the newfound inhabitant squatting on his land and consented to leave Gaber to his own devices. However, the farmer was a caring man and made frequent trips to the cave to check on Gaber's well-being. It was evident to the farmer that Gaber wasn't very skilled at living the life of a hermit; within a month he had been transformed from a strong young man to a gaunt skeleton. The farmer often brought food to the cave, but the hermit always refused to eat. Instead, he survived on a meager diet of berries and plants.

At last the hermit grew so weak that he lacked the strength to leave his cave for a drink of water from the nearby spring. The farmer reported the malnourished misanthrope to the county home in Meadville (in present-day Crawford County), and a few days later three men from the home ventured to the cave. The hermit was so weak that he offered no resistance. When Gaber arrived at the poor farm in Meadville, he refused to eat. Eventually, he was coaxed into eating something, and in a matter of hours the hermit's strength and vitality seemed to return. Within days he was eating regularly and appeared to be rational and sane, much to the amazement of his caretakers, who initially assumed that Gaber was a lunatic.

Although Gaber appeared to have recovered from his malnutrition, he refused to answer any questions, only permitting his caretakers to learn of his name and nothing more. The hermit was apparently quite vocal in his sleep, however, and every night curious workers from the county home would gather around his bed in the hopes of learning a few details about the mysterious and secretive Edward Gaber. "I'm so unhappy," Gaber frequently muttered in his sleep. Some attendants claim that the man occasionally spoke of Switzerland in his sleep and, on several occasions, uttered the words "she was too cruel." One attendant claims to have heard Gaber mumble the name of a woman once, which led everyone to believe that Gaber's troubles started with a love affair in Switzerland.

Once recovered from his illness, Gaber begged to return to his cave. The workers at the county home in Meadville had been anticipating an escape attempt, and the superintendent made it a point to keep the hermit closely guarded at all times. At four o'clock on the morning of July 6, 1886, the hermit finally saw an opportunity to flee when one of the attendants drifted off to sleep while guarding his room. The moment the caretaker closed his eyes, Gaber bolted out of his chair and dashed to the window, hurling himself to the ground with a banshee-like scream. He fell two stories and died from his injuries two hours later, never once revealing the details of his past, and forever leaving unsolved the mystery of his troubled life.

7. The Hermit of Buckingham Mountain

A mere 520 feet in height, Buckingham Mountain is a bit of a misnomer. Although it is the second highest point in Bucks County, it is neither imposing nor majestic, yet this verdant hillock rising above the rolling farmlands has struck a chord of fear into the hearts of many locals for generations. Atop Buckingham Mountain is a deserted church, known once as the Mount Gilead African Methodist Episcopal Church. Built in 1835, the church was founded by runaway slaves and was considered to be one of the more important places of refuge for escaped slaves in southeastern Pennsylvania. A spooky little cemetery, overgrown with vegetation, can be found next to the old abandoned church. The entire mountain is rumored to be haunted, and it is here they say you can race the devil, if you so desire.

The rules of the footrace vary, depending on who is telling the tale, but they say that winning the race will bring a year of good luck, while losing the race will bring grave misfortune. Runners never see their otherworldly opponent, but it is said that you can tell by the wind whether you're winning or losing the race against the devil. If you feel a gust of wind after completing the sprint from the church to the cemetery, it's the devil trying to catch up to you. But if you feel a gust of wind *before* reaching the cemetery, it's the devil brushing past, and you best prepare yourself for a terrible misfortune. It's unclear how this legend began. Some claim that some of the slaves were practitioners of black magic, and this so angered God that He cursed the church and the hill on which it stands. Others claim that the spooky legend was manufactured by Albert Large, a hermit who once called Buckingham Mountain home.

Little was known about Albert Large until 1858, when the hermit was discovered living beneath the "Wolf Rocks"—an outcropping of boulders near the summit of Buckingham Mountain. On his way home from work one evening from the nearby quarry, a free slave had decided to take a shortcut by passing over the mountain. When he approached the Wolf Rocks, he was frightened by a menacing voice, which seemed to emanate from beneath the ground. Believing that he had heard the angry growls of something sinister and demonic, the young man took off running as fast as his feet could carry him. Once off the mountain, the young man sprinted back to the quarry and related his experience to the workers. The men at the quarry decided to investigate, and the group proceeded to the spot of the otherworldly emanations. Upon reaching the rocks, the men heard a booming voice warning them to leave at once or else they would be killed. The men were also threatened with death if they so much as told another soul about what they had seen. One of the bolder fellows in the group thought he recognized the voice and inched closer to the rocks, in spite of the repeated warnings.

"Why, it's Albert Large!" the quarry worker remarked. "Albert, just what in the world are you doing under those rocks? You come on out of there!" insisted the quarryman. The menacing voice replied, rather defiantly, that he wasn't Albert Large. The group of men tried to convince the strange fellow to come out of his hiding place, but the man adamantly refused and told them to go away.

The men returned to town and paid a visit to Large's friends and relatives who lived in the neighborhood, and they agreed that they should ascend the mountain and try to talk some sense into Albert. Even though the hermit continued to deny that he was Albert Large, enough of the villagers recognized his voice, and they needled him until the hermit finally confessed that he was, indeed, Albert Large. Once the townsfolk had talked the stubborn recluse out of his hiding place, Albert confessed that he had been using the shallow cave as his private hideaway for nearly thirty years, sleeping in his rocky habitation by day and sallying forth into town for food during the night. At first, he only went to the cave whenever he needed to get away from life's troubles, but, over time, he spent more and more time there until he decided to make it his permanent home. The curious villagers demanded a tour of Large's secret hideaway, of course, and they pestered Large until he agreed to show them around.

Albert's cave, which had a well-hidden entrance, consisted of two small rooms; one of which was used as the hermit's living quarters, while the other served as a pantry. The walls of the cave were paneled with boards, upon which hung various utensils, pots, pans, and cooking implements. An iron kettle, inside of which was found a cooked chicken, stood in one corner of the room. The intruders also found a pot of butter, a few bottles of whiskey, a pile of clothes, and a handful of other objects that made the hermit's confinement bearable. All in all, it was a very comfortable, little cave, and some of the visitors remarked, in a jealous tone, that they wished they had a private getaway like Albert's, some cozy, little place to which they could escape after a hard day of work or an argument with the wife.

At the time of his discovery, the hermit presented a shaggy appearance and some of the locals convinced Albert to make himself a little more presentable. He reluctantly agreed to a shave and a haircut. His old friends and neighbors, figuring the old hermit could use some company, made frequent visits to the cave, much to Albert's chagrin. As his celebrity spread throughout the countryside, even strangers began to journey to the cave in order to catch a glimpse of the celebrity recluse. Throngs of visitors showed up unannounced, inviting themselves inside and laying their hands all over the poor recluse's property. Some even demanded some sort of souvenir they could return home with, to show off to their friends. The poor, old hermit could not stand this invasion of privacy, and he soon abandoned his beloved hideaway in search of a new cave. By this time, however, he had become such a local celebrity that newspapers began reporting his every move. As a result, everywhere the hermit went, crowds followed. Realizing that the life of hermitry occasionally required one to play the role of social butterfly and gracious host, Albert Large gave up his life of seclusion—it was just too darn noisy.

One of the last newspaper articles about the hermit of Buckingham Mountain appeared in the April 29, 1858, edition of the *Bucks County Intelligencer*, which reported,

"We are informed that Large, the hermit, has returned to this county and is now staying with some of his friends in Buckingham. He has again assumed the habits of the out door world, having cut off his long hair and shaved his face, and seems happy and contented among his fellow creatures."

Somehow, we get the impression that Mr. Large might disagree with that statement.

8. The Hermit of Blue Hill

When residents of Sunbury or Northumberland cast their eyes westward across the Susquehanna River, they see a large hill that overlooks the confluence of the east and west branches of the river. Atop this craggy bluff sits the Shikellamy State Park scenic overlook, a popular spot for love struck teenagers by night and amateur photographers and bird watchers by day. However, locals would have seen a much different sight 150 years ago at the summit of the hill. That's because the summit of this promontory, formally known as Blue Hill, was the home of one of the most unusual and eccentric men in the history of Pennsylvania, a man by the name of John Mason. In 1839 Mason designed and built a strange octagonal-shaped tower on the top of Blue Hill. The tower, which was two stories tall, projected at an odd and precarious angle over the rocky edge of the hill's summit, inspiring many locals to refer to the bizarre structure as the "Leaning Tower of Pennsylvania."

Mason, who became known as the "Hermit of Blue Hill" for his eccentric behavior and solitary existence, was enamored with astronomy. It is believed that he constructed the tower as his own personal observatory. The structure stood until 1864, sixteen years after the hermit's death, when it was destroyed by a handful of railroad employees in an act of mischief. The vandals loosened the tower's moorings, causing the enormous structure to topple into the Susquehanna River below. Sadly, the tower was said to contain hundreds of rare and priceless Old English books and centuries-old illuminated manuscripts, which, as a result, were destroyed. Had the books survived, the hermit's library would be worth a considerable fortune today.

John Mason's eccentricities were as well-known as the tower he had built. Born in Philadelphia to Quaker parents on December 7, 1768, the hermit relocated to the town of Northumberland and opened a general store, which he operated for a few years before relocating his business across the river, along the banks of Turtle Creek near present-day Lewisburg. Mason, who never expressed an interest in women or marriage, would be what society called a "confirmed bachelor" in those days. Mason was known to walk all over the area, sometimes to places as far away as Williamsport, carrying an umbrella, even on the sunniest of days. Accounts say that he was the fidgety sort who always had to be in motion, and he was considered to be a fine athlete in his youth. Even in his older years, he was well-known for ice skating down the frozen Susquehanna during the winter, and it has been said that Mason often skated to Harrisburg (almost fifty miles away) and back in a single day.

On April 25, 1849, John Mason, "The Hermit of Blue Hill," died on a farm owned by Colonel Meens outside of Williamsport, in present-day Newberry. His friends brought home the body of the eccentric hermit, and Mason was buried atop Blue Hill on the ninety-acre farm, which he owned, within sight of his leaning tower. Unfortunately, Mason's marble tombstone was vandalized and later stolen in the years following his death and, to this day, the Hermit of Blue Hill lies in an unmarked grave somewhere on the summit of the hill.

A close personal friend of John Mason was Pennsylvania author Juliet Lewis Campbell who, in 1857, published a novel entitled *Eros and Anteros* under the pen name Judith Canute. The novel makes several references to the strange tower and John Mason. On January 1, 2012, a portrait of Juliet Lewis Campbell was donated to the Lycoming County Historical Society, along with one of the few surviving copies of *Eros and Anteros*, which was largely based on the life of John Mason, the Hermit of Blue Hill.

MASSACHUSETTS

9. Arthur Carey

The town hall building in Leicester is a handsome, red-brick structure with gleaming white pillars and a stately bell tower. Designed more than a century ago, it is the ideal example of a New England town hall building, as though the sole intention of its architect was to someday have his creation grace the front of a post card, or serve as a model for a Norman Rockwell painting. Inside this building can be found the Town Clerk's office, and inside this office can be found historical documents pertaining to a man named Arthur Carey: early settler, wealthy entrepreneur, and hermit.

Arthur Carey once owned 550 acres of land, upon which the town of Leicester would later be platted. Carey was the first white man to settle in the area, back when the wild region was known as Towtaid to the native Nipmuc tribes. When the first group of explorers from Worcester arrived in Towtaid in 1699, they were shocked to discover Arthur Carey living in a cave and were even more shocked to discover that he had been living there for twenty-five years.

According to these early settlers, the man they encountered living in a cave had no flint or steel, and had learned to start a fire by watching the Indians. In order to cook or to keep his cave warm, Carey created fire by whirling a dry, pointed stick of hardwood in a mass of tinder until the heat of the revolving stick set the material ablaze. Carey only had to master this skill one time; he managed to keep the same fire blazing and smoldering for forty years without once allowing it to flicker.

When the explorers found Arthur Carey, they found it nearly impossible to converse with the hermit. He had lived in solitude for so long that he had forgotten how to speak, and every utterance that left his mouth sounded like confused gibberish to the men from Worcester. Astonishingly, the hermit seemed to be able to converse with members of the animal kingdom, and it was said that Carey, for several years, kept a tamed black bear as a pet and companion.

Once Carey had brushed up on his English, he was able to tell the men from Worcester the story of his life. Carey had been born in Ireland and was an outlaw under England's rule in his homeland, having been accused of being a pirate. This story aroused the interest of the explorers; recently a pirate vessel had been sunk by a warship off the coast of Cape Cod, and her crew was taken to Boston and put to death by hanging on Corn Hill. One member of the pirate crew managed to escape and had never been found. The hermit neither admitted nor denied being the fugitive pirate who managed to escape from his stone cell by befriending and seducing the jailer's daughter.

It soon became evident that Carey could not have been the wanted pirate, as the story of his arrival predated the sinking of the pirate ship on Cape Cod by many years. According to the story Carey had told the explorers from Worcester, he had left Boston in the middle of the night and hiked through miles of forest until he arrived at Long Pond. This he crossed in a dugout canoe he borrowed from an Indian. A short distance later he encountered another white man, who was dressed in furs and armed with a musket and an axe. This strange, white man took Carey to his log cabin and gave him food. Carey remained there for several weeks and learned that the name of the man was Ephraim Curtis. The name of Ephraim Curtis was well known to the explorers; for he was the legendary pioneer who settled Worcester and built his hut on the site of present-day Lincoln Street. It was Curtis who suggested that Arthur Carey make his home on the steep hill seven miles west. This is how Carey came to settle in Towtaid country.

When Carey found the steep hill, he dug a small cave into the hillside with sharpened sticks until it was thirty feet deep. He then fashioned crude supports for the ceiling from fallen timbers. Armed with only an axe, he made bows and arrows and managed to build snares in order to catch rabbits and fowl. He managed to survive by his wits and the sweat of his brow, but even the native Nipmucs looked upon the hermit and shook their heads in pity; so crude and primitive were Carey's methods. The hermit told his visitors that it took him over a week to make a fire using the stick-twirling method and, once lit, he treated it as his most precious possession, making sure the flame was never extinguished.

The hermit was approximately forty-odd years old when he was discovered by the men from Worcester, with sandy hair that streamed in tangled wisps over his rugged shoulders. His long, matted beard was brown, matching the color of his animal pelt wardrobe. He showed his visitors the rest of his possessions, which he had obtained by trading with the natives. He owned a set of rudimentary dishes made from soapstone, and a great supply of arrows, which he used for hunting and spearing fish. The hermit's clothing was made from tanned hides and fur pelts of the animals he had hunted. A table crafted from pine planks, a simple chair, and a cot made of spruce boughs completed his collection of material possessions. Carey had no gunpowder or shot and was eager to trade some of his most prized furs with the new arrivals for these luxuries. Carey became increasingly industrious and also began to trade more freely with the natives. Eventually, he managed to cultivate a field of maize and taught himself how to smoke meat and fish for his winter provisions. However, as more and more white settlers arrived in Towtaid, the hermit once again grew uncomfortable and, abandoning his cave, fled deeper into the wilderness.

He must have grown homesick for Towtaid country and his hillside hovel, because one day, not long after fleeing into the wilderness, he returned. Inexplicably, Arthur Carey had traded his primitive fur loincloths for fine European clothing and had on his person an abundance of gold coins. The locals were flabbergasted and were eager to learn how the former cave-dweller had suddenly become so wealthy.

In June of 1714, after a survey conducted by John Chandler, fifty lots of thirty to fifty acres apiece were allotted and put up for sale. This land would become the town of Leicester. Chandler had set the price at a shilling an acre, which, at the time, was a tidy sum, since the hardy early settlers rarely had two shillings to rub together. One can easily imagine the spectacle that must have erupted when Arthur Carey, the shaggy recluse, paid for 550 acres with gold coins, as shiny as if they had just been minted.

On this expansive tract of land, Carey built a log house, the rear end of which backed up to his cave. The hermit didn't purchase much of anything else, but anytime he bought something, he paid for it in gold, much to the bewilderment and jealousy of the impoverished villagers. When Carey last made an appearance in Leicester, he was dressed in expensive, finely tailored clothing and carried a gold-headed cane. He remarked that he was going to Worcester and then to Boston. In Worcester, he took a room at the Stears Hotel and in the morning caught the coach for Boston, never to be seen in Leicester again. Where he went or how he obtained his wealth has always been, and continues to be, a mystery.

10. The Hermit of Melrose

Originally named Ponde Fielde for its abundance of ponds and streams, the city of Melrose can trace its history back to 1628, when the area was first explored by Ralph and Richard Sprague. Since that time, the verdant valley north of the Mystic River has continued to expand in population, making Melrose one of the busiest suburbs of Boston. Though the city has been home to many notable residents, such as artist Frank Stella and geneticist Sewall Wright, there has only been one resident in Melrose's storied history who can make the claim that he had once been the classmate of a king.

In the winter of 1907, a dying pauper was brought into the hospital in Melrose, where he soon died from pneumonia. An effort was made to identify the body of the dirty and disheveled tramp, and a few days later a woman from Dorchester identified the hermit as Charles Frederick Powell, the mysterious cave-dweller known throughout the Mystic River valley as the "Hermit of Melrose." Powell had been taken to the hospital from his piggery, where the aged hermit was found dying among his herd of swine. Only after Powell's death would the remarkable story of his life be uncovered.

Until his death, Powell was regarded by the villagers as a cranky, old misanthrope who shunned the human race and preferred to surround himself with swine. The amazing secrets of his life were known to nobody but himself and, like most hermits, Powell vehemently refused to delve into his past. It was said that he especially loathed children, and whenever they approached his cave near Middlesex Fells (or, "The Fells," as the area is still known to the locals), he growled and contorted his features to such an extent that the children would run back to town in terror. Yet, if it hadn't been for a child, who discovered the dying hermit after hearing tortured groans from the cave, he would've died among the hogs.

No man was known better by sight to the residents of Melrose than the hermit, whose birth name was known only to the woman who later identified his corpse at the hospital. Every few months he would hobble into town in his filthy rags for the bare necessities of life, causing frightened children to rush indoors and curious villagers to peep out their windows at the odd recluse in their midst. Whenever he made a purchase at the general store, he would sign the bill with a simple "X," and thus his true identity remained a mystery for decades.

When the mystery of the wild man's identity was solved, a remarkable portrait of a remarkable man began to emerge. Charles Frederick Powell had been born in Plymouth, England, fifty-seven years earlier. As a young boy, he was surrounded with every possible luxury and comfort. His father sent him to Trinity College at Oxford, where Powell expressed an interest in music. He sang in the choir, and his solo performances were often attended by a fellow classmate who also loved choral music. This classmate would go on to become King Edward VII.

Powell was a bit of a prankster in his youth, and his mischievous streak and rebellious antics soon landed him in hot water with his professors. He was expelled from Oxford and he later enrolled in a German university. While he was away at school, his father married a second wife, and she didn't take much of a liking to Charles. When the youth returned home, he and his stepmother had a violent quarrel and Powell's father took the side of his new wife, which so enraged the son that he raised his fist to his father and struck a blow that knocked him out cold.

Charles never forgave himself for that act, and the disgraced, young man left home and boarded a ship to

America, where he tried his hand at various occupations before deciding to become a sign painter. He relocated to Massachusetts and lodged at the home of a Mrs. Lynd in Dorchester and, though he tried to act like a typical workman, Mrs. Lynd could tell that he was a well-educated man with superior intelligence. He could quote Plato and Virgil from memory, and in his room he kept books that were written in Greek, French, and Italian. Mrs. Lynd took a liking to the young man, and in the lonely of hours of night they would sit around the fireplace and discuss everything from politics to philosophy. Had Mrs. Lynd been unable to form a bond with Charles, the story of his life would have followed him to the grave.

Charles eventually quit his job as a sign painter and drifted to Canada. Due to his excellent education, he obtained work as a reporter for newspapers in Montreal and Toronto. For reasons known only to himself, he returned to Massachusetts and wandered the wilderness until he found a small cave near the granite cliffs of "The Fells." In this primitive shelter he remained until the day of his death, occupying his time by raising swine and writing poetry. Before his illness he confided to an old married couple from town that he had written a trunkful of poetry, which he later buried beneath a large rock on the Melrose-Malden line. After his death, a search was made for the hermit's buried poetry, but the trunk couldn't be found. All he had left behind were his pigs and books and two faded photographs, which were found in his pockets after he died. They were the portraits of his mother and sister. According to Mrs. Lynd, Charles had kept the photographs in his pockets ever since he arrived in America, never allowing them out of his possession.

VERMONT

11. Old Gold Toes

The second highest summit in the state of Vermont, Killington Peak rises to an elevation of 4,235 feet, looming majestically over the neighboring Green Mountain peaks like an ancient giant. Today, this mountain is home to

Killington Ski Resort. Known as the "Beast of the East," Killington features the largest vertical drop in New England. But a little more than a century ago, before scores of summer tourists and winter adventurers flocked to Killington, the region was vast wilderness, accessible only by a few rugged wagon trails and Indian paths. Around this time, at the dawn of the twentieth century, Killington Peak was the home of a curious hermit, known to the locals as "Old Gold Toes."

In 1903 a trapper and fisherman named Homer Weston was fishing for trout on one of the pristine streams on the eastern slope of the mountain when he discovered Old Gold Toes. This discovery was a newsworthy event; for while the aged hermit had been locally famous for decades, he had since disappeared from his haunts in the forests of the Green Mountains. Given up for dead, the hermit's existence was eventually forgotten, his legendary name relegated to fire-side tales told by the old-timers who had once stumbled across his grizzled countenance while hunting or hiking in the lush, emerald Vermont forests.

When Old Gold Toes was found by Homer Weston, the hermit was over eighty years old. Realizing that the hermit's time was growing short, Weston decided to spend two days with the peculiar fellow, determined to learn everything he could about the shaggy man who seemed to be as much a part of the local scenery as Killington Peak itself. This is what Homer Weston learned:

Old Gold Toes had been an unknown until the 1880s, when a severe drought impacted the region, resulting in the drying up of most of the mountain streams. Faced with the possibility of death by thirst, Gold Toes went to the Killington House spring for water. As to the origin of his name, Gold Toes had been a prospector for much of his life and, according to local legend, was supposed to have concealed gold dust in his shoes and nuggets between his toes. Once his shoes were filled with gold, he would hide them inside his cave, where he spent much of his time with his pet dogs and owls.

Like most prospectors, Gold Toes was understandably hesitant to reveal too much information about his hidden treasure to Homer Weston, and Weston had no desire to pry. He wasn't after the hermit's wealth; he was far more interested in his story. Once Weston had earned the aged prospector's trust, Gold Toes consented to show him the cave. The two men started up the mountain. Once the men reached the vicinity of the cave, the hermit made Weston swear upon three crossed hedgehog quills that he would never reveal the cave's location to another human being. Weston agreed.

Escorted by the prospector's dog, Gold Toes led the way through the dense timber to a remote part of the mountain rarely visited by hunters or fishermen. Here, the trails ceased and the vegetation grew so thick that it seemed to shut out the sun. It was rugged terrain for even the most physically fit outdoorsman, but the eighty-year-old hermit traversed the course with the ease of a ghost. The much younger Homer Weston, growing exhausted, had to stop and catch his breath on more than one occasion. After a brief rest, the dog led the way, and the two men followed and, after about thirty minutes of hiking, the trees began to disappear and were replaced by large lichen-crusted boulders. A little further on, the ground itself fell away between the sides of a treacherous ravine, forming one hundred-foot-tall cliffs on either side. The walls of the steep canyon narrowed and, much to Weston's surprise, Gold Toes explained that they must descend into the dangerous ravine and continue along the narrow passageway between the cliffs.

"The rocks were covered with running pine, and I could see by the way the moisture hung to them that the ravine extended north and south," Weston later explained, relating his spectacular story to the press. "The sun never struck the place except at noon, and it had an uncanny, moist smell. There was not a trace of a pathway, which was accounted for by the fact that the old man continually stepped on the rocks. I didn't notice this until I was cautioned to do the same.

"Finally we came to a narrow slit in the rocks that went off at right angles from the main passageway. A thin slab of shale, about four feet by five feet, leaned up against the main rock, and before this the hermit stopped. He then removed the slab, disclosing a narrow opening. Gold Toes got down on his hands and knees and, motioning me to follow, crawled in. The dog had already gone, and I heard him with half a dozen other animals growling and snarling somewhere down in the depths. How far we crawled I don't know, but it seemed about fifty rods. There were several turns and twice we passed through chambers of considerable size. The old man explained that these were his ante-rooms, and that the dogs guarded each while he was absent.

"We finally came to the main cave, which was about thirty feet in diameter and nearly round. It was carpeted with spruce needles, and the walls were hung with the skins of bears and minks. There was a couch in one corner made of sticks, skins, and moss, and hunting implements stood in the corners. A stove constructed out of several pieces of sheet iron and rocks held together by clay completed the furnishings.

"I was as hungry as a bear, and began to pull some hardtack and bacon out of my kit, when old Gold Toes laid his hand on my arm and smiled. He thought a minute for words that were rambling about in the back of his head and then said that as I was his guest he insisted on doing the providing. With that, he removed a rock in the side of the cave, disappeared into a recess, and brought out some flour, a partridge, and a little meal. The dogs all set up a united howl and circled around to be fed, but the old man kicked them into a corner and built a fire. He then cooked as dainty a meal as I have eaten in many a day.

"In all, I was at the place two days. We dined well. The old man showed me some excellent runways for deer and some trout brooks that I had never discovered. He showed me how he blocked the cave in winter and explained that he could keep as snug as a bug in a rug. I shall carry out my promise regarding the provisions, and shall keep the location of the cave a secret. The old man was well and seemed to love his solitary life."

Homer Weston remained true to his word and never revealed the precise location of the hermit's cave, which may contain, to this very day, several pairs of decaying, leather boots hidden away on some rocky shelf, brimming with gold that had once belonged to Old Gold Toes.

12. The Hermit of Hoot Owl Pond

In January of 1889 two hunters were following a trail of blood left by a wounded bear, when they passed by a tiny hut. It was a hut the two men had passed by countless times during their many years as hunting partners, and they knew the occupant well. What caught their attention on this particular winter afternoon was the pristine layer of snow, untrampled by the foot, on the ground in front of the door. The hunters' thoughts departed from the wounded bear and turned toward the occupant of the tiny shack, a kindly, old hermit named Pierre Grévy, better known in those parts as the "Hermit of Hoot Owl Pond."

Although the hunters, like every other hunter and woodsman in that part of Vermont, respected the hermit's preference for privacy, they feared that some terrible fate may have befallen old Pierre, and so they proceeded to break down the door. Inside, they found Pierre lying dead on the floor, sprawled across a bearskin rug. He had the appearance of having been dead for quite a while; his flesh had become purple, and the unmistakable odor of decay filled the stagnant air with its sickening smell. Very little had been known about the Hermit of Hoot Owl Pond, but all of that would change shortly after the discovery of his lifeless body. The information gleaned from old letters and papers found inside the dead hermit's hut painted a portrait of a remarkable man, and without the discovery of these old letters, the story of Pierre Grévy might still remain untold.

Pierre Grévy departed Quebec and arrived in the unspoiled wilderness of Vermont in September of 1832. He built himself a hut against a large outcropping of rock and settled into a life of seclusion. He was a fixture of the forest, and many hunters, who came to know the hermit as Old Man Grévy, frequently spotted Pierre on the pond fishing for trout, which served as his primary source of food. He never allowed a razor to touch his face, or scissors to touch his hair. His beard was his most notable feature, reaching well below his waist, and the hair on his head had grown to a length of nine feet by the time of his death. Hunters remarked that Pierre often wore his hair in a braid, which he wound around his neck and tied into a bow. Pierre also refused to cut his fingernails, and it was reported that his claw-like nails were nearly three inches in length.

Twice each year Pierre would stumble into the village and purchase enough tobacco to last him for six months, paying for his purchase with French silver coins. After the hermit's death, several of these old coins, minted during the reign of Napoleon Bonaparte, were found in a rusted, metal box inside of Pierre's cabin. An expensive signet ring was also found in the box, along with a silver pocket watch. The hermit's cabin, though crudely constructed, contained very little furniture, but the hermit had displayed three magnificent oil paintings on the wall: one of Napoleon, one of Josephine, and one of French military hero Marshal Ney.

The papers tucked inside the hermit's metal box revealed Pierre's true identity, but failed to describe the sad circumstances that had led him into the Vermont wilderness. A birth certificate was found, announcing that Pierre Grévy had been born in Marseilles, France, on January 24, 1779. A marriage certificate was also found, indicating that the hermit had married Marie Gauthier on September 21, 1802. A journal found in the hermit's cabin contained an entry that read: *Thank God, Jules Grévy is now President of the French Republic*! Based upon subsequent journal entries, it became clear to the local citizens that the shaggy old hermit with the long beard and claw-like fingernails was the uncle of the president of France.

13. Jeff Bryant

In a crooked shack erected years earlier in the yard behind the family home lived old Thomas Jefferson Bryant— eccentric hermit, hypnotist, inventor, and jack-of-all-trades. "Jeff," as he was known to the people of Richmond, preferred a primitive life, even though he lived in the shadows of his son's commodious home. Born in 1821, Jeff was one of the oldest residents of Richmond and had been the town's most colorful citizen for nearly nine decades, even when he occupied the handsome family home with his wife, who died a dozen years before Jeff took up the life of a recluse.

After his wife died, Jeff's son and his family moved into the home, where they could keep a watchful eye on the aged patriarch. They were thrifty and practical people, but were also well-educated and up to date on the current events of the early 1900s. This was too much for the old man, who believed that the world was heading to hell in the proverbial handbasket. He couldn't make much sense of the younger generation; the young women with Gibson Girl haircuts and wide-brimmed hats adorned with feathers, the men with their fancy short trousers and bowler hats and the music they referred to as "ragtime" all conspired to rub old Jeff the wrong way. When he overheard his son talking about such nonsense as electric lighting and indoor plumbing, Jeff decided he had had enough. He declared that unless they abandoned their wild ideas and conformed to his simple way of living, he would pack up his belongings and move out.

The Bryant clan had no desire to return to the nineteenth century, and they tried, in vain, to extol the virtues of modern technology. They told old Jeff about all the amazing things they had seen while traveling to the city; moving stairways that they called escalators, lights that glowed dazzling colors from a gas called neon, and a dirt-swallowing machine known as a vacuum cleaner. The Bryants may have been impressed by such things, but to old Jeff they sounded more like dangerous and bizarre monstrosities. Jeff promptly gathered up his personal effects and moved into his little wooden workshop in the backyard.

The dilapidated shack, which had never seen a coat of paint in its lifetime, may have made a luxurious home for a beagle or a bloodhound, but was less than ideal for human occupancy. There were no windows to open during the sweltering days of summer, and the shack offered no protection from the bitter Vermont winters. In spite of not having a stove or a fireplace, Jeff braved the sub-zero temperatures and, in time, even grew accustomed to the cold. The shanty was divided into two small rooms; one served as a kitchen and workshop, while the other was used as a bedroom.

Jeff's move to the shack in the backyard didn't exactly surprise his neighbors, as the old man's eccentricities had been the topic of local gossip for decades. In his early days, he had been very much like his son, impressed by gadgets and gizmos. He was labeled a genius, at least when it came to mechanical ability. Even those who shunned Jeff had to admit that he possessed marvelous ingenuity and might have been worth millions if only he had money enough to put some of his ideas into execution.

Half a century earlier, while boys from the towns of New England fought the rebels on the bloody battlefields of Dixie, Jeff could be seen whizzing around Richmond without a care in the world, riding a velocipede of his own design. The queer vehicle, constructed from three carriage wheels, drew stares of astonishment from the confounded locals. Jeff propelled his velocipede through the streets not with pedals, but by levers, which he operated by hand. Jeff's velocipede may have earned him nationwide fame if it hadn't been for a near-death experience, which so badly frightened its inventor that he gave up on his idea. After shooting down a steep hill, he narrowly avoided colliding with a speeding locomotive at the Jericho Road crossing of the Central Vermont Railroad.

For more than half a century Jeff also spent his time perfecting his surgical skills. As a self-taught veterinary surgeon, his success rate was so remarkable that no other veterinarians wanted to hang up a shingle in Richmond. After attending a few years of school as a child, Jeff abandoned formal education and became an apprentice to a blacksmith and wheelwright. Over the years he also learned the carpentry trade. He was a quick learner with a keen business sense, and just about every citizen of Richmond was a customer at one time or another, whether to have a calf delivered, a wagon repaired, or a pair of shoes cobbled.

While the old hermit appeared to be perfectly rational to the villagers, his habits became increasingly strange as he grew older. He claimed that he possessed more than a million dollars' worth of diamonds, which he had found in the mountains of Vermont. These gems, he said, were stored in more than sixty cigar boxes. Each box of stones was securely wrapped up, but Jeff would open a box on occasion to give some of the shiny pebbles to his closest friends. "I have a million dollars' worth of these stones," he once said, "and I am the only man in Vermont who knows where to find them. When I go to New York or Boston this year to sell them I will make a mint of money. I am the luckiest man in the state today, but I think that if others kept their eyes open they could find some." Jeff pointed to a nearby house. "See that farm over there? Well, my friend Hogan paid fifteen thousand dollars for the houses and land, and the very day he paid for it I found this stone worth fifty thousand dollars on the street in front of that place." He then pulled a few small pieces of quartz from his pocket and fawned over them as if they were the Crown Jewels of England.

Old Jeff was never happy unless his time was occupied. He spent the dull months of winter confined to his shanty, reading, writing, or mending shoes. When he grew tired of being indoors, he would hobble into town and find somebody to tell his stories to. He loved to engage in neighborhood gossip, although his mind tended to remember facts much more differently than the others. Then he would thank the person who made time to talk to him by reaching into the pocket of his threadbare trousers and bestowing upon the patient listener one of his precious "diamonds."

NEW JERSEY

14. The Hermit of Avalon
Avalon is a beachfront community on Cape May, dotted with sprawling estates and quaint cottages, which overlook

one of the finest beaches in the mid-Atlantic. In the late nineteenth century, Avalon was a playground for the rich and famous, who flocked to the luxury resorts on Seven Mile Island in order to frolic on the sands in diamonds and designer swimsuits. The barrier island upon which sits the community of Avalon was purchased in 1722 for the sum of $380. Today, it is the site of some of the most expensive real estate in America.

Back in those early days before the upper crust took over, the island was home to a colony of peculiar people. The story of that colony has been handed down from generation to generation, and it is a rather interesting one.

In the spring of 1792 a man of unusual appearance arrived on the island. His hair was long and tangled, a shaggy beard covered his breast, and he was wearing little more than threadbare rags. He looked like a seafarer, due to his craggy features and weather-beaten face, but he refused to speak to anyone who asked him about his identity and intentions.

The island was uninhabited at this time, but it was visited frequently by fishermen, who dragged their nets along the shore and harvested turtle eggs from the sand. The eastern shore was covered with a sparse growth of stunted pines, and in this pitiable grove the stranger constructed a crude, wooden house from the driftwood and wreckage that had washed upon the shore. The man had a tiny boat, a handful of tools, and some bare necessities, and, as he appeared to be of a peaceful disposition, he was seldom bothered by the fishermen or adventurers who visited the island.

Before long, word of the stranger's existence had spread to the mainland, resulting in a great deal of gossip. The prevailing theory was that the man had jumped from a passing ship for some reason known only to himself and, hoping to avoid capture, made his home on the deserted spit of land. The fact that he refused to speak only added credence to this theory. The mainlanders dubbed him the "Hermit of Avalon," and by that title he was known throughout the remainder of his life. The hermit was renowned as an expert fisherman who was also skilled in finding turtle eggs, which he carried to the mainland and sold to the markets. All of these business transactions were carried out in writing. The merchants were impressed by the hermit's handwriting, which was remarkably clear and signified that the hermit was a man of exceptional intelligence and education.

One day, in the fall of 1797, the hermit made an appearance at one of the village markets. He appeared highly excited and motioned for the proprietor to give him a sheet of paper. Eagerly taking the paper, he proceeded to write:

Death and destruction in the wind! Let no man venture upon the water tomorrow. The spirits say that danger is at hand.

The storekeeper, looking over the message, thought the hermit had lost his marbles. But to satisfy the warning's author, he pinned the note to the wall so that other customers would be able to see it. This seemed to placate the excited hermit, who then left the mainland and returned to his shack on the island. Customers came and viewed the warning but they, too, thought the hermit must be crazy. Someone suggested rowing to the island and taking custody of the hermit, fearful that he may devolve into a state of complete lunacy, but the mainlanders eventually decided that, as long as the hermit didn't pose any immediate danger to himself or others, they would let him be.

The following morning, fishermen went about their business as usual, ignoring the hermit's warning. For it was a splendid morning, without the slightest hint of unpleasant weather. However, around noon the sky grew dark and ominous. The wind blew in salty, angry gusts, and in a matter of moments a terrible storm fell over the coast. Many of the fishermen, caught between the storm and the mainland, were unable to return home. All day long they were forced to wait out the storm from their positions miles away from shore in the calm and open sea. Meanwhile, the storm grew in size and intensity, punishing earth and sea alike with sheets of rain and sleet. Of all the fishermen who went to sea that day, only a handful returned. More than thirty men were lost.

About a year after the terrible storm, the hermit again ventured to the village store, where he overheard a conversation between two villagers who were discussing the case of a seriously ill man. One of them, a doctor, feared that the sick man would not last through the week; he had been stricken with a strange malady and was bound to waste away before the illness could be identified. The hermit visited the sick man the following day. As he entered the room, the patient groaned in agony, and an attempt was made to get the hermit out of the house. The hermit wrestled his way to the patient's bedside, threw back the covers, and began to knead the man's stomach with his hands. The friends of the sick man tried to drag the hermit away, but he refused to relinquish his grip on the invalid's hand. To everyone's astonishment, the sick man begged his friends to let the hermit stay. All night long the hermit massaged the sick man's stomach and the next morning the patient sat up for the first time in days. A few days later, the man was back to his usual routine; all symptoms of his affliction had vanished.

Word of the mysterious hermit's healing powers spread like wildfire. Before long, dozens of families from the mainland relocated to the island. The wealthiest among them offered to build the hermit a palatial home, but the hermit declined. He continued to heal the sick, asking nothing in return. Every few weeks, the hermit would fall into a deep sleep, which lasted for days, and it was said that he gained his healing powers during these times from spirit guides.

For ten years the residents of this colony lived on the island, near the hut of the healing hermit. They treated him with maniacal devotion, and his legend spread far and wide. Sick people from all over the country made the pilgrimage to Avalon, in the hopes that they would be healed by the hermit's touch. In all this time the man was never heard to speak a word.

In 1808 the hermit fell into one of his protracted sleeps and did not awake. The residents of the island refused to bury him until they were certain he was dead. His body was eventually carried to the summit of a small hill on the center of the island and buried, and a huge pile of stones placed over his grave. The colony remained on the island for several more years, until all of the native timber had been cleared away. This proved disastrous for the colony, since the trees acted as a windbreaker. The winds blew sand across the narrow island, and the drifts smothered the colonist's gardens which, in turn, depleted their supply of food. One by one the villagers left Avalon, leaving their homes to ruin. Sand eventually covered every remnant of the colony, and Mother Nature eventually reclaimed what was hers.

15. The Tramp of West Hoboken

Union City, in Hudson County, New Jersey, is known as "the embroidery capital of the United States" because of the city's importance in lace manufacturing. Although it is a city with nearly 70,000 inhabitants, Union City didn't appear on maps until 1925. Before that time, much of the land upon which the present-day city sits was known as West Hoboken. From the rocky cliffs known as the Palisades, where the old trolley road made its wide, sweeping horseshoe curve, one could look across the Hudson and behold the thriving metropolis of Manhattan. Near these cliffs, in the closing years of the nineteenth century, was a shallow cave where a hermit once lived. Forgotten by the world, the only surviving records that prove this man existed are faded and timeworn newspaper articles from the 1890s.

The checkered and mysterious life of this hermit, a German immigrant, may be completely unknown if not for his discovery in the summer of 1896 when he was approached by police officers. The policemen from the West Hoboken station visited these cliffs regularly, since the area was a haven for ruffians, fugitives from the law, and an assortment of other tough and unsavory characters. In September, during a routine patrol of the area, two plainclothes policemen named McCartney and Suhr discovered the hermit's cave.

The officers were exploring the cliffs at the foot of Fulton Street, where they had nabbed a group of pickpockets the day before. McCartney's attention was attracted by a pile of bones lying on the rocks. He approached the bones and spotted the remains of a cat hanging from a bush. Intrigued, the officers clambered down the rocks and discovered the mouth of a tiny cave. Inside the cave sat a man smoking a pipe. The officers took one look at the hermit and, holding their noses, retreated. The stench from the cave was overpowering.

"Come out of there," demanded one of the officers. "We want to talk to you."

When no answer came, the officers took a deep breath and ventured into the cave. Sitting cross-legged on the floor was the most unusual man they had ever seen. He was large and powerfully built and looked to be around forty years of age, though it was impossible to tell because of the dirt that encrusted his features. His beard and hair were indescribably dirty and matted; his clothing consisted of ragged trousers and a threadbare army overcoat. "What are you doing in here?" asked McCartney. "You'll have to give an account of yourself," explained Officer Suhr. "You've got no right here." With a thick German accent, the hermit declared that he had as much right to the cave as anyone. The officers, nauseous from the stench, told the hermit to be out of the cave by the following day. "You take me and I'll show you what I did to them in California!" threatened the hermit.

The following day the two officers returned with Sergeant Usher and a patrol wagon, and the hermit, failing to make good on his cryptic promise, went without a struggle. The wagon carried the hermit to the station house for questioning, but the mysterious German refused to answer questions. But the officers were relentless; after hours of interrogation, the hermit began to open up. He admitted that his name was Paul Carl Seidel and that he was from San Francisco, where he had worked as a barber.

"Why did you leave California?" asked the detective. The foul-smelling stranger once again grew silent and refused to answer any more questions. After a long discussion with each other, the officers came to the conclusion that the only offense they could charge Seidel with was vagrancy. He did his thirty-day stint in the county jail and then returned to his life as a tramp, abandoning his cave and wandering into the unknown.

What circumstances had brought the barber to West Hoboken? Had he really murdered someone in San Francisco as he had hinted? Or were these merely the incoherent ramblings of a delusional vagabond? Nobody knows, and the world no longer cares. Thus, it is unlikely the mystery of Paul Carl Seidel will ever be unraveled.

16. Kneeling Francis

The history of Nutley stretches back to 1693 when a Dutch painter by the name of Bastian Van Giesen settled in the region. At the time, the land was a rough patch of uncultivated woodlands, but, before long, a handsome village sprung forth from the wilderness. By the close of the eighteenth century, Nutley was the location of a brownstone quarry, which provided jobs to Irish and Italian immigrants who settled in the area. Numerous mills were built along the Third River, shops were opened, and Nutley quietly came into existence.

The growth of Nutley was slow and sporadic; by 1920, the entire population of the township numbered well under ten thousand, with most of the citizens residing in the hamlets of Avondale, Belleville, and Franklinville. While the nearby city of Newark grew into a transportation and manufacturing center, Nutley remained a menagerie of quaint and rural villages. Because Nutley had managed to escape from development, much of the woodland surrounding the town remained intact. It was in this undeveloped patch of wilderness where a hermit known as "Kneeling Francis" once lived.

When Francis arrived in Nutley in the 1870s, no one knew from where he had come. His accent led many to believe that he had emigrated from Belgium, and since he knew Latin, it was supposed that he had once been trained for the priesthood. Francis was frequently seen in the village of Belleville, where he regularly attended services at

St. Peter's church. After the church of St. Mary's was built in Avondale, Francis began attending services there. Every Sunday, rain or shine, the hermit could be found kneeling reverently in the back of the church, close to the door.

Many of the congregation in Avondale raised an objection to Francis's attendance, on account of the hermit's unkempt appearance. While others worshipped in their Sunday best, Francis knelt in dirty rags. The priest, bowing to the objections of the parishioners, told Francis that he was no longer welcome at St. Mary's. From that point forward, whenever the church bells would ring on Sunday mornings, old Francis could be found at the edge of the woods, kneeling on the hard ground and praying in silence.

The hermit aroused much curiosity among the villagers, and his life story was the topic of much gossip and speculation. People attempted to ask him about his past, but the old hermit refused to answer any questions. Some wondered if he had fled into the wilderness because of some horrendous crime he had committed; that would certainly help explain his mournful expression and constant state of penitence. For everywhere the old hermit went, he carried with him a crucifix, with one of its arms broken off. Some wondered if perhaps he might be the legendary "Wandering Jew," said to have taunted Jesus on the way to the Crucifixion and thus had been cursed to wander the Earth until the Second Coming.

Someone in the neighboring village of Belleville, who knew of Francis before he took up the life of a recluse, finally told the story of the old man's sad life and put the rumors and gossip to rest. Thirty years earlier, Francis had been engaged to a beautiful girl from Belleville. The wedding date had been set, and it was to be a splendid ceremony. Sadly, on the day of the wedding, tragedy struck. His beloved bride, while standing at the altar, collapsed and could not be revived. The wedding turned into a funeral, and the bride was laid to rest in her flowing, white bridal gown.

After the funeral, Francis decided to leave Belleville because everything there reminded him of the girl he loved.

Not having any other place to go, Francis roamed the forests and countryside until he arrived in Avondale, where he found a small hut in the woods. The hut had been abandoned for several years and was built for a wealthy socialite from New York who had been stricken with consumption. The socialite's physician believed that the fresh, country air would improve her condition, but the wealthy socialite refused to live in such a humble abode. Francis arrived at the hut with nothing more than the clothes on his back and a one-armed crucifix, which served as an eternal reminder of his lost love. Wherever he roamed he carried the broken cross, and he lived his life in a state of constant prayer and penance, hoping that one day he would be forgiven for whatever sin he had committed that resulted in the death of his bride.

Adding insult to injury, Francis's hut was later burned to the ground by a group of mean-spirited boys who disliked the strange inhabitant of the Nutley woodlands. Undeterred, Francis resumed his wanderings and found a cave in the woods near Belleville, where he lived until his death.

17. The Killer Mosquitoes of the Hackensack

When the first Dutch settlers arrived in the Meadowlands in the seventeenth century, it was not the arrows of the Lenape they feared most, nor the fangs of the venomous water moccasin. It was the monstrous, savage, blood-thirsty mosquitoes. For hundreds of years people have known that Jersey mosquitoes were menacing, but it wasn't until 1908 that they were reported as having beaks that were long enough to run a man through from his breastbone to his backbone. At least that's the story an eccentric old hermit told Judge Kelly after appearing in his court room dressed in a woman's corset.

Robert O'Brien, who was originally from Rhode Island, had been dwelling inside a small cave on the banks of the Hackensack, directly across the river from the Snake Hill penitentiary, when he was arrested by an officer named Cuthbert and charged with disorderly conduct. According to Patrolman Cuthbert, his wife and children had been walking along the meadows in the vicinity of the hermit's cave when O'Brien popped out of his hole and frightened Mrs. Cuthbert's children half to death by growling like a wild man and jumping up and down. Patrolman Cuthbert went out to look for the hermit with another officer, and the two men eventually apprehended O'Brien after a furious wrestling match.

O'Brien was arraigned before Judge Kelly, but the magistrate was more concerned about the hermit's costume than the charge of disorderly conduct. The hermit with the dirty and tangled hair and gray, bushy beard arrived for his hearing wearing a woman's corset. The magistrate demanded to know why the defendant was dressed in feminine garments, unaware that he was about to receive a bizarre lecture on entomology.

"It's to keep off mosquitoes, Judge," explained the hermit. "Unless I wore something of the sort, they'd take my heart's blood. They're terrible in the meadows. I've seen 'em big as broilers, and when they get through making a meal off a man, they're fat as squabs. What's more, they've got *sense*. They're not like those low-browed, Staten Island mosquitoes. We think we have pretty sporty skeeters in Little Rhody, but alongside these Jersey fellows they're pikers."

Judge Kelly, amused by the girdled wild man, allowed O'Brien to continue his tirade. "You know the difference between a rattlesnake and a moccasin, don't you?" asked the hermit. "Prod a rattler with a stick and he'll strike at the stick. Do the same to a water moccasin and he'll strike at your hand. That's the difference between ordinary skeeters and the Jersey kind. Common mosquitoes bite the first part of a man that comes handy, but the Jersey skeeter strikes for the heart.

"The Jersey skeeter seems to know blood fresh from the heart is the best, and that to get it good and strong he has to pierce the arteries in the cardiac region. I found that out by living in the swamps. Lucky thing for me I ran across this old corset. If I hadn't, those Jersey skeeters would have stabbed me to the heart in the first week after I moved into the cave."

Although the judge reminded the hermit that only the female of the species sucks blood, and that no mosquito known to man has a proboscis strong enough to pierce the breastbone, old Robert O'Brien held strong to his beliefs. The hermit's little lecture on natural history may have elicited a smirk from the judge, but it didn't save him from commitment to the county jail. The hermit couldn't defend himself against the charge of scaring the Cuthbert children and engaging in a donnybrook with Patrolman Cuthbert and another officer. The hermit was stripped of his corset and taken to jail, where he cooled his heels for a few weeks before returning to his life of seclusion in the marshlands along the Hackensack River.

CONNECTICUT

18. The Highwire Hermit

Even those who are only mildly acquainted with the circus may have heard of Charles Blondin, considered by many to be the greatest tightrope walker of all time. After crossing Niagara Falls on a high-wire in 1859, the French-born Blondin became one of the most famous celebrities in America. His name was so well-known throughout the United States that Abraham Lincoln, prior to the 1864 presidential election, made a speech in which he compared himself to Blondin on the tightrope.

Jean François Gravelet (who used the stage name Blondin in deference to the color of his hair) was born in the French town of Saint-Omer in 1824 and began training as an acrobat at the age of five. Blondin was such a prodigious talent that he made his performing debut after only six months of training at the École de Gymnase in Lyon. Blondin soon became dubbed "The Boy Wonder." He arrived in America in 1855 for an engagement at the famed Niblo's Garden theatre on Broadway. It was around this time when Blondin began to toy with the idea of crossing the gorge at Niagara. After his first crossing in 1859, Blondin repeated the feat several more times, with many different variations; he crossed the falls blindfolded, he crossed the falls while pushing a wheelbarrow, and he even crossed the falls on stilts. During one of his Niagara crossings, Blondin prepared a meal on a portable stove while walking the tightrope and then served it to the guests aboard the Maid of the Mist by lowering it down with a rope. Charles Blondin was, without a doubt, the most famous entertainer in America during the Civil War era, and arguably the most famous circus performer who ever lived.

Shortly after Blondin first arrived in New York, he met and married his wife, Charlotte. The Blondins had three children: Adele, Edward, and Isis. They bought a house in the town of Niagara. The tightrope prodigy was also becoming equally as famous in Britain during this time; he made his first London appearance in 1861 at the legendary Crystal Palace, where he dazzled onlookers by crossing the high-wire while performing somersaults on stilts. From London he went on to Scotland and then to Ireland, where he suffered a temporary setback. Blondin's rope snapped during a performance at Dublin's Royal Portobello Gardens, and although he was not injured by the fifty-foot fall, the collapse of the scaffolding resulted in the loss of two lives. As if to laugh in the face of disaster and tempt the hand of fate, he returned to the very same venue the following year and repeated his routine, but increased the height of the tightrope to one hundred feet.

Blondin contemplated retirement a few times over the course of the following decade, but even when he wasn't performing, he enjoyed worldwide popularity. After a few years of life outside of the "sawdust circle," he staged a short-lived comeback in 1880 and performed for a while on Staten Island. Charlotte died in 1888, and the tightrope walker married a woman named Katherine, who bore him no children. However, it has been claimed by many experts and circus historians that Blondin may have fathered several illegitimate children.

The Great Blondin's final performance was given in Belfast, Ireland, in 1896. He was sixty-eight at the time of his last tightrope walk. Charles Blondin died at the age of seventy-three at his home in London in February 1897 from complications related to diabetes and was buried at the Kensal Green Cemetery.

Or was he?

In September of 1907 a veteran circus manager named Abe Totten was visiting Cheshire, Connecticut, where he encountered a man going by the name of Michael Todd. Todd was a hermit carpenter who lived west of town who earned his living by performing odd jobs around Cheshire, and Totten immediately recognized him as the tightrope legend who had supposedly died ten years earlier in England.

"Ah, yes, I know they think me dead," explained the hermit, "and perhaps I had better be dead." The disheveled old hermit continued to tell his story to Totten: "I made money fast and spent it faster in the maddening pleasure of life, and I certainly have felt the need and the value of money since. My oldest son knows where I am. He is with Whitney's Circus in the west."

Those who knew Abe Totten also knew that, like P. T. Barnum, he was a showman with a penchant for exaggeration. Did Charles Blondin really die in 1897? Or did the greatest tightrope walker in history also manage to pull off one of the greatest disappearing acts of all time?

NEW HAMPSHIRE

19. English Jack

Near Crawford Notch, one of the most famous landmarks in New Hampshire, lies Mount Willard, which provides thousands of tourists each year with breathtaking views of the White Mountains. The summit of Mount Willard is accessible by a hiking trail, serving as a pathway to the peak since the eighteenth century, when the first European settlers arrived in Carroll County. After a sharp climb over the rough and rocky landscape, the trail leads to a little clearing that looks like a shelf set into the mountainside. In the latter half of the nineteenth century, those who arrived at this tiny clearing would have encountered a crude hut surrounded by a small but well-tended vegetable garden of potatoes, corn, and cabbage. Here, amid the somber firs and beeches, lived a hermit known as English Jack.

Jack's cabin had three rooms, the first of which contained pens of pigeons and cages filled with a menagerie of woodland creatures. The room also contained a large amount of pet snakes, which English Jack would allow to crawl all over him and wind themselves around his neck and limbs as a form of entertainment to his visitors, of which there were many. The adjoining room, which was used as a kitchen and pantry, held a goodly supply of homemade root beer, which brought the hermit nearly as much local fame as his snake handling. The third room, off limits to all but his dearest of friends, featured walls adorned with photographs sent to him by admirers and well-wishers. This room also served as Jack's armory, housing a well-used shotgun, some odd-looking Spanish pistols, and several menacing knives.

English Jack, being a rather colorful character, became something of a tourist attraction during his many years on the mountain. He presented an odd appearance; his unkempt hair and beard, whitened by age, cascaded over his torso in a matted mass, and his nondescript apparel garnered curious stares from his visitors, many of whom stopped by on their way to the summit of Mount Willard to hear the old hermit tell stories of his Robinson Crusoe life.

English Jack, born John Alfred Vials in 1827 and orphaned at the age of twelve, had lived an adventurous and eventful life. As a young man he answered the call of the sea, and for twenty-four years sailed the world, a soldier of fortune, under the flags of many different governments. He was shipwrecked five times during his career, and once spent two years living on an uninhabited island where he survived on a diet of snakes and frogs. If any of his visitors doubted the veracity of this claim, English Jack would respond by grabbing a lively frog from his collection and swallowing it whole.

While in China, in the service of the British Royal Navy, he was shot through the arm. During the Crimean War he was in the Army Transport Service, becoming friends with Colin Campbell, the brave military commander who later became the commander-in-chief of India. English Jack fought under Campbell during the

English Jack, "The Hermit of Crawford Notch."

Indian Rebellion of 1857 and was among the eight hundred recruits aboard ship during the Sepoy Mutiny, which killed 150 British soldiers. Jack was present at the taking of Delhi and assisted in capturing Bahadur Shah Zafar, the last Mughal emperor. During the Siege of Delhi, English Jack received two gun-shot wounds in the side and a bayonet wound in the face.

The hermit's romantic life was every bit as remarkable as his military career. He met his one true love when he was a homeless youth on the streets of London. He encountered a little girl who was lost and had wandered the streets of the great city until she collapsed from exhaustion. The orphan revived the girl, asked her where she lived, and, with great difficulty, carried her all the way home. The girl's father, Bill Simmonds, took a liking to the boy and took Jack to sea with him. The romance between Jack and Mary Simmonds endured for years, and at last a wedding day was fixed. Jack returned from one of his voyages with an exquisite wedding gown, only to find that his betrothed had died while he was at sea. He never loved another woman after her. This event is what inspired Jack to leave his native land and come to America, where he lived the life of a hermit on the side of Mount Willard for over thirty years. Though he entertained numerous visitors, he preferred the company of his pets, which included a pig, a lamb, a dog, and deer—all of which he taught to enjoy his famous root beer. It was said that English Jack had, on several occasions, searched for and found lost hunters and hikers in the mountains, and that his services as a guide could always be commanded by anyone who sought his help.

During the final years of his life, the old and frail hermit spent the winter months living with the McGee and Fahey families in Twin Mountain. When winter passed and it was time to return to his ramshackle hut, Jack would take the new clothes that he had been given and poke holes in them and rub them in dirt in order to make them look worn and tattered so that the visitors to his shack wouldn't be disappointed. He passed away in April of 1912 while staying with the McGee family. John "English Jack" Vials was so well-loved by the citizens of Carroll County that they set up a fund for the upkeep of his cemetery plot at Straw Cemetery, which still attracts visitors from all over the Granite State.

MAINE

20. Edward Young: The Socialist Hermit

In the lush forests of northern Maine, inside of a wooden shanty built and abandoned by lumber men, lived a man by the name of Edward Young. Years earlier, Young had been a school teacher in New York City. The circumstances that induced Edward to abandon the comforts and conveniences of city life and take up residence in the lonesome Maine wilderness, miles away from the nearest neighbor, would be peculiar to the average man, but not to other hermits.

In the 1870s the teacher became the subject of much gossip in his New York neighborhood when he abruptly resigned his position and disappeared like a thief in the night, without leaving behind any indication of his future plans. Twenty-five years later, a writer found himself vacationing near Moosehead Lake, tucked among the Longfellow Mountains, when he and a friend stumbled across the hermit and, after spending several days with Edward Young, learned of his unusual story.

When the visitor met Young, the hermit was over seventy years of age but still vibrant and hearty, often walking up to thirty miles in a day in order to obtain the bare necessities of his monastic existence. But the hermit's acquaintance had been made under circumstances that were a little bit trying. The writer and his friend had gotten off the Bangor and Piscataquis Railroad train at the Katahdin Iron Works, which was a small settlement scattered about the furnaces. Anxious to find lodging for the night, the two men knocked upon door after door in a seemingly futile search for a place to rest their heads. Finally, they came to a backwoodsman, who remarked that they ought to try lodging with the old hermit. If the two visitors followed the old logging trail, they were told, they would be sure to find the shack belonging to Edward Young. The only problem was that the hermit's shack was dozens of miles away.

Since there would be no train out of the village for two days, the two men decided that they had no other alternative than to make the journey to the hermitage. The pair had only gone a short distance when they encountered Edward Young, who was making his way into the village. As he had walked the great distance from his shack, the hermit was more than a little tired and told the men that he did not intend to return home for a couple of days.

The two visitors looked at each other dejectedly, aware that the hermit's shack was the only place where they might find lodging. As they prepared to resign themselves to a night of sleeping on the muddy streets, the hermit offered his humble abode to the travelers. "He assured us that there was plenty to eat at his place, and no end of comfortable bunks to sleep in," the writer later remarked. "Then he set us a bit on the road, which, by the way, was a trail very faint in its outlines."

A curious thing happened later that night, which caused the travelers a bit of alarm. It was some time after midnight when the two men reached a point in the woods where all the lake and the surrounding trees began to glow an otherworldly shade of white. The two men decided to build a fire and rest for the night, but were aroused a few hours later by savage cries and howls. The men looked across the lake and saw a line of lights that moved in a straight line, shadowy and spectral, and disappeared into the dark forest. As the lights disappeared, the savage howls turned to ghostly laughter. The startled men abandoned their plan to sleep and high-tailed it down the path until they finally reached the hermit's cabin the following morning.

When the hermit arrived home later in the day, the visitors described the harrowing scene of the previous evening. Young explained what the men had witnessed. He told the visitors that they had passed through a portion of the forest known as the White Wilderness. The cries they had heard were made by the loons, and the lights were the result of will-o'-the-wisps. Also known as "foolish fire," these ghost lights are often seen in marshy and swampy areas. Today, these lights are written off as "swamp gas."

The hermit, noticing his empty bean pot, excused himself, explaining that he had to step out to his garden in order to gather more. Four hours later, Young reappeared, much to the surprise of his guests, and apologized for the delay. As the visitors later discovered, the hermit's garden was located six miles away from the cabin. The hermit presented a striking appearance as he prepared a dinner of brook trout and green beans for his guests, one of whom later wrote, "Nearly six feet in height the old man, inured to all kinds of hardships by his out-of-door life, is a perfect picture of health. In appearance he is just what any one would desire or expect a hermit of the regulation sort to be. His hair is long, and his matted whiskers almost cover his bronzed face and reach to his waist. He says himself that the clothes he wears have served him for over twenty years. Perhaps they have. It would be hard to tell what their original color was. He has absolutely no wants that the rest of humanity is called upon to fill, and for all he cares the rest of the world may go to smash just as soon as it likes, which, he predicts, will be before long."

The hermit's home, a relic of the old lumber camps of Maine, was described as being a roomy structure with six bunks stacked atop each other at one end of the room. The door to the cabin bore a number of deep scratches, which the hermit said had been made over the years by wolves and bears seeking shelter for the night. Young, who despised firearms, had a "live and let live" philosophy, and wished the critters no harm. The hermit had not a stick of furniture, and his possessions were limited to a frying pan, in which he cooked his fish, and a few jars, which he used to store vegetables. Young didn't even own blankets or pillows for his bed. "His cabin is surrounded by dense woods," wrote one of the visitors, "and two or three hundred yards off is a stream which supplies him with fish and water. Fish, with the beans from his garden, form his only diet. He drinks no coffee, tea, or spirits."

The two visitors wondered why a man living in a region noted for its abundance of game should limit himself to such a diet. The hermit explained that he had a horror of taking the life of anything with fur or feathers, and believed that they had as much right to live in peace as man. However, Young insisted that fish were lower and "less-evolved" creatures, and, thus, he saw no harm in eating them. This conversation about food led to the exposition of the shaggy hermit's philosophy, which finally explained why Edward Young had run away from civilization nearly thirty years earlier.

Young had a well-defined notion that civilization was a failure of the worst kind. He then produced a worn copy of Wordsworth's poems, from which he recited:

> Oh! what a joy it were, in vigorous health,
> To have a body (this our vital frame
> With shrinking sensibility endued,
> And all the nice regards of flesh and blood)
> And to the elements surrender it
> As if it were a spirit!—How divine,
> The liberty, for frail, for mortal, man
> To roam at large among unpeopled glens
> And mountainous retirements, only trod
> By devious footsteps; regions consecrate
> To oldest time!

"This is the only book I possess," said the hermit, "and it is quite enough for me." He got nearer to nature than any of those court poets and society rhymers who never breathed the free air of the forest.

"How did I come to make my home here? Well, that is a strange story, and I doubt if many people would understand it even if I should try to tell it. I told you I was a teacher in Grammar School No. 1. Most of the scholars were the children of the very poor, those who lived in the Five Points and similar localities of old lower New York. The misery I was compelled to witness daily oppressed me sadly. About this time I began to read works on socialism and became a convert to its doctrines. There is nothing new about socialism, although the rich and powerful say it is a new and dangerous doctrine. Well, I grew unpopular with my superiors and was forced to resign.

"A year, or perhaps two, before this I became interested in a work of Thoreau's. It was called, I think, 'The Maine Woods.' He had made a canoe excursion in this very neighborhood a little before that time and described the locality. I forgot to say that all the money I had saved was lost in the suspension of the savings bank in which it was deposited. I came to Bangor and just walked on until I came to this place. It suited me and I remained. Since then I have never been farther than the iron works at Katahdin, and I don't expect I ever shall."

Fascinated by the socialist hermit, the two men remained for several more days. They admired his rugged simplicity and the primitive, unfrivolous manner in which he lived. He demonstrated to the visitors how he caught fish, how to plant beans, and a variety of other chores. Although the visitors were impressed by Edward Young, it came time for them to return to the city. As the men prepared for their departure, the hermit explained that there was a second cabin abandoned by the lumbermen a short distance from his own, and he offered to sell this cabin to the men for five dollars. "Think it over," said the hermit, "and when you get sick of the world you will have a place to come to. The offer remains open."

PART II
HERMITS OF THE SOUTH

GEORGIA

21. Wild Man of the Chattahoochee

For over 430 miles the Chattahoochee River meanders through Georgia and Alabama before joining with the Apalachicola and flowing lazily to the Gulf of Mexico. The Chattahoochee is a fabled river and the source of many legends inspired by its importance in American history. The river was of immeasurable importance to Native tribes, such as the Muscogee and the Cherokee, and was of prime strategic importance to General Sherman during the Civil War, as the land along the river had been heavily fortified by the Confederacy.

Fifty years after Sherman led his troops into Atlanta, the banks of the Chattahoochee was the home of a peculiar hermit who lived in Heard County, near the Georgia-Alabama border. In August of 1917 this strange fellow was captured by Sheriff Taylor and turned over to federal authorities. Though he was harmless and innocent of any wrongdoing, the authorities were intrigued by the wild, hairy creature, and they took it upon themselves to discover all they could about the man's past. They were to be very disappointed.

The hermit was a tiny man with a back bent by time, who needed a cane to get around. His face was covered with hair, shaggy and matted, giving him the appearance of a strange half-human beast. Sheriff Taylor attempted to speak to the hermit, but the hermit evidently didn't speak a lick of English. Communication was impossible; the sheriff didn't know any other languages, and the odd language spoken by the hermit was not understood by anyone in town. Not knowing what to do with his "prisoner," the sheriff decided to hand him over to federal agents in Atlanta.

In Atlanta, the hermit aroused much curiosity. The best linguists in the city were called upon in order to communicate with the odd fellow, but to no avail. The authorities even summoned Dr. F. E. May, the French consul, who was a highly-educated diplomat fluent in dozens of different languages. After many hours of interrogation, Dr. May threw up his hands in frustration. "He understands nothing I speak; he speaks nothing I understand," lamented the diplomat.

The federal authorities couldn't hold him, since the hermit had done nothing wrong, so they gave him back to Sheriff Taylor, who remarked, "The government doesn't want him. I don't want him, and he won't run rabbits, so what am I going to do with him?" The old hermit was taken to a poor house, where he lived out the remainder of his life before being buried in an unmarked grave in a potter's field. Since no one was able to understand his peculiar language, the identity of the tiny hermit with the wooden cane remains a mystery.

22. An Inventive Hermit

From the cradle to the grave, Charles Howard lived in the Okefenokee Swamp of southern Georgia. For the better part of his eighty-two years, until his death in 1900, Charles lived alone in a small, log hut. He was a pauper, dependent on the county for support during his final thirty years, but always believed that his ship would come in one day—once he finally got around to solving the problem of perpetual motion.

In this secluded existence he spent countless hours of his life obsessed with solving this problem, employing an old spinning wheel as a machine and two large swamp rats as a power source. Charles fastened his rats to the rim of the wooden wheel to prevent their escape, and he kept the wheel spinning at a rapid speed night and day. Once the wheel was set in motion, the rats would continue to run on the rim until they expired from sheer exhaustion. So intent was the old hermit on solving the problem that he hardly ever diverted his eyes from the wheel. He would awake from his slumber several times each night to make sure that the rats remained running and the wheel remained spinning.

The major obstacle that stood in the way of the hermit's pursuit of scientific immortality was the biological mortality of his furry, little workers. Charles found that the life of the rats did not exceed a week after he put them to work on his wheel. When one team of rats expired, another pair was put into harnesses and tethered to the spinning wheel. Charles realized that if he wanted the wheel to spin indefinitely, he would need a constant supply of varmints. The old man spent many a day out on the swamp wrangling up volunteers, hunting for the rats in the ruins and foundations of ancient cabins and hunting camps, and often returning to his hut with a burlap sack filled with a dozen or more critters. He experimented with various species of rodents, but found that muskrats tended to stink up his humble abode and the giant, swamp-dwelling nutria, brought from Argentina by enterprising fur breeders in the nineteenth century, tended to be somewhat lazy and unmotivated. Beavers were just plain mean, deer mice were wimpy, and weasels just didn't seem very trustworthy, so old Charles settled upon the humble *Rattus norvegicus*, the brown rat, which famously inhabits the wharves and sewers of New York and were abundant throughout the blackwater wetlands of the Okefenokee. Charles once estimated that his perpetual-motion machine consumed over one hundred rats per year.

Although Charles preferred to avoid unnecessary interaction with his fellow man, every once in a while a hunter or fisherman would spot the old hermit gathering up rats and feel compelled to ask the strange fellow what he was planning to do with his quarry, and the hermit never hesitated to elaborate on his plan to solve the age-old mystery of perpetual motion. When asked why he decided to undertake such a project, the hermit once replied, "I hain't a losin' er gainin' up nuthin' by passin' off the time with my wheel an' rats, an' if I hit on per-pet-chee-yule motion yit hit ain't ner wuss'n a lot of yer edicated folks is done in ther way an' failed. Hit's mighty purty a seein' my rats a chasin' one anudder on my spinnin' wheel, an' I thinks as how I'll git a way to feed 'em after awhile so as ter keep 'em a runnin' durin' their natcherl lives. Then I'd be nearer to per-pet-chee-yule motion than some people what knows more'n I do. I thinks I'll git things a workin' fer per-pet-chee-yule motion atter I gits a way to feed the rats while they's a runnin'."

With a smile he added, "An' if I do, I'll juss rake in a million dollars as easy as fallin' off a log."

TENNESSEE

23. Mason Evans

The Great Smoky Mountains have been the home of many a hermit in Tennessee, but few of these wild men have attained the level of notoriety as Mason Evans, known throughout the Volunteer State as the "Wild Man of Chilhowee." When he died in the spring of 1892, word of his demise was printed in hundreds of newspapers across the nation. He is the rarest type of hermit; one whose name continues to live on, long after his body and bones have turned to dust.

The colorful life of Mason Kershaw Evans began in 1824 in Monroe County, on the land that the Cherokees had signed away to the United States government just a few years earlier. Though he was born into a modest Quaker family, Mason attained a fair amount of success in early life, first as a captain of the state militia and then as a brilliant school teacher. He eventually landed a position as the principal of a small school in McMinn County. Little did Mason know at the time that his future would be determined by a young teacher he would soon hire.

Mason became attracted to the beautiful, young woman whom he had hired as a teacher. She was the daughter of a wealthy landowner, and the girl's stern father was one of the most powerful and influential men in the county. In order to prevent scandal, the pair met regularly in the shade of a large white oak, carrying on their romantic tryst away from the prying eyes of the pupils and villagers. The romance blossomed like a cherry tree in springtime, and before long, their conversations turned toward marriage.

As was the custom of the time, the bride-to-be went to her father for his permission and blessing. He was, to put it mildly, less than satisfied. Mason was just too common, her father tried to explain. The daughter of a retired doctor and wealthy landowner deserved more than a bookish school principal and part-time soldier, he explained. But the more the young woman professed her deep love for Mason, the angrier her father became. He did not support the government's plan to remove the Cherokee from their God-given territory, and he certainly would not allow his daughter to marry a militia man who would be duty-bound to slaughter innocent Cherokee women and children if the order was given.

The following morning, Mason saddled up his sleek, black horse and raced to the school in order to await the appearance of his future bride. Mason was certain that the girl's father had given her permission to marry, and he was so excited that he found it difficult to focus on his duties as principal. The bell rang and children filed into the classroom, but still there was no sign of the young teacher. Growing worried, he taught class as best he could. As soon as class was dismissed, however, he got back on his horse and raced like lightning to the farm owned by the teacher's wealthy father. Along the way he spotted a buggy owned by the wealthy landowner and, as the young schoolteacher climbed down from the carriage, Mason raced over with arms wide open. She refused his embrace and turned away, and though she refused to explain her sudden change of heart, Mason knew by the iciness of her tone that it was over. Heartbroken, Mason returned to the home he shared with his parents, put his horse in the barn, and, without speaking a word, disappeared into the mountains. He made his new home in Panther Cave, on Starr Mountain, where he would spend the better part of the last forty years of his life.

His hair grew long, his clothes disintegrated into rags, and he subsisted on nuts, berries, and rattlesnake meat, which he consumed without cooking. After a few years of solitude Mason discovered that there was another hermit living on Starr Mountain. The rival hermits initially fought with each other, each believing that the other was an intruder in his kingdom. Finally, the two men reached an armistice and both occupied the mountain in peace. It was around this time when Mason witnessed something very strange.

The crackle of gunfire was nothing new to Mason; he had been chased by angry farmers during his midnight raids of their chicken coops and had encountered countless hunters traipsing through the forest. But he was startled to discover that the gunfire came from the rifles of gray-clad soldiers. Mason wondered if America had been invaded by a foreign enemy; for he had no way of knowing that Tennessee had seceded from the Union. For months, Mason lived in a state of despair, fearing that he would be arrested for desertion and hanged as a traitor.

Not long after the war, construction began on a hotel, which was being built on his beloved mountain. Known as the White Cliff Springs Hotel, this resort was touted as one of the most commodious in the Smoky Mountains, able to accommodate up to four hundred guests per night. The hermit was initially angered at this intrusion upon his private kingdom, of which he was *de facto* emperor. But as time went on, Mason convinced himself that it would be in his best interest to use the resort to his advantage. He wasn't getting any younger, and being a hermit was hard work, what with the need to hunt down every meal and scavenge for the vital necessities that would allow a hermit to survive season after season and year after year. Mason befriended the cooks who worked at the White Cliff, and these cooks would leave buckets of food for him outside hanging on tree limbs.

The hotel brought all kinds of new faces to the region, among them a Yankee who decided to start a newspaper in the sleepy county seat of Athens. The Yankee editor, who had a soft spot for sensationalism and a hard time selling newspapers, learned of the hermit and began to print numerous stories about him, many of which stretched the limits of credulity. The editor called for the capture of the "wild man," speculating that he was a deranged individual who posed a threat to the public's safety. Thanks to the Yankee's sensational stories and far-fetched fabrications, Mason Evans was hunted down, captured, and taken to the jail in Athens.

The deputies dragged the shaggy mountain man to jail in 1890, cuffed and shackled to prevent him from escaping. Once word spread that Mason was in Athens, hundreds of curious locals flocked to the jailhouse. The frightened hermit cowered in his cell, attempting to hide himself from the curious crowd that pointed their fingers in his direction and jeered. He managed to escape at some point during the night.

Knowing that it was too dangerous to return to Panther Cave, the hermit roamed the mountains for days until he decided to visit a brother-in-law named J. Horner Coltharp, who owned a large parcel of forested land. Coltharp built a shack for the hermit on this land so that he could live the rest of his days in peace. On January 11, 1892, Coltharp found the body of Mason Evans frozen to death on the side of Starr Mountain. His body was placed in a simple, wooden casket and buried at Hickory Grove Cemetery, where a stone marker still bears the hermit's name and an inscription, which reads: "The Hermit, 40 Yrs in the Wilderness."

24. The Tree Dweller

Although Daniel West died in 1860, his name is still remembered in the Cumberland Plateau region of central Tennessee, where the lovelorn hermit spent the last decades of his life living inside a hollowed-out poplar tree. West was a North Carolinian by birth and, as a young man, had a successful career in the military. He was a soldier in the War of 1812 and fought bravely in the Battle of New Orleans. When he returned home he married a woman whose husband had abandoned her years earlier and had been given up for dead. Daniel and his wife had one child together, and the couple lived a quiet life filled with harmony and happiness—that is, until the long-lost first husband came back into the picture.

Mrs. West's first husband was determined to win back the hand of his former bride. Daniel assured his wife that, if she chose him, she would never be forced to question the decision a day in her life, because he was determined to give her the moon and the stars if it would make her happy. Daniel also told her that if she chose her first husband, he would respect the decision and leave them alone to live in peace. Mrs. West looked at Daniel and his love-filled pleading eyes, which always seemed to sparkle every time he gazed upon his beloved wife. Then she looked into the beady eyes of her first husband, the shady character who had abandoned her without giving a reason, and who had led her to believe that he was dead. Without blinking, she leaped into the arms of her first husband.

At the time, Daniel was a man of means. He had shrewdly invested his money in stocks and bonds and had considerable money in the bank. But after his wife deserted him, Daniel became dejected and filled with despair. After his wife gathered her belongings and moved out, the West home, once a cozy and quaint haven of happiness, fell into disrepair and ruin. The child went to live with the mother and Daniel. Believing that he had no good reason to stay, he abandoned his property and took up a life of wandering.

He eventually found his way to Warren County, Tennessee, and made his home in the wilderness, inside the hollow of a large American poplar. Daniel affixed a door to the tree, and the hollow cavity behind the door was large enough to meet all of Daniel's simple needs. Daniel didn't require much space because he was known to sleep in a sitting position, with his back reclined against the wall of his extraordinary home.

The hermit didn't live in this peculiar manner because of necessity; for he had made several friends in Tennessee and they offered to open their homes to him. He also had his stocks and bonds and other investments in North Carolina, and could've lived a life of ease if he so desired. Daniel chose to live inside a tree because he wanted to. It was as simple as that, he explained to those who happened to encounter him. When questioned as to why he preferred the life of a hermit, he answered, rather vaguely, "The world had not used me well."

Until his death at the age of seventy-eight, Daniel kept himself busy by working in his shed, which he had constructed next to the hollow tree, where he built chairs and tables and other pieces of furniture that he would take to town and trade for food. According to those who knew him, Daniel never appeared to be sour in his disposition or embittered in his feelings. The past was past, and what can anyone do about it? Some folks make lemonade when life hands them lemons, while others wallow in self-pity. Daniel West, on the other hand, moved into the trunk of a tree.

25. From the White House to the Wilderness

Many presidents have gone from the log cabin to the White House, but few individuals have left the comfortable confines of the White House to dwell in a crude cabin perched atop a mountain of wilderness. In fact, there may be only one man who could make this claim, and that man was Andrew Stover, the grandson of President Andrew Johnson.

As a child, Andrew played and frolicked on the well-manicured White House lawn. As an adult, Andrew lived the life of a hermit in the mountains of eastern Tennessee, where he died a penniless recluse. His remarkable life story presents a striking illustration of the contrasts that color the lives of the American people. Many "rags to riches" stories have been written throughout the generations, but Andrew Stover's story is different. It is a story of riches to rags.

Andrew's mother, Mary, was the youngest of the President's two daughters. The President's eldest daughter, Martha, served as the official White House hostess in place of her mother, who dreaded making public appearances. Mary had married a fellow named Dan Stover, who served as colonel of the Fourth Tennessee Union Infantry during the Civil War. Stover died the year before Andrew Johnson became President, so Mary and her young son moved to Washington.

The life of a president's grandson was not always filled with prestige and glamour, however. The nation was still mourning the loss of Lincoln and trying to patch itself together after a prolonged and ghastly war between the states. At any rate, little Andrew Stover saw first-hand the most splendid society of the era; he was petted by foreign emperors and fawned over by wives of ambassadors. He reveled at the sight of military heroes in uniforms bedecked with medals and was enchanted by the loveliest women of the era floating in crinoline gowns as they gracefully danced the waltz. With uncomprehending childish eyes he watched the great events of American history unfold.

Perhaps the young boy comprehended more than anyone guessed. Perhaps he discovered the hollowness of glory and grandeur, or the misery that goes hand in hand with political distinction. Perhaps the gilded ballrooms and the pretentiousness of high society awakened in him a desire to seek happiness in the simple life, away from the hustle and bustle of the nation's capital.

Andrew built himself a cabin near the summit of Holston Mountain and never regretted his decision to trade the lush White House gardens for the wildflowers of the forest. Instead of following in his grandpa's political footsteps, he followed the tracks of wild game, armed with his trusty rifle, an assortment of traps, and his faithful dogs. He acquired the unmistakable appearance of the rugged self-sufficient mountaineer, dressed in furs and animal skins. He let his hair and beard grow long and never looked back.

Perhaps it was something in the Johnson family blood. Before becoming the governor of Tennessee, Andrew Johnson was a simple and self-educated country tailor who had been born on a farm in Greene County. Johnson ran for the position of alderman in the village of Greeneville, then became its mayor. He went on to the state legislature and then onto Congress. He was later chosen as the vice presidential nominee, not because of his ability or accomplishments, but merely because he was a Union sympathizer who lived in a Southern state. Had it not been for this geographical abnormality, Andrew Johnson might have been the one who ended up in a log cabin on a Tennessee hillside. The hills and mountains of Tennessee always held a special place in the hearts of the Johnson family; Andrew Stover's mother, three uncles, and aunt— all children of the President—lived the majority of their lives in the Volunteer State.

Sadly, the serenity which he had found in the wilderness slowly dissipated in his later years, and it was said that the hermit lost his mind after the death of his mother in 1883. From that point forward, he became withdrawn from society and seldom welcomed visitors to his cabin, and his health rapidly declined. The death of Mary Johnson Stover was the last in a string of tragic events involving the Johnson family. The hermit's father had died when Andrew was a boy, his Uncle Charles had been thrown off a horse and killed, his uncle Robert became an alcoholic and committed suicide, and another uncle, the youngest of the President's children, died mysteriously at the age of twenty-seven. Andrew Johnson Stover, the hermit of Holston Mountain, died on January 25, 1923, at the age of sixty-two, and rests in eternal slumber at the Andrew Johnson National Cemetery in Greeneville, Tennessee.

KENTUCKY

26. Mum the Meat-Eater

At the extreme western end of Kentucky lies the land that locals call the Jackson Purchase, so named because the territory belonged to the Chickasaw until 1818, when Andrew Jackson purchased over 2,300 square miles of land flanked by the Mississippi River to the west, the Ohio River to the north, and the Tennessee River to the east. Today, the cities of Paducah, Murray, and Mayfield are located on "The Purchase." In the days of Mum the Meat-Eater, however, much of the land was rugged wilderness.

Mum was first discovered around 1870 living in the wilds surrounding Paducah, and the hermit earned his name because whenever anyone attempted to talk to him, he would invariably respond by putting his finger to his lips and saying, "Mum's the word." Since he never spoke anything other than that one sentence, the nickname stuck.

Mum lived in a dilapidated pine shack in the forest for a period of five years, seldom seen by anyone except for the occasional hunter. As more settlers arrived in the region, Mum decided to abandon his wooden hut and made a new home in a small cave beneath a rocky overhang known as Lizard Rock. There he lived for five or six years, managing to avoid encounters with other human beings, until he was spotted by a party of three hunters from Paducah, who witnessed the hermit running into his cave without a single stitch of clothing.

Naturally, it didn't take long before word of such a spectacle had spread throughout the purchase and many other hunters came forward claiming that they, too, had seen the wild man during their excursions into the Kentucky wilderness. According to these accounts, Mum had a body covered in shaggy brown hair from head to toe. The hermit was also known to steal farm animals in the middle of the night; one farmer claimed that he had followed the tracks of a missing calf and two sheep to the hermit's cave. Though the cave was abandoned at the time, it was said that not a single trace of the animals remained. The hermit, who once lived in a shack and hushed his interviewers with a raised finger to his lips, had apparently devolved into a beastly, bloodthirsty maniac.

Raymond Boyd and James Harvey—two hunters who lived in McCracken County—were so aroused by the stories of the wild man that they decided to capture him. The men located his cave, and nearby, they found the skeletons of dozens of small animals and the skins of more than fifty snakes, most of them venomous. Boyd and Harvey decided to construct a trap in order to capture the hermit, baiting it with a big hunk of freshly killed beef. Concealing themselves in the woods, the hunters waited three days until Mum entered the trap.

It took two days to accustom the wild man to the presence of his captors. At first, he shrieked and howled incessantly, fear glinting in his savage eyes. A tinkle of a small dinner bell had great influence over the hermit, however, and the hunters used the tinkle of the bell to "train" the shaggy creature. Knowing that he would be fed whenever the bell tinkled, Mum became as tame as a golden retriever.

In March of 1883 Boyd and Harvey purchased three second-class tickets to New York City. The two hunters, along with the hairy hermit, boarded the train and took their seats in smoking car No. 153. Their destination was

Bridgeport, Connecticut, and the two men from McCracken County prayed that there would not be any delays, for they had an appointment in Bridgeport with P. T. Barnum, who was rumored to be looking for a new "wild man" for his circus.

27. Thirteen Years in Darkness

In the spring of 1880, during the construction of the Cincinnati Southern Railroad, it became necessary for workers to blast tunnels through the rugged Cumberland Mountains of northern Kentucky. The task of excavating one of the largest of these tunnels was left to a pair of men named Riley & O'Neal, who employed a large force of men to blast and dig into the bowels of the Earth. On a Thursday morning in April, after a heavy blast rattled the ground, the workers were surprised to discover that they had blasted away an opening to a large cave. The curiosity of the work crew induced them to explore the cavern.

The cave proved to be quite large and contained several chambers of remarkable, natural beauty. Armed with miners' lamps, the explorers had little difficulty traversing the depths of the cavern and meandering through the wide subterranean passageways. One of the men in the lead emerged from a narrow passageway into a spacious room, screamed in fright, and beat a hasty retreat. He claimed that he had seen a monster. This, of course, drew hearty laughs from his colleagues, who were determined to investigate the cause of the workman's shrieks of terror. The workers entered the chamber and were shocked by what they saw in the light of their lamps. Their frightened friend hadn't seen a monster, but a human being—a human being who hadn't seen the light of day in thirteen years!

The alarmed cave-dweller crouched behind a rock in abject horror, unaware that the workers were about to rescue him from a confinement worse than a thousand deaths. The caveman, naked as a jaybird, had hair and a beard that hung down to his waist in a tangled mess. His hair and beard, as well as his skin, were as white as the driven snow. The man's emaciated body was also unnaturally covered in milky-white hair, which made him appear to glow like a ghost in the beams of the miners' lamps.

The man's voice seemed at first to have left him, and it took several minutes before he could speak. It was as if he had forgotten how to use his voice, which initially manifested itself in quiet groans and wheezes. He finally said his name was John King, and when he first saw the light from the miners' lamps he was certain that his hour of death had finally arrived. Once he recovered from his shock, King said that he had been born in Jefferson County and in 1860 had bought a fine piece of land in the valley above their very heads. He had never been married, and he lived a hermetic life in peace and quiet until about the time of the Civil War.

According to John King, he had raised a good crop of corn and other grain and had a smokehouse in which he cured a large amount of bacon. Then along came the war, and armies from both sides foraged upon his lands, trampling his fields of grain and raiding his smokehouse. Even worse, deserters from the military continually showed up on his rural property in the hopes that John would shelter and feed them. Fearing that he would himself starve to death because of the war, John decided to stockpile his grains and cured meats inside of the cave he had found on the side of the mountain. After many months he had succeeded in placing the entire crop from his farm into the cave, along with many provisions and supplies he feared would be stolen by the uninvited military guests.

Once all of the crops and provisions had been moved to the cave, John realized that he didn't have much need for his cabin. Whenever he heard the approaching footsteps of soldiers, John disappeared into the cave and remained hidden until the intruders left his property. In December of 1862, John heard the soldiers' footsteps one final time. As usual, he retreated to the safety of his cave and waited for the uninvited guests to depart. The soldiers, however, thinking that the farm had been deserted, decided to linger. Then the clouds grew heavy and dark and a fearsome storm commenced. The soldiers sought shelter in

John King's empty house, and John was forced to spend the night in the cave, unaware at the time that he would not be able to leave for thirteen excruciatingly long years.

The tremendous rains relentlessly pounded the earth as John waited into the lonesome hours of night for the storm to abate. He eventually grew tired and drifted off to sleep. In the morning he opened his eyes and saw nothing but inky blackness. At first he feared he had been stricken blind, but he soon discovered that his fate was far more perilous; the torrential rains had caused a landslide on the side of the mountain, closing off the opening to the secret cave. John was trapped, and the cave would have been his tomb were it not for the building of the Cincinnati Southern Railroad.

For John King each day became an exact replica of the day preceding, or one continuous night, depending on one's point of view. Not a speck of light remained, and if John wished for a quick and painless death, he would be sorely disappointed. He had stockpiled enough food to last until the Second Coming, and the coolness of the cave kept his provisions well preserved. Even a man determined to starve himself to death cannot accomplish this task while in the presence of such a large quantity of edibles. Even the strongest of wills and the most steeled of minds cannot compete against the rumbling of the stomach, at least not in the long run. The belly wins every time.

John's death would have occurred in a matter of days if not for the small stream that trickled through the cave. The hermit must've imagined that it was both a blessing and a curse. On the plus side, the water sustained him and kept him alive. On the down side, well . . . the water sustained him and kept him alive. Every time he took a sip from the cool stream or ate from his enormous stockpile of grain, he knew that his misery of eternal blackness and total isolation would be prolonged.

The hermit had lost all concept of time, not knowing what year it was when the railroad workers found him, but his mind was little affected. Even the most depraved of criminals are spared from long bouts of solitary confinement, because it would be deemed as cruel and unusual punishment. Yet, John King spent thirteen years entombed in inky blackness, an experience that would make death row seem like paradise in comparison.

28. Pig Jack

One of the most peculiar fellows to ever call Edmonson County home was a moonshiner known as Pig Jack, who earned his nickname because he lived in a cave with a herd of swine. Pig Jack's cave was located several miles from Brownsville in a lonesome and wild part of the county. He had taken up residence inside the cave because, in his own words, he "liked animals better than men." He occupied his time by raising the swine that furnished his two most pressing needs—companionship and food. Pig Jack had a marked distaste for fresh produce; smoked pork and bacon constituted the entirety of his everyday diet. His long, matted hair and unkempt beard, along with the ragged clothing that appeared to have been made by his own hands, lent him the outward appearance of a veritable wild man.

One day in 1886 the thirty-five-year-old hermit ran afoul of the law. Though Pig Jack was as harmless as a newborn kitten, he was also a moonshiner, and Edmonson was a dry county. The hermit found himself hounded relentlessly by Deputy United States Marshal John Rule, and the beguiled lawman had a devil of a time trying to capture the elusive hermit. Rule tried time and time again to apprehend the notorious moonshiner, but Pig Jack had exceptional hearing and knew every nook and cranny of the woods like he knew the hairs on his favorite pig's chin. Whenever the deputy marshal managed to get within sight of the hermit, Pig Jack would take off running into the wilderness and remain expertly hidden until the danger passed. It was like trying to catch a greased pig (no pun intended). As a result, the long arm of the law always ended up getting the short end of the stick.

Deputy Marshal Rule was determined to apprehend the moonshiner, however, and it became an all-consuming passion. From behind his desk he gathered his men and planned and plotted his attack, drawing maps and devising traps as if he were a general staging an invasion of a foreign land. The fruitless pursuit dragged on until winter and when the snows came, Deputy Marshal Rule set out once again to bring the wily hermit to justice.

Rule and his men canvassed the area until they discovered the whereabouts of Pig Jack's well-hidden cave. Rule knew that the winter would be the ideal time to hunt for the cavern since it would no longer be concealed behind lush, thick vegetation. The hermit's cave was abandoned, but Rule and his officers were able to follow Pig Jack's footsteps. They mounted their horses and followed the moonshiner's tracks for quite some distance until they found the man they were looking for. Pig Jack had been out shooting squirrels and, stopping to rest, had dozed off against a tree. Rule raised a finger to his lips to hush his colleagues, and the lawmen slowly and stealthily approached Pig Jack. One of the officers pounced upon the hermit, but the moonshiner wriggled his way out of the lawman's grasp and took off running. The authorities followed on horseback in hot pursuit, but the nimble hermit outstripped his pursuers since the ground was too rocky and uneven for the horses. The lawmen considered waiting for the moonshiner to return to the cave but soon realized that the hermit, who was far more accustomed to the cold weather than the officers, would be able to outwait them.

Foiled once again, Deputy Marshal Rule went back to the drawing board and, after much brainstorming, the lawmen believed they had finally thought up a way to catch the hermit. Since Deputy Marshal Rule knew that he couldn't catch Pig Jack on foot, he decided that he would smoke the hermit out of his own hiding place. Rule returned a few days later and directed his men to build a large fire at the mouth of the cave. When the flames had grown to sufficient height, damp leaves and sulphur were thrown onto the blaze, producing a thick cloud of foul, noxious smoke. The officers fanned the smoke into the mouth of the cave. The strategy worked, but perhaps it worked a little *too* well. A few moments later the hermit darted out of the cave and into the waiting arms of the authorities. Unfortunately, the hermit's hurried exodus from the cave was followed by a stampede of dozens of frightened razorback pigs. What a sight that must have been; surprised lawmen scrambling for their lives, some of them frantically climbing up trees in order to avoid being trampled by hundreds of pounds of maniacal pork.

Once the mayhem died down, Deputy Marshal Rule breathed a sigh of relief. After months of hard work, he had finally caught his man. On the 18th of December, the notable moonshiner and swine herder arrived at the county jail, in a state of wide-eyed amazement. Pig Jack had never been in a town before, and he marveled at the sight of Brownsville (pop. 1,000), which must've seemed like Midtown Manhattan at rush hour. Pig Jack, whose real name was Charles Meredith, was described as being "a genial, comical fellow" by his jailers, who also remarked that the hermit was full of reminiscences, and that, in spite his alleged disdain for humanity, he was a capital favorite among the prisoners at the jail.

29. Polly of the Pines

Twelve miles east of Bardstown, in the depths of the forests divided by the Rolling Fork River, once stood a log cabin occupied by a hermitess by the name of Polly Blake. For half a century Mrs. Blake lived in this tiny shack, her only companions a flea-bitten dog and a couple of cats. While the cabin may be long gone, its crumbling and forsaken foundation can still be found deep in the Kentucky woods, and its weathered remnants tell a tale of undying love and betrayal.

Fifty years earlier, Polly Andrews was a vibrant young girl living with her parents on a modest farm near Springfield. Her father was a successful farmer and a respectable gentleman who provided his family with a comfortable life, but instilled within his children the values of hard work and simple, honest living. Polly was an unusually pretty girl and, as a result, had many suitors for her hand. Among her suitors was Stephen Letton, a prosperous young farmer who lived down the road. It was generally accepted by all that Stephen and Polly would someday be married.

The Andrews home was situated along the public highway, and travelers frequently stopped there for a place to rest. During the summer of 1835 a stranger named Thomas Blake was entertained by the Andrews, who gave him a place to stay for the night. Blake stated that he was from Boyle County and was passing through the area in a quest for mules, which he was buying for a market deep in the South. Blake was a handsome man, and he gave all the appearance of being a gentleman of high social standing. When Blake met Polly he was smitten, and over the course of the summer he became determined to win her hand in marriage. Polly and Thomas Blake were married the following spring, but not before Polly's father was satisfied that Blake was all he had represented himself to be. Though he was quite fond of Stephen Letton, Mr. Andrews encouraged his only daughter to follow her heart and choose the man she loved the most.

After the wedding, the bride and groom took up residence at the Andrews farm and Blake went out of his way to smooth things over with the rejected beau, Stephen Letton. If Letton felt any resentment toward Thomas Blake or Polly, he gave no evidence, and the Letton and Andrews families continued on the friendliest of terms. In fact, strange as it may seem, Blake and Letton became very close friends.

In the fall of 1836 Letton sold his property and announced that he was moving to West Virginia, stating that he had purchased an interest in a coal mine there. Around this time, Thomas Blake decided to return to Boyle County to settle some business matters and then proceed to eastern Kentucky in search of mules. As the routes of both men led in the same direction, the two friends decided to travel together. On arriving in Boyle County, Blake and Letton stopped to rest at the home of a wealthy rancher, who was a friend of Thomas Blake, and here their trails parted. Before Letton took his leave, he asked to borrow some money from Blake, which he promised to repay once he reached West Virginia. Letton sheepishly explained that he had all of his money invested in the coal mine and needed some extra money in order to get to his destination. Blake was happy to oblige.

The following evening, after both men had departed from the rancher's house in Boyle County, the property was entered by a thief who murdered the residents of the home and stole a box containing $1,800 in bank notes. In order to conceal the crime, the killer set fire to the property. The building burned slowly, and this allowed the neighbors to extinguish the fire and discover the dastardly deeds that had been committed. The killer, before leaving the scene of the crime, had torn open one of the bundles of money and tossed the wrapper on the ground. This bit of evidence was found by one of the neighbors, who turned it over to the authorities. The paper wrapper had been stained with blood.

Shortly after arriving in Springfield, Blake received the money that Letton owed him. Unbeknownst to Blake, detectives suspected that he might have been the killer. He was known to have done business with the rancher many times over the years, and had been seen at the home of the deceased the day before the crime had been committed. Blake, unaware that he was considered a prime suspect, was kept under constant surveillance by law men for four months.

Polly Blake's health began to fail around this time, and her husband decided to take her on a trip to the Deep South, in the hopes that the climate would improve her condition. The detectives followed every step of the way, like determined hunters stalking their prey. Whenever Blake paid a hotel bill, a detective would seize the note from the proprietor and examine it. Eventually, Blake paid with a $20 bill, which had been marked with a red splotch, and the detectives immediately arrested him.

At Blake's trial, the torn and bloodied paper wrapper was presented as evidence, along with the marked bank note. The location of the bloodstain on the paper wrapper corresponded with the red splotch on Blake's $20 bill. Blake vehemently denied the accusation, insisting that the $20 bill was part of a loan repayment sent to him by Stephen Letton. Witnesses testified on Blake's behalf, asserting that the accused had plenty of money of his own and had no reason to steal from the wealthy rancher.

Others testified that Blake and the victim had been close friends for several years, and still others testified that Letton and Polly Blake had once been sweethearts before Blake came along. Nonetheless, Blake was convicted of murder and given a life sentence.

Polly never once doubted her husband's innocence and made numerous efforts to secure his pardon. She searched high and low for Letton, but he could not be found. The story he had told everyone about owning an interest in a West Virginia coal mine was a creation of his own imagination. Ten years after his conviction, Blake died in prison of consumption.

A few years after Blake's death, Polly received a letter with a San Francisco postmark. The letter, which was signed by a notary public and a minister of the Gospel, would have been the piece of evidence that proved her late husband's innocence—had it not arrived over a decade too late. The letter stated that Stephen Letton had been fatally wounded in a bar-room brawl. The unexpected letter was his deathbed confession. Letton admitted to the killing of the wealthy rancher and had caused the crime to be pinned on Blake, because he had deprived him of the girl he loved. Money was only a secondary motive; Letton's primary motive was revenge.

Shortly after Polly received this letter, her parents died, and the widowed bride was left without a dollar to her name. She had spent every last dime trying to prove her husband's innocence. Polly Blake retired into the wilderness, where she would spend the remaining fifty years of her life mourning the loss of her wronged husband.

30. Basil Hayden
Settled by European immigrants shortly after the Revolutionary War, Bardstown is one of the oldest cities in the state of Kentucky. It is a city with a rich history and friendly people, and most of Bardstown's twelve thousand residents would be happy to stop and tell you about it, if you were inclined to ask them. They might tell you about Judge Rowan's plantation, which inspired Stephen Foster to write "My Old Kentucky Home," or the fact that Bardstown

is known as the "Bourbon Capital of the World." They will be happy to tell you about the Old Talbott Tavern, which offered shelter to the likes of Abraham Lincoln and Daniel Boone, or that the bullet holes in an upstairs wall are reputed to have been made by Jesse James. They may even tell you about one of the most unforgettable characters who ever lived in the area, a hermit named Basil Hayden.

If the name sounds familiar, it's because Basil Hayden's is a well-known brand of whiskey named after the hermit's grandfather, who was one of the region's early settlers. The Hayden family, which can trace its roots back to the Norman Conquests of the eleventh century, were also pioneers in the distillery business; Old Grand-Dad, another popular brand of whiskey, was started in 1840 by the hermit's brother. Nobody who knew Basil in his youth would ever have imagined that the popular boy from one of Bardstown's wealthiest families would grow up to become an ornery old recluse.

When the war broke out, Basil left his farm and joined the Confederate Army. He made a good soldier, but when he returned home he found that his slaves had been freed and his long-unattended property had been ransacked. The emancipation of the slaves greatly distressed Basil, and he brooded over it constantly. He became bitter and melancholy and declared that the Lord had dealt harshly and unjustly with him, as if the Lord had freed the slaves for the sole purpose of causing the ruination of his enormous farm. In his anger, he swore that he would never again set foot on the Lord's earth or allow the sun to shine on his face, and Basil was true to his word until the bitter end. This, however, caused a great rift in the family; it was Basil's legendary grandfather who had led twenty-five Catholics from Maryland into Nelson County in 1785, becoming the region's first settlers. It was the hermit's grandfather who had also donated the land for the first Catholic church in Kentucky.

Basil gradually reduced his level of contact with the outside world until he became a recluse, seldom seen by anyone other than the overseer he had appointed to manage his finances. Basil's business interests extended well beyond his farm, and under the watchful eye of the competent overseer the recluse became wealthier and wealthier as the years went by. Although the farm continued to operate, Basil rarely made a sale, since he insisted upon charging pre-Civil War prices, when his crops commanded a high price. As a result, his harvests were left to wither and rot. He insisted upon living in the past, and refused to read any newspapers or books that had been printed after 1863. It was said that he had never laid eyes upon a female since the beginning of his self-imposed exile, and refused to hire or do business with women. Other than his business manager, the only other person who was permitted into the Hayden home was a banker from Bardstown, who visited Basil twice each year in order to settle the hermit's financial matters with the outside world.

In his youth, Basil was a fine-looking man, and the few who encountered him in his old age remarked that the hermit hadn't lost his looks. Except for the full beard and flowing hair, which were white as snow, the old miser was still handsome and debonair. As he preferred to keep his home in a state of darkness, decades of confinement had made him pale as a ghost and years of inactivity made his hands as soft as raw cotton. How he spent the lonesome hours in his darkened room no one knew, but it was said that his only diversion was counting and recounting his money, of which there was a vast amount.

As an old man, Basil once had an auction of mules at his farm and a number of the animals fetched high prices. Though a large number of people were present at the auction, none of them caught a glimpse of the hermit. His written instructions to the auctioneer were sent out by his overseer. In the summer of 1909 Basil Hayden finally passed away, after four decades of refusing to leave his house. After his death, Mr. Borders, the man who had been the overseer of the hermit's estate, remarked that the total number of words he exchanged with the recluse over the years could be counted on his fingers. It wasn't until after Basil's death that the true reason behind his eccentric behavior was revealed. The reason why he had refused to acknowledge the outside world since 1863 had nothing to do with slavery or the war between the states; for it was the year that the girl he intended to marry had tragically died.

ALABAMA

31. The Hunchback of Chulafinnee Mountain

When Billy Holden died at the age of 108 in the summer of 1890, many children around rural Cleburne County breathed a sigh of relief. For forty years, the hunchbacked hermit had been the bogeyman of many a tale told by parents, designed to frighten disobedient children into submission. If the children continued to misbehave, they were told that "Uncle Billy" would come and get them.

It was an effective story, since the old hermit's physical appearance was described, at best, as grotesque. Long and tangled hair and beard, gray as smoke, covered his entire head. Only his beady eyes were visible beneath the matted mess of hair, making him look more like a wild gorilla than a human being. His gnarled body was bent almost double, lending him the appearance of the famed bell-ringer of Notre Dame.

Unlike Quasimodo, however, Billy's back was perfectly normal at birth. In fact, as a young man, Billy was broad-shouldered and well-built as the result of his work as a cooper. Billy made wooden barrels and buckets and pails, which he would then string onto a pole and carry on his strong back. He would set off on foot and visit all the villages at the foot of the Chulafinnee Mountains, selling his wares to farmers and blacksmiths. Decades of carrying heavy barrels on his back had turned the once young and handsome man into a hobbled and humped monstrosity.

Billy lived in a small shack near the top of Chulafinnee Mountain, with a mean-tempered black cat as his only companion. The disposition of the cat was said to have perfectly matched the old hermit's ornery demeanor. Inside this simple cabin Billy lived for forty years, making his bed on a pile of wood shavings swept into the corner. Because of Billy's peculiar lifestyle, he became the subject of much gossip, and the topic of many a scary story told around the dancing flames of a backwoods campfire.

Billy's regular customers paid little attention to these wild and outrageous stories. They had been buying Billy's barrels and butter churns for decades and knew perfectly well that the "wild man" of Chulafinnee Mountain was as harmless as a kitten, even though the cranky old-timer shunned society and avoided conversation as much as possible. Up until a few weeks before his death he would place upon his shoulders a load of barrels that would break the back of a man one-third his age, and day after day he would wander the countryside until the last of them had been sold. Billy Holden was never known to remove the immense burden from his shoulder when he stopped to negotiate a sale, and he never demanded payment in cash. Money held little value to the hunchbacked cooper; instead, he traded his wares for sacks of flour and cornmeal. These provisions, weighing nearly as much as the barrels, he would carry on his back until reaching his cabin atop the mountain. Most days, Billy's wanderings carried him thirty or more miles away from home.

Once when he was asked why he refused to lay down his heavy burden when he stopped to rest or make a sale, the elderly hermit replied that if he put it down it would feel heavier than before when he picked it up again. This was just one of Billy Holden's explanations for his seemingly super-human strength. He also explained that he would begin each journey by filling the barrels and buckets he intended to sell first with stones. He said he did this because his load always felt so much lighter when the extra weight was removed after the first few sales.

Near the end of his life Billy Holden became more sociable, and the elderly hermit described the events that led him to a life of solitude in the mountains. He had grown up in North Carolina and eventually won the hand of the girl he loved since they were both children. They got married and lived in happiness for a year, until Billy's wife found someone she liked better. Billy learned of his wife's infidelity and was blinded by jealousy. When he discovered his wife in bed with another man, he killed them both in a fit of rage and then fled into the wilderness of Alabama. By the time Billy's whereabouts were discovered by the North Carolina lawmen, most of whom weren't even born when the slayings took place, they made no effort to apprehend the old hermit. They took one look at his disfigured form and decided that he had, in his own bizarre way, repaid his debt to society.

Billy could've given up his heavy load as he grew old and withered, but he knew that as soon as he put the weight down, the guilt he carried on his back from the days of his youth would overpower him. As long as Billy Holden was still alive, he was determined to carry the weight of the barrels upon his hunched back, imposing upon himself the punishment that he had avoided by running away from the scene of the crime so many years earlier.

NORTH CAROLINA

32. A Lesson in Karma

The strange story of John Armstrong is a drama, which countless hermits know all too well. It is a story about one woman's infidelity and behavior so cold that it drove a man to the life of self-imposed exile deep in the wilderness. It is also a story with a plot twist so amazing that it seems nearly impossible to believe.

The strange story of John Armstrong begins in 1838, when the only son of a well-to-do farmer from Wilmington fell in love with Carrie Scott, the beautiful daughter of a neighbor. On the morning of their wedding, Armstrong and a group of his friends were riding to the home of Miss Scott when they were met by a servant of the Scott family, who informed John that his betrothed had just gotten married hours earlier to a northern gentleman named Samuel Opdyke.

Armstrong was dazed by the news. Without saying a word to his companions, he spurred his horse and disappeared into the distance. He was never again seen in that neighborhood, and gossip soon spread that John Armstrong had become so distraught over Carrie's betrayal that he committed suicide. Years passed by and John's father and mother died. The family farm fell to ruin, before being handed over to distant relatives who had barely known John and his family. The unexplained disappearance of the young man with the broken heart was soon forgotten.

Thirty years later, a party of hunters from New Berne was chasing game in the forests of Craven County when they stumbled upon the cabin that had been Armstrong's home since the day he ran away from Wilmington. The hunters spent a few hours at the cabin listening to the hermit's sad story. He told his visitors that on the fateful morning when he learned that his bride-to-be had broken the promise, which John held sacred, he resolved to forever turn his back on humanity. Unlike Carrie Scott, the hermit was true to his word.

Though Armstrong told his story to the band of hunters, he was greatly annoyed that his hiding place had been discovered. However, the hermit saw no need to find a new place to live and tried his best to discourage future visitors to his cabin. In 1893 a gentleman from the North sought out the hermit and remarked that John Armstrong was vigorous and healthy in spite of his seventy-six years. His silky hair and long, flowing beard were as white as snow and were clean and free of tangles and knots. He walked proudly with his back erect and with a spring in his step, and appeared to be as strong as an ox. Unlike most wilderness dwellers, he was keen on cleanliness and kept his simple cabin in a state of good repair.

Armstrong told his visitor that he had not set eyes on a woman in over thirty years, and to this he attributed his vigor and vitality. The visitor asked the hermit about railroads and steam boats, but Armstrong confessed that he had never heard of such things. The doings of the outside world were of little interest to the hermit, but Armstong was well-versed in theology and science, thanks to the numerous books that he hoarded in his cabin. The hermit was also an ardent student of natural history and impressed his visitor with his bug collection. According to the visitor, Armstrong could tell you the proper scientific name and habit of every insect native to the North Carolina woods.

The aforementioned visitors to John's cabin found the hermit to be sociable and pleasant but, during the Civil War, one unfortunate soul accidentally encountered the hermit and didn't find him to be nearly as jovial. John Armstrong told the story of the unfortunate visitor to the man from the North who came to see him in 1893, nearly three decades after the war's final shot had been fired. One day, a Union officer took flight into the forest in order to escape a scouting party of Confederate cavalry. The Yankee wandered into the deepest and darkest section of the forest and eventually stumbled across John Armstrong's cabin. The fugitive pleaded with the hermit to give him shelter and a place to hide from his horsebacked pursuers. Armstrong asked the soldier his name.

"Samuel Opdyke," replied the Union officer.

"Are you the man who married Carrie Scott?" inquired the hermit, as he cocked his gun and pointed it at the soldier.

"Yes, but why do you ask that question?" pleaded the bewildered officer. "Who are you?"

"I am John Armstrong, whom she promised to marry and vowed that she loved better than any one else in the world. But she deceived me; her heart was hollow. She was false to me. You stole her from me, and now I have my revenge."

The Yankee officer knew he shouldn't have gotten out of bed that morning. What had begun as a bad day was about to get much, much worse. John Armstrong, with his gun still pointed at the soldier, smiled and pulled the trigger.

33. Robert Harrill

Few hermits throughout history have achieved the fame of Richard Harrill, who took up a life of hermitry in 1955 at the age of sixty-two. Harrill's path to solitude was long and hard; he had been a failure at everything he tried, and after working a string of unsuccessful jobs he also had to deal with a failed marriage and the suicide of his son. After his wife filed for divorce, Richard sunk into a state of deep depression and his in-laws had him committed to a mental institution in Morganton.

While institutionalized at the State Hospital at Morganton (renamed the Broughton Hospital in 1959) Harrill discovered the writings of Dr. William Taylor, a controversial psychiatrist from Spruce Pine who became rich teaching courses in something called "Bio-Psycho-Genetics." Taylor's writings had a profound impact on Harrill, who was determined to enroll in Dr. Taylor's course as soon as he earned his freedom from the state hospital. When Harrill discovered that the hospital had no plans to release him, he escaped by fashioning a key from the handle of a soup spoon.

Harrill then hitchhiked to Spruce Pine to enroll in Dr. Taylor's course, and he spent the following few years pursuing a degree in "Bio-Psycho-Genetics." One day, the doctor told Harrill that he should try to discover his true self, and said that this could be done by starting a new life from scratch. Harrill's thoughts immediately turned to a place he had once visited as a child with his parents, a peaceful place that brought back fond childhood memories —the beach surrounding Fort Fisher. He packed a small bag and hitchhiked 260 miles across the state until he reached the Carolina coast.

Robert Harrill made his home on a stretch of beach near Fort Fisher, which was once a Confederate stronghold that was overrun by Union forces in 1865. There, he was arrested for vagrancy and taken back to his hometown of Shelby. Harrill returned to the coast the following summer and found refuge inside an abandoned World War II-era ammunition storage bunker near the salt marshes among the Cape Fear River. The oyster beds and shellfish of the marshlands provided Harrill with more than enough to eat, and Harrill settled into a life of hermitry.

Harrill wasn't a hermit in the truest sense of the word, however. Although he was distrustful of people, he harbored no resentment or ill will toward them. He simply wanted to live life on his own terms, in a place where he could get back in touch with nature. Over the years the hermit became viewed as a guru of sorts, and many other people who hungered for a simpler way of life journeyed to his peculiar abode and sought his advice. "Everyone has

Robert Harrill, "The Fort Fisher Hermit."

the desire from time to time to be a hermit, to be alone, to relax and perhaps converse with your Maker," Harrill once remarked. "I represented the hermit in them."

This wisdom struck a chord with hundreds of thousands of men and women across the globe, and Robert Harrill soon became the second greatest tourist attraction in the entire state of North Carolina, behind only the *USS North Carolina* in number of visitors. His guest registry had been signed by over one hundred thousand visitors from over twenty different countries. He placed a frying pan near his bunker for donations, and it was always overflowing with cash. When asked about his cult-like following and his international fame, the hermit replied, "Everybody ought to be a hermit for a few minutes to an hour or so every twenty-four hours, to study, meditate, and commune with their creator . . . Millions of people want to do just what I'm doing, but since it is much easier thought of than done, they subconsciously elect me to represent them, that's why I'm successful."

After years of preaching his philosophy to people from every corner of the globe, the Fort Fisher Hermit died under unusual circumstances in June of 1972. His bloodied body was found by a group of teenage boys on a Sunday morning, laid spread eagle atop a pile of trash. Some people believed, and still believe, that he had been murdered for his money. Others believed that Harrill was murdered out of hatred. The coroner from New Hanover County ruled that the hermit had died as a result of a heart attack. Although this remains listed as the official cause of Robert Harrill's death, dozens of investigators and biographers who took an interest in the old hermit are still pursuing the truth, since an official investigation into the strange death of Robert Harrill has never been conducted.

SOUTH CAROLINA

34. The Coward of Blacksburg

Around the time of the outbreak of the Civil War, a man named John Starnes lived in the South Carolina town of Blacksburg, a stone's throw away from the battlefields of Cowpens and King's Mountain where, during the Revolutionary War, the Americans gave a sound thrashing to the British. The close proximity of these hallowed fields of war did little to inspire patriotic fervor in the heart of John Starnes, however, and neither did the fact that his own ancestors had fought valiantly at King's Mountain.

Starnes was a strong and able-bodied fellow, and when the war broke out the conscription officers did everything in their power to muster him into service. Starnes, having no taste for a military career, took off running into the woods. Although the officers chased after him, Starnes was a better runner than a fighter, and thus managed to avoid not only conscription but the whole entire war. He had taken with him an old musket and some ammunition, which enabled him to hunt for game. After deciding that the quality of the fare in the wilderness was better than that in town, Starnes grew fond of the hermit lifestyle and chose to stay hidden away in the wilderness of York County, even long after the war had ended and he was no longer in danger of being drafted.

Starnes's home, a tiny windowless cabin, is said to have been either the very model of simplicity, or a monstrosity built by someone with absolutely no knowledge of the "manual arts." Shaped like an igloo, the curiously-constructed hut had no door, but an opening of about two feet in height, which served as the entrance and exit. In the wintertime, Starnes built fires at the entrance of his hut, there being no stove or fireplace inside his ramshackle hermitage.

The hermit was well-known throughout the county, but very few details about his life have ever been ascertained, due to the fact that Starnes grew angry whenever anyone attempted to converse with him. In his later years, he was described as having long, white hair, a snowy beard, and a thin, lanky frame; a sharp contrast to the broad-shouldered, young man who had fled into the wilderness when the war broke out so many decades earlier.

The hermit was visited occasionally by relatives, many of whom tried to persuade Starnes into leaving his crude shack. Some even offered to build him a house so that he could live comfortably and alone, without fear of attack from the wolves and rattlesnakes and other creatures of the woodlands. The hermit declined all of these offers and chose to remain in the woods for the remainder of his days, and his legend spread from the lips of fathers into the ears of sons, who anxiously listened to the stories about "Wild John Starnes." It was a title that the old man had always disliked, having been known to vehemently state that he was "not so damned wild as you might suppose." According to some local legends, Starnes became a hermit after being rejected by a lover. Some legends even went so far to claim that Starnes fled into the woods because he had been the soldier who accidentally shot and killed Stonewall Jackson.

After forty years in the wilderness, John Starnes finally died as the result of a lingering illness. In the summer of 1911, word spread that the old hermit has fallen ill and a party of relatives took him, against his will, to the county poor house in Gaffney where he drew his final breath a few days later, succumbing to complications from pneumonia.

WEST VIRGINIA

35. Cole Carrington

Since the time of the Revolutionary War, the county of McDowell in West Virginia's coal country has been an impoverished land whose hearty occupants live on small salaries and large amounts of faith. Throughout most of the county's history, the way of life of its citizens has remained largely unchanged. Folks were born, lived, and then died, many without ever setting foot outside of the county. So when a mysterious stranger arrived in the county seat of Perryville in 1864, it was an event that raised many eyebrows.

The reason why the arrival of this particular stranger garnered so much attention was because when Cole Carrington came to Perryville he was wearing a frayed uniform of Confederate gray with a black-plumed cavalry hat drawn over his face. The shadow from the hat made the stranger's dark, deep-set eyes appear even more menacing. The mere presence of a Confederate in Perryville was cause enough for alarm; McDowell was one of the counties that had seceded from the state before the war. It was an uncomfortable moment in history for the villagers, many of whom weren't even sure where their loyalties had stood during the fighting. Were they living in the southernmost of the Northern states, or the northernmost of the Southern states? At the time of his arrival, it was unclear whether or not the lone Confederate knew that he had strayed into dangerous territory.

The stranger asked no questions and refused to answer any in return. When interrogated by one of the overly inquisitive locals, the man in gray would turn toward his questioner with an icy stare, inevitably causing the inquisitor to mumble an apology before quickly retreating from the scene. The newcomer silently walked into one of the village stores and purchased powder, lead, and a small assortment of cooking utensils, which he placed into a sack and then rode off in the direction of the mountains. This event resulted in a tremendous amount of gossip around Perryville. The locals wondered what deep, dark secret was hidden behind the stranger's piercing stare and aloof demeanor, but when the outsider arrived in town the following week to make his purchases, no one dared ask any of the questions that had been on their minds. After this second public appearance, three or four of the more coura-geous spirits in town, perhaps emboldened by whiskey, grew determined to see where and how this mysterious Confederate lived. They attempted to follow the stranger's trail, but to no avail. It was as if the dark-eyed enigma had disappeared like a phantom into the underbrush.

A few days later two young men named Andrew and Eson were out hunting deer when one of their dogs gave chase to a wounded doe. The young men followed the dog to a deep gap between the mountains. With daylight fading, the boys were just about to abandon their search for the wounded deer when they were startled by the thunder of a rifle shot. Hurrying as fast as their legs could carry them, Andrew and Eson scrambled to a clearing in the woods, where they encountered the mysterious stranger. He was standing over the carcass of the deer that they had been following all afternoon. Without uttering a sound, the stranger pointed his finger in the direction from which the boys had come. One look was sufficient, and the young hunters, bold as they were, saw that there was something cold and deadly in the man's dark eyes. They returned to town and told the villagers what they had seen.

The stranger would not be seen again until the summer of 1870, when a band of hunters from Ohio found themselves in the deepest pocket of McDowell County wilderness. One of the hunters, James Hall, had gotten himself separated from the group and the others spent nearly a week looking for him. They were ready to give up their lost friend for dead when Hall stumbled into camp with his arm in a sling and his head bandaged. Hall then proceeded to tell his companions a most remarkable story.

Hall had lost his way on the day of the hunt and strayed several miles away from the group. Unfamiliar with his surroundings, the hunter scurried up the side of a steep mountain in order to survey the terrain. On his descent, Hall lost his footing, fell off the cliff, and was knocked unconscious when he hit the ground. When he regained his senses he found himself in the arms of a strange, dark-eyed man, who carried him up the side of the mountain until he reached a deep cave. Inside the cave, the stranger laid the injured hunter down onto a bed of pine needles. With the skill of an experienced physician, the mysterious man in gray set the hunter's broken arm and dressed the wounds on his face. Hall remained in the cave for about a week, where he fed upon venison and bear steaks. During this week not a single word passed from the lips of the stranger. When he felt that the hunter was well enough to travel, he signified to Hall with the gesture of a finger that he must go. The silent hermit escorted Hall through the wilderness until they got within sight of the hunting camp. Hall turned to thank the dark-eyed hermit, but he was gone.

Years passed, and the hermit was not seen for months at a time. The villagers, still curious about the identity of the stranger, feared that he could be dangerous, and thus, he was permitted to live in peace without undesired contact from the outside world. Fears about the stranger's nefarious intentions abated in 1875, when a severe drought threatened to cause famine and starvation throughout McDowell County. The stranger would be seen lurking in the shadows of evening near the homes of those most affected by the famine. Without a sound, he would leave a leg of deer, a few squirrels, or a turkey on the doorsteps of the hungry.

Around that time a man by the name of McCormick received an accidental gunshot wound, which threatened to be fatal since the nearest doctor was over twenty miles away. A messenger was dispatched, but the villagers feared the man would be dead before the doctor arrived. Before long, the stranger showed up at the house with a rifle over his shoulder. Based on his appearance, he had been out hunting when he overheard the commotion over McCormick's condition. The stranger walked into the home, turned down the bedsheets, and examined the wounded man. Family members of the wounded man were astonished by the ease with which the stranger worked. He probed the wound with his fingers and in no time at all managed to extract the lead ball. He then closed the wound with the precision of a practiced surgeon. The stranger visited McCormick twice more, and after he was convinced that the man was out of danger, he returned no more.

That was the last time the stranger was seen in town. Ten years later, the life of the dark-eyed stranger was brought to a close by a bizarre accident, and only then was the mystery of his identity explained. A party of fishermen had been exploring one of the numerous mountain streams for trout when they came across the body of a man lying on the bank. It appeared as though he had stumbled and struck his head on a rock when he fell to the ground. He was alive but unconscious. One of the fishermen dragged the body into the shade, propped him up against a tree, and drew the mouth of a canteen to the parched lips of the wounded hermit. Color began to return to his face, and his muscles began to twitch as if coming to life for the first time. He opened his eyes, glanced wildly and wonderfully about, and asked, "Where am I?"

The fishermen, all of whom recognized the stranger as the mystery man of the mountains, were flabbergasted. For twenty years no one had heard him speak. Upon being apprised of the situation, the stranger appeared confused and confessed that he had no recollection of his surroundings. After being told that he had been a hermit in the mountains for twenty years, the stranger's eyes grew wide in astonishment, and the menacing, icy stare, which had been his signature since the day of his arrival, was gone. He sighed, sat up with a groan, and spoke to the fishermen.

"I feel that I have but a few minutes to live and I want to say that I have no remembrance of the past twenty years. My name is Cole Carrington, and I was a surgeon in the Confederate Army. On the twentieth of June, 1864, I was wounded in the head while attending a wounded soldier. Since that time I remember nothing—"

The exertion was too much for the weak old man, and the poor fellow fainted. A sip of whiskey brought him back, but it was evident he didn't have much time left. He gasped, "I live in Georgia. Tell my mother to . . . write . . . to grand—," and he died.

After his death an examination of the body revealed that Cole Carrington had received a terrible injury many years before, which fractured his skull and had driven shards of splintered bone into his brain. This was deemed the cause of his amnesia and peculiar manners. The final blow to the skull on the day of his death must have provided him with a brief moment of clarity, allowing him just enough time to tell his story. The villagers attempted to track down Carrington's relatives in Georgia, but his mother was long dead, and no other relatives could be found. The hermit was buried by the side of the stream where he had fallen, beneath the shady branches of a maple tree near the foot of the mountain.

MISSISSIPPI

36. Miss Jennie Senkhart

Throughout its history, Waynesboro existed as a sleepy Southern town near the eastern edge of Mississippi. It was the type of place one might expect to find in a William Faulkner novel, a town whose most prominent citizens are referred to as "Colonel," and wide-hipped housewives sit on their porches and politely argue with neighbors about the best way to fry a chicken. It's the kind of town where a hound dog could spend his day lazing in the shade beneath the spreading arms of a magnolia tree and where children could play safely in the streets. It was the kind of small town in which everybody knew everybody else. Or so they thought.

In the spring of 1953, a recluse known throughout town as Miss Jennie Senkhart died at the age of eighty.

Jennie rarely left her shack on the outskirts of town and never entertained visitors, yet the genteel residents of Waynesboro tolerated her peculiar behavior with a polite bow or the tipping of a hat on the rare occasions when she strolled into town in order to buy groceries or mail a letter at the post office. During Jennie's thirty-one years in this rural Mississippi town, not one soul could ever remember hearing her speak.

After Miss Senkhart died, her body was taken to the mortuary by Sheriff Westover, where it was discovered that the spinster had been leading a secret life: Miss Jennie wasn't a woman at all, but a man. The sleepy town soon became a buzzing hive of gossip, and everybody clamored to know more about the recluse who had been living a secret life in their very midst. Sheriff Westover conducted a search of the shack and rummaged through three decades worth of old letters in the hopes of learning the story of Wayne County's most peculiar resident. Though the sheriff thought that he had seen all there was to see in his long career, nothing in his career could have prepared him for what he uncovered: Miss Jennie was a Communist spy!

The sheriff found papers that indicated that the hermit was a man by the name of John Hushler, who had been born in Austria and became a naturalized citizen in San Francisco in 1902. Letters found in the shack dated back as far as 1922, and most of the letters had been sent from the infamous New Llano co-operative colony in Louisiana. Established in 1917 by Job Harriman, a leader of the American Socialist Party, New Llano was said to be the longest surviving socialist community in the United States, surviving until the winter of 1937.

Although the residents of New Llano lived a peaceful existence and nothing nefarious ever occurred there, the death of John Hushler occurred right in the middle of the McCarthy era, when American distrust of Communism reached its peak. During the McCarthy era, thousands of American citizens were accused of being Communist sympathizers, and many became the target of aggressive questioning and interrogation. It certainly didn't help the hermit's reputation when Sheriff Westover found several letters inside the shack that were addressed "Dear Comrade." He immediately turned the matter over to the FBI.

Federal agents from Meridian, fifty miles to the north, quickly took charge of the hermit's papers and announced that they included Communist letters and literature. However, nothing was found in the hermit's letters that implied that he had been sent to rural Mississippi as a Communist spy. The matter was soon forgotten and nothing ever came of the federal investigation, except for the revelation that police had once visited the shack of "Miss Jennie" in the early 1940s and confiscated nine hundred gallons of liquor from the basement.

Perhaps Sheriff Westover said it best when he told the papers, "If he was spying, for the life of me, I can't see what there was here to spy on." Perhaps John Hushler was sending secret fried chicken recipes back to Germany. Perhaps the Russians had sent him to Waynesboro in order to conduct top secret research on farm equipment. In all likelihood, John Hushler was probably just an eccentric, old recluse who liked to dress in women's clothes. But every year, when the dog days of summer come to the Deep South and folks pass the time by telling stories of days gone by, some of the older residents of Wayne County still spin yarns about Miss Jennie Senkhart, the spy who never was.

FLORIDA

37. The Storm King

Lake Eustis is one of the lakes comprising the Harris Chain, which includes several magnificent lakes linked together by rivers and man-made canals. From Lake Eustis flows the Ocklawaha, a narrow and crooked river shadowed on both sides by swampy marshes and hardwood hammocks as it loafs lazily past the hill and lake region of Florida. The Dead River links Lake Harris to Lake Eustis, while the St. Johns River links Eustis to Lake Griffin. The hills sloping down to these lakes are dotted with handsome villas and citrus groves and the homes of both permanent settlers and winter residents.

Lakes Harris and Eustis are the twin jewels in the Lake County crown. Fishing, boating, and sailing are the preferred pursuits of the local population, who proudly announce that it is darn near impossible to find better bass fishing anywhere else in the country. Because of its ideal climate and recreational opportunities, the region has experienced tremendous growth in recent decades. The city of Eustis, which was a small spattering of cottages and vacation homes less than one hundred years ago, is now a thriving city of nearly twenty thousand.

Much of the region was unspoiled wilderness in the years immediately following the Civil War, however. Back then, when the county was sparsely settled and everybody knew everybody else, the appearance of a stranger often resulted in much gossip and speculation. One such stranger arrived at Lake Eustis around this time, and this fellow was only ever seen on the lake fishing from his boat. He never appeared in town and never spoke to a soul. Many efforts were made to discover something about the newcomer, but every effort failed. He would answer no questions, and he would not even look up when he was being addressed. It was as if he had taught himself to ignore the human race altogether.

The stranger appeared to be around seventy years of age, with a wiry build and long, white hair that cascaded over his shoulders. A snowy beard reached to his thin waist. The man appeared to have only one set of clothes, gray in color, which he wore until they grew threadbare. His boat was a long canoe, reminiscent of the type of boat an ancient tribe of natives may have constructed from the trunk of a tree. It was thought to be hollowed out of a tree by the hermit's own hands. Though this boat was crude, its captain managed it with consummate skill; when curious fishermen became too bothersome, the bearded stranger would speed away from them like a frightened fish.

At night the stranger would become even more mysterious, his actions even more peculiar. He would rig his canoe with a sheet of canvas, and was able to out sail the fastest craft on the lake. The pleasure boats, out on the water for a romantic, moonlit sail, would greet the stranger's homely craft with jeers and laughter. But the stranger paid no attention to the insults. When thunder was heard rolling across the lake and the skies poured down rain, all of the other boats would dash for shore, but the old man was in his glory. Those fleeing the scene, eager to seek shelter from the storm, would remark that the old man seemed to revel in the tempest. His canoe would sweep through the blinding sheets of rain, sometimes disappearing for a split second beneath the waves, before reappearing again. At these times, the aged hermit would stand up in his canoe, wave his arms wildly, and curse to the heavens between fits of maniacal laughter. And the more severe the storm, the more the hermit would shriek and laugh.

Numerous efforts were made to track the hermit to his hiding place, but the old man knew that his simple canoe was able to venture into streams and canals too narrow and shallow for other boats. He knew the maze of waterways as though he had designed them himself. One evening in 1886, a party of men who had been determined to find the hermit's hiding place managed to follow him for quite a distance. The hermit paddled his canoe out of the lake and into the Ocklawaha River, with his pursuers following stealthily at a safe distance. They were confident that the hermit had no idea that he was being tailed but then, all of a sudden, the hermit made an abrupt turn and disappeared from sight. The pursuers reached the spot where the stranger disappeared and saw only tall marsh grass. The hunters couldn't navigate their boat through the muddy swamp and, accepting defeat, they returned home.

A week passed, and the hermit didn't return to the lake. When a second week passed, the same young men who originally mocked and laughed at the old man became determined to find him, this time not because of their curiosity, but because of a feeling of compassion and humanity. They feared he might be sick and in great distress, and they wanted to apologize for their previous actions. They wanted to tell the old hermit, the mysterious Storm King, that he had won their respect and admiration.

The young men procured a much smaller and lighter boat and set out to find the enigmatic stranger. When they reached the tall grass where the hermit had disappeared, they pushed their flat-bottomed johnboat through the reeds with a pole. After what seemed like hours of pushing forward through the tall, matted grass, they came to a clear creek that was easily navigable. Two hundred yards downstream they encountered a clump of hammock, and there the search ended. The hermit's shack stood before them in all its primitive glory like the lost kingdom of Shambala.

The young men tied their johnboat to a large exposed root of a bald cypress and quietly approached the shack. It was about eight feet long and four feet wide, constructed of saplings thatched together with grass, the sides covered with the dried hides of alligators. As the two men approached the shack, they were overcome by a powerful stench, which turned their stomachs. They opened the door to the shack and looked inside, where they found the hermit dead upon the floor, his body badly decomposed. The dead man's fingers clutched at a book, which he must have been reading at the moment of death. The young men took the book and then respectfully covered the hermit's body with an alligator skin. After bowing their heads and saying a prayer, they pulled down the supports of the hut and collapsed the structure, burying the old man beneath a pile of timber and reeds. Though the hermit was a stranger, the two young men felt as if they had lost a lifelong friend.

Their feelings for the mysterious stranger only deepened after they returned home and read the book that had been in the dead man's hands. It was a diary, and its pages contained the sad story of the hermit's life. His name was Frank Walton, and he had come from Savannah, Georgia. Though everyone presumed that the hermit was around seventy years old because of his grizzled appearance, he was not yet fifty at the time of his death.

Forty years earlier, Frank Walton and Minnie Jeffcott lived a few miles outside of Savannah on adjoining farms. As neighbors, the two had grown up together and were as inseparable as a pair of best friends could be. It was only natural that Frank and Minnie would fall in love and get married, even though there was a six-year age difference between them. They became engaged, and the wedding was set for June of 1861. At the time, he was a young man of twenty-three, and she was barely seventeen. When the war came along, Frank enlisted and served under Francis Stebbins Bartow, who would later be killed at the Battle of Manassas. Minnie agreed to postpone the wedding until his return and, emboldened by this promise, the young man marched gallantly into battle. Bartow's troops were obliterated at Manassas, with half of the men under his command either killed, wounded, or captured. Frank Walton was among the captured, and he spent the next three and a half years in a Union prison camp.

In the spring of 1865, ragged, dirty, and half-starved, Frank returned home. Stopping to rest in Savannah, he ran into an old friend and immediately asked about Minnie. He was informed that Minnie had just gotten married about a week earlier, to a coward of a man who had escaped military duty by hiding out in the woods for the duration of the war. The news stunned Frank so much that he turned as pale as a ghost and left Savannah without saying a word. That night, Frank left Georgia and was never heard from again.

38. Silas Dent

More often than not, hermits end up taking their untold stories to their unmarked graves. But every so often a hermit comes along whose name becomes permanently woven into the fabric of the local tapestry. Silas Dent, the "Hermit of Cabbage Key," is one such fellow. Just about every resident of St. Petersburg has heard of the colorful hermit, whose name now graces a famous steakhouse on St. Pete Beach.

Silas Dent was born in 1876 and grew up in Georgia, where he lived on a farm with his father, Will, and his brother, Noah. The Dent clan relocated to Florida in 1900 and operated a dairy farm on Cabbage Key, the largest of the fifteen islands that make up Tierra Verde. The Dents, along with a sea captain from Maryland by the name of William Bunce, were the island's first homesteaders. The dairy farm was a dismal failure, and after a few years the Dents moved to the mainland, but young Silas loved the island and eventually returned there, building the palm-front hut that would serve as his home for the next forty years.

Although he lived alone in his hut on the island, Silas became a familiar sight to the tourists and locals alike. Twice a month or so, he would row his boat over to the village of Pass-a-Grille and sell handmade fly swatters and other knick-knacks to the tourists, who likened the bushy-bearded hermit to Santa Claus with a sun tan. Unlike most hermits, Silas didn't harbor any resentment toward others, but he preferred the unspoiled solitude of his palm-frond shack to any place in the world. Cheerful in disposition, he never drank alcohol or smoked tobacco, and spent much of his alone time reading from his well-worn Bible or playing his banjo.

"I ain't been blue since 1912," he once remarked to a newspaper reporter who had paid a visit to the seventy-year-old hermit, "and I forget now what worried me then." When asked about the inevitable boredom that surely must befall a man removed from civilization, the hermit replied, "If I get to feeling restless, I just take one of the hairs from my beard between my fingers and try to split it. Sometimes I can split it clear up to my chin!" As old Silas had a long and bushy beard, this must have kept him quite busy.

The hermit had a soft spot for children, who in turn smothered him with hugs every time he rowed over to the mainland to sell his souvenirs to the tourists. He kept the children entertained with ghost stories and tales of pirate treasure, and dazzled both adults and children alike with his bizarre method for catching stone crabs, which involved dangling his feet over a crab's lair and waiting for it to attach itself to his toes, which had become callused and rugged from decades of walking around barefoot. He also impressed the tourists with his weather prognostication; it was said that he could estimate the temperature within two degrees based on the frequency of cricket chirps. These feats turned old Silas Dent into as much of a tourist attraction as Tierra Verde itself, and in 1948 *LIFE*

Silas Dent, "The Hermit of Cabbage Key."
Courtesy of St. Petersburg Museum of History.

magazine wrote a story about him, titled "The Happy Hermit of Cabbage Key."

As Silas grew older, his relatives on the mainland expressed a deep concern for his safety and well-being. Once, a niece of the hermit managed to convince him to spend some time with her family. On his first evening on the mainland, the niece prepared Silas a hot bath against his wishes. Reluctantly, he stepped into the gleaming porcelain tub and promptly fell, breaking five ribs. As soon as he recovered from this mishap, he hightailed it back to his beloved island, insisting that "civilization is too dangerous."

By the 1950s others had settled on the island, but the hermit didn't object to their presence. Claude McCall, a shrimp fisherman, moved to Cabbage Key with his wife and their infant son, and Mrs. McCall would often look in on the elderly hermit to make sure that he was in good health. She later remarked that Silas was something of a fatalist, who lamented annually that each winter would be his last. "I have made my peace with the Lord," he would say, "and I am just sitting here waiting for Him to take me in His own good time."

Silas Dent's time came in 1952 when he passed away at a hospital in St. Petersburg at the age of seventy-six. Hundreds attended his funeral, and the "Happy Hermit of Cabbage Key" was laid to rest at Greenwood Cemetery. To this day, visitors still leave shells next to his grave marker. Shortly after his death, when relatives removed Silas's meager possessions from the hut, they found a sign that the hermit had carved with his own hands hanging from the wall, which simply said: *It is nice living alone with God.*

We can only hope that there is a special place, perhaps a palm-frond bungalow on an enchanted island off the southern coast of Heaven, set aside for hermits like the loveable Silas Dent.

DISTRICT OF COLUMBIA

39. From Riches to Rags

Is the District of Columbia in the North or in the South? While the native-born citizens of Washington enlisted with the Union during the Civil War, the *de facto* border that separates the Northeast from the South, the Mason-Dixon Line, seems to suggest that the District of Columbia resides in Dixie. Even Washingtonians are divided on this issue; in D.C. there's a saying that goes "the further south you go, the more northern D.C. gets, and vice versa." Many others refuse to take sides at all, insisting that the District of Columbia isn't in the North *or* the South, but exists in a state of non-statehood limbo. However, based solely on geography, the District of Columbia *should* be in the South by virtue of the fact that if you drive more than a few miles in any given direction, you'll find yourself in Dixie.

Regardless of the District of Columbia's geography, in January of 1906 one of the most remarkable characters in Washington passed away—a hermit by the name of Henry M. Martin. His story is remarkable because Henry was a man whom fickle Fortune placed high upon the pedestal of wealth and fame, only to fall into the deepest abyss of anguish and poverty. Though he lived the better part of his life in grandeur and comfort, his final days were torture, as old Henry the hermit drained the last bitter drop from his cup of calamity.

Henry M. Martin was born in the city of New York in 1833. He received his education at Dr. Middleditch's Seminary in England and was noted for his academic and intellectual brilliance. While still a teenager, Henry returned to New York and obtained a position as a clerk with the Franklin Insurance Company. Henry quickly climbed the ladder of success on account of his business sense, amiable personality, and integrity. He earned the trust of prominent and influential businessmen and, as a result, was offered the position of assistant secretary at the Washington Insurance Company. A few years later he resigned his position and went into business for himself, establishing the firm of Martin & Stonig. He soon became one of the most prominent men in the business world of New York.

The outbreak of the war temporarily dissolved the business partnership, and Henry, along with a number of his friends, enlisted in the New York State militia. Henry's regiment, under General Daniel Adams Butterfield, sailed from New York to Annapolis, where the regiment camped for a short while before heading to Georgetown. Henry had risen to the title of commissary officer by this time, holding the rank of second lieutenant. After discovering that the regiment's entire store of food was spoiled and rancid, Henry immediately rode into Washington and demanded to see Secretary of War Edwin Stanton. Secretary Stanton, offended by the brazenness of a lowly second lieutenant, made it clear that he had no interest in such trivial and unimportant matters. Undeterred, Henry sought out President Lincoln. Unlike Secretary Stanton, however, Lincoln was impressed by the young officer's determination, and he gave the necessary order to correct the condition. The half-starved men under General Butterfield came to view Henry as a hero.

At Harper's Ferry Henry was thrown from his horse and suffered a severe head wound, which became infected. Though he was feverish, weak, and in excruciating pain, he refused to seek treatment. After a few weeks his condition worsened to such an extent that he was discharged from military service and sent back to New York. Upon recovering from his injuries and illness, Henry went back to the insurance business and once again rose to prominence. As a hobby, he took up chemistry and devoted his leisure time to studying the properties of various gases. His interest in illumination led him to the vice presidency of the Equitable Gas Light and Construction Company.

Within a few years of the war's end, Henry had become the nation's foremost expert in the manufacture of gas and began construction of a large gas works in Baltimore. In 1876 he went to Havana and built a chemical plant there, as well as the island's first ice manufacturing company. While in Cuba, Henry contracted malaria and was ill for several weeks, but he rallied against the disease and turned his attention to bigger things: supplying the entire city of San Francisco with gas and water. It was an ambitious dream that would soon turn into a nightmare.

Henry's project was so ambitious that it would require tens of millions of dollars and involve virtually every major financier in Europe and America. After purchasing several large tracts of land north of San Francisco, construction got under way. Henry was so confident, that he invested every dime he had into the venture. One of Henry's most important backers was Baron Emile de Erlanger, who was perhaps the wealthiest man in France at the time. Construction grinded to a halt when the baron grew skittish; the project could not proceed without his financial backing. After several months of sitting on the fence, the baron decided to pull out of the project. Other investors soon followed. Within weeks, Henry Martin was penniless.

Broken in spirit and faced with poverty, Henry returned to New York and accepted a position as the European agent for a large New York banking firm. But all was not lost; Henry had met a beautiful Prussian woman while he was in San Francisco. They were married, and Henry's wife soon gave birth to a son. Henry's new family accompanied him to Europe. He was making a name for himself in London when the stock market panics of 1890 and 1893 hit, and once again Henry found himself penniless. With his head bowed in shame, he took leave of his wife and son and returned to America, only to become critically ill on the return voyage. Henry slipped in and out of consciousness for weeks but eventually regained his strength. Once he recovered, he was informed that his son had died of typhoid fever. A short time later, Henry's grief-stricken wife decided to visit friends in Paris. On her voyage to Paris she was swept off the deck by an angry sea and drowned. The strain was too much for Henry, and his mind became blank. He couldn't remember his own name for a period of days. If not for the watchful eye of a faithful friend in those darkest hours, Henry surely would have died.

After recovering from his breakdown, Henry wandered into Washington and secured a pension for his military service. Since he had only spent a short time in the army, he was awarded the paltry sum of $12 a month. In a stretch of marshy wasteland outside of the Washington neighborhood of Langdon, beyond the railroad tracks and decaying factories, Henry rented a decrepit shack. He became a hermit and spent his remaining days amassing a respectable library of second-hand books, which he read from morning until night. As he grew older his health began to fail, and in the fall of 1905 he was removed from his dirty, mosquito-infested shack and taken to the Homeopathic Hospital, where he quietly passed away the following January. Through the efforts of his old acquaintances, Major Carson and William Jennings Bryan, the hermit's body was interred at Arlington National Cemetery.

40. Aunt Nancy

When Nancy Green died in the summer of 1896, it created quite a stir in South Washington. The colored hermitess was said to be a practitioner of voodoo, and her powerful potions and curious concoctions were reputed to be so powerful that folks of all races and backgrounds came to see her. "Aunt Nancy" may have been known to many, but very few people knew any details about her life; the old recluse was as mysterious as the incantations she murmured whenever she mixed up one of her potions.

The old woman's shack was located at the junction of Half and M Streets, on the banks of the odoriferous James Creek Canal, which, in those olden days before the advent of indoor plumbing, was teeming with raw sewage. Aunt Nancy's shack may have been a crude one-story structure that had seen better days since the day it was built, but the interior was a den of mystery and magic. Jars of teeth, scales, feathers, claws and fangs, and other ingredients of her craft adorned the shelves of her shack. Aunt Nancy had a panacea for every conceivable trouble or woe, whether mental, physical, moral, or imaginary. The hermitess would fill a small, silk pouch with hair from black cats and teeth from snakes as an amulet against bad luck, and there was a time when many of the residents of the Bloodfield neighborhood could be seen walking downtown with silk purses tied around their necks. After her death, Police Sergeant John C. Daley, who was familiar with the hermitess, stated in the July 7, 1896, edition of the Washington *Evening Times*: "You would be surprised to know how many people in South Washington are wearing Aunt Nancy's silk bags today."

For fifty cents a bottle (the equivalent of roughly thirteen dollars in today's currency), Aunt Nancy sold a blood-red liquid guaranteed to restore positions of power to those who had lost them. This "folk medicine" landed the hermitess in trouble one day. She had sold a bottle of the red liquid to a man who had lost his job as a stableman for the sum of ten dollars, and the buyer was instructed to place a few drops of the potion in front of his former employer's door each morning. Aunt Nancy assured the buyer that his position would be restored in time. Of course, the magic potion failed to produce the desired result, and the disgruntled stableman had the voodoo priestess arrested. Judge Miller dismissed the case, caustically remarking that any man who was foolish enough to invest his money in such voodoo deserved to lose it.

After Aunt Nancy's death her shack of mystery was searched by the local authorities, and the search turned up many strange articles related to necromancy, as well as a blind dog that the hermitess regarded with particular reverence. A bottle of her famous red liquid was confiscated and sent to a chemist at the Department of Agriculture to analyze. The mystery substance contained nothing of any medicinal value. The rest of Aunt Nancy's effects were claimed by her grandson, who was employed on Hermann Stutz's dairy farm near Tenleytown.

PART III
HERMITS OF THE MIDWEST

KANSAS

41. Hugh Cameron

No book on hermits would be complete without the tale of Hugh Cameron, one of America's best-known hermits. Cameron, who came to be known as the "Hermit of Kansas," earned his fame as an abolitionist, teacher, and military commander. However, he is perhaps best remembered for his eccentric behavior; behavior that included living inside of a wooden piano crate.

Born in 1826 on a farm near Saratoga Springs in Upstate New York, Hugh was the son of a Scottish immigrant, and was one of eight children born to Catherine Frazier. Almost entirely self-educated, Hugh didn't set foot inside a classroom until he was eighteen years old. Despite his late start in the world of academics, his intellect and perseverance allowed him to excel in his studies and a few years later, at the age of twenty-three, Hugh was hired as a mathematics teacher by the Rittenhouse Academy in Washington, D.C.

While in Washington, Hugh formed friendships with many influential people, some of whom would become loyal, lifelong friends. These friends included prominent men of the era, such as Daniel Webster and Stephen Douglas. Because of his strong opposition to slavery, Hugh Cameron became a very polarizing figure within Washington's social circles, where he made powerful friends as well as powerful enemies.

One of Hugh's closest friends was Gen. William Chaplain, who created a major stir in the 1850s when he was arrested for attempting to free the slaves belonging to a congressman from Georgia. Cameron was accused by his enemies of being an accomplice in this crime (which he was, in all likelihood) and was fired from his teaching position as a result of the rumors. A few days after losing his position, Cameron was attacked by a pro-slavery mob on the streets of Washington. It has been said that Hugh would've been killed during the attack if not for Henry Clay, the senator from Kentucky who intervened and saved Cameron's life.

Shortly after this incident, Cameron was appointed to a position within the Treasury Department, but his promising political career in Washington was cut short after he developed serious health problems stemming from a lung hemorrhage. Cameron was able to support himself during this time by obtaining employment as a door-to-door salesman. While selling subscriptions for *Harper's Magazine*, Cameron met and eventually befriended a group of New England abolitionists. The abolitionists planned on going to the Kansas Territory, and Cameron was invited to join them.

In 1853 Cameron set out on foot for Kansas. He walked to St. Louis, where he rejoined his friends from the Emigrant Aid Society from Massachusetts. Cameron and his party made their way from St. Louis to Kansas City, where he once again set out on foot and followed the Kansas River upstream. He set up camp near a bend in the river, on the site of present-day Lawrence.

Cameron was later appointed judge of Kansas Territory by Governor Redder who, like Hugh, was a close friend of Stephen Douglas. Under the next governor, Wilson Shannon, Cameron was appointed justice of the peace for the settlement of Lawrence. It has been written by many historians that Hugh Cameron, as a judge, played a pivotal role in preventing Kansas from becoming a slave state. During the territorial elections, many outlaws from the neighboring slave state of Missouri crossed the border into Kansas in the hopes of swaying election results by casting fraudulent ballots. Thanks to Cameron's efforts, these fraudulent voters had their ballots disqualified by the governor. This was no easy feat, since the other two territorial judges from Kansas had been elected to their posts thanks to illegal ballots cast by the same Missouri outlaws during previous elections. In William G. Cutler's 1883 *History of the State of Kansas*, it is written:

"When the polls were surrounded by more than 1,000 ruffians, he (Cameron) did not abandon his post, although others fled. In making out the returns, he secured a certificate from the two Judges elected by the ruffian invaders that the votes cast at his precinct were not all by legal resident voters; and the returns being made in this form, furnished the Governor valid grounds on which to declare the election void, which he did."

During the Civil War, Cameron enlisted and served two years in the 2nd Kansas Cavalry, earning the rank of captain. He then served four years in the 2nd Arkansas Cavalry, where he rose to the rank of lieutenant colonel. After returning from the war, Cameron was a changed man and, for one reason or another, decided that he wanted to live the secluded life of a hermit. He spent his later years making his home inside of a wooden piano crate mounted to a tree a-

Hugh Cameron, "The Kansas Hermit." From the Philipsburg Herald (KS), October 1, 1896.

long the banks of the Kansas River, three miles northwest of Lawrence. To this day, this area is still known as Cameron's Bluffs.

Although Hugh Cameron chose to live in a wooden treehouse, he was a veritable national celebrity in his day. Until his death in 1907 at the age of eighty-one, the snowy-bearded hermit would walk from Kansas to Washington on foot in order to attend special events paying tribute to Civil War veterans. Locals recalled that he would often be seen embarking on these journeys attired in his faded and crumpled blue military jacket with brass buttons.

42. Rudolph Myers

Alone on the barren prairie, toiling beneath the sweltering summer sun, a man and his mule team are inching along at a snail's pace. Behind them, across the shadeless plain, runs a long, brown scar carved into the ground that stretches on as far as the eye can see. It is a marvelous scar, its cuts and fills level and true, and it extends backward in a perfectly straight line before vanishing in the prairie grass somewhere on the horizon.

The man talks to himself as he works. Sometimes he hums a tune, sometimes he laughs. He is bearded and dark-skinned, his hide having been tanned to a deep bronze from endless hours of outdoor labor. Dirt-caked overalls, worn down to rags, struggle to keep from falling off the man's lean and wiry body. His name is Rudolph Myers, and he is building a railroad to nowhere.

For the better part of two decades Rudolph Myers has been the enigma of Hodgeman County. In 1908 he decided to build himself a railroad, beginning at the base of some low bluffs a few miles away from Jetmore, a town of but a few hundred souls. He has purchased twelve miles of right-of-way, and has thus committed himself to single-handedly building a railroad extending from no place in particular to someplace even less in particular, in a general south-westerly direction.

Rudolph Myers, the son of German immigrants, lives alone on the right-of-way, in a tiny shack of rusted corrugated iron. His mules live in a pen constructed of broken and discarded boards. The mules, much like the locals, have no idea why Rudolph engages himself in such a futile endeavor but, unlike the locals, the mules keep their mouths shut and don't ask questions. At any rate, Rudolph has grown tired of responding with the same answer. With every new shout of "Hey, what are you doing out there?" the bronze-skinned hermit replies, "I'm building a railroad!" Then he shakes his head and worries about the state of civilization, since it's obvious that he's building a railroad, and anyone with eyes in their head should be able to discern as much.

Year after year he works on his railroad, which no one ever asked him to build. Every once in a while he buys another mile of right-of-way, paying for the land with checks that never seem to bounce, much to everyone's amazement. The residents of Jetmore remember when Rudolph Myers first arrived, sometime around 1907. Bids were being taken for the grading of an approach to a bridge, with bids ranging from $800 to $1,000 having been made. "I'll do it for five hundred," offered the stranger, and the city, smiling in its sleeve, awarded him the contract. He finished the job in ten days, turning himself a nice profit in the process. Shortly thereafter, he made the decision to build the railroad.

From that time forward he became a hermit. As the years pass, Rudolph loses track of time, and he often goes into town on Sundays for his household necessities, forgetting that the stores are closed on Sunday. He argues that the shop owners have conspired to close their doors either a day early or a day late. On only one of his visits to town did the hermit ever elaborate on his project. In 1920, when asked about his railroad's destination, the fifty-five-year-old hermit merely shrugged and said, "Somewhere north of Garden City. I dunno just where."

"It's the best route for a railroad anywhere round here," he then added as an afterthought. He wistfully gazed to the southwest. "I figured I'd have money enough to buy the right of way, and I could do all the work myself, just me and the mules. I thought maybe I could sell stock and be a stockholder. I've got about all the grading done now, the rest will be level ground. But I won't have money enough to put down the ties and rails and get the trains running. And nobody seems to take any interest. They come round and ask a lot of questions, but they don't do nothing. Some railroad fellows came and looked at it once, but they never came back."

Myers eventually graded the final stretch of right-of-way, linking his railroad to the old Nickel Plate Road, an old railroad that had been abandoned before its construction was ever finished. This finally connected Jetmore with Garden City, and shortened the existing Santa Fe route by several miles. The people of Jetmore had long sought a western connection with Garden City, over fifty miles away, but various attempts at making this connection failed. Dozens of Santa Fe workmen had attempted this feat in the 1880s, but didn't come close to the hermit's accomplishment, giving up after a few short miles. This important connection established a link between the Kansas wheat fields, the corn fields of Nebraska, and the wheat fields of the Dakotas.

Railroading magazines of the era marveled at the hermit's achievement:

It is an unusually good railway grade, as good as any standard-gauge railroad anywhere in a prairie country. It has been built without surveyor's lines being run, without the use of levels or other mechanical devices, yet the top of the grade is absolutely level and ready for the track to be laid . . . Nothing has been left undone to build a perfect railway grade, fourteen feet wide on top, with standard slopes for all fills and cuts and standard drainage through all the cuts and level places. Real railroad engineers have been over the grade at various times and have pronounced it as good as any grade in the country. (The Railway Conductor, Volume 38, 1921)

Sadly, the hermit never saw any of the profits from his important contribution. He continued living as a hermit for twenty more years, until he was removed to a hospital for the mentally ill. He died on January 20, 1943, and was buried in an unmarked grave on the grounds of the Topeka State Hospital—a facility with a notorious reputation for abuse, neglect, and cruelty. One newspaper reporter wrote of seeing a patient at the hospital who had been confined in leather straps for so long that the patient's skin was growing around the straps. It had been alleged that some patients were chained or strapped to chairs and beds for years at a time. Other newspapers condemned the institution for losing thousands of patient records.

Unfortunately, due to the hospital's ineptitude, the details surrounding the final years of Rudolph Myers's unusual life have been lost to history. However, a measure taken by the Kansas Legislature has restored a small amount of dignity to the long-forgotten pioneer of the prairie. In 2006 a monument was erected on the northeast corner of the old hospital grounds, engraved with the names of 1,157 people who died at the asylum and were laid to rest in unmarked graves. Rudolph Myers's name appears on the monument, a small but noteworthy reminder of the eccentric hermit who built himself a railroad to nowhere.

43. Fred Kupler

Situated on the Arkansas River, the city of Derby is the largest suburb of Wichita. During the time of Fred Kupler, however, it was a rapidly growing village on the Atchison, Topeka, and Santa Fe Railway line known as El Paso. In the middle of the river is a tiny island, which is still marked on maps as Kupler's Island. Though the small island itself is ordinary and unremarkable, the man who settled there was anything but.

Fred Kupler was Swiss by birth and drifted into the territory of Kansas when the banks of the Arkansas River were occupied only by natives. He made his home on the island and lived a life of peaceful seclusion, even as the nearby settlement known to the locals as Cowtown grew into the flourishing city of Wichita. Kupler was a frightful sight, with his tangled mass of long, black hair, but had one friend in the city—a Dominican priest named Father Nicholas. The priest was the only human being who seemed to have any influence over the wild man of Kupler's Island.

One day in the spring of 1892 two boys out on a hunting trip landed on the island and, curiosity getting the better of them, decided to investigate the hermit's shack. It was a bold decision, and one they would soon regret. By the end of the day, the two young hunters probably wished that they had heeded the words of their mothers, who warned them to never set foot on the mysterious island. Although nobody knew a thing about the hermit, it was popular opinion that he was dangerous and quite possibly deranged.

The two boys tip-toed across the island toward the hermit's crude, wooden shack. The air was filled with the booming voice of a man speaking in a strange tongue, as though trying to cast a magical spell or conjure up the dead. One of the boys, feeling his nerve slide down his leg and into his shoe, voiced his concerns in a hushed tone and said that he wanted to turn back. "He's just a harmless old man," explained his friend, and with a rolling of his eyes decided to press on. "You're probably right," the nervous hunter whispered. The two boys continued toward the shack.

Approaching the window they saw the old hermit inside silhouetted against a blazing bonfire, which sent curls of putrid black smoke up through the rusted pipe that served as a chimney. Pressing their foreheads against the pane of glass, they saw Kupler dancing some variety of ghost dance never seen before and howling the tune of some curious song. The boys weren't sure whether the bizarre scene was grounds for concern or laughter. Their minds were made up a few moments later, however, when the old hermit suddenly stopped dancing. The boys heard Kupler proclaim, in a pleading voice, "Oh, for a sacrifice!"

Just then, the hermit caught a glimpse of the two boys peeking through his window, and, evidently thinking that one of them would be just the right kind of material for an offering to some dark god, the black-bearded hermit dashed out of the cabin and chased after the two young men, all the while hollering that he needed somebody to sacrifice. The boys dropped their guns and took to their heels. Kupler followed them to the edge of the river. The boys, who didn't have a boat, waded across the shallow waters, but were closely followed by the mad hermit, who was whooping in delight and laughing like a maniac. The chase continued through the woods and, at times, the hermit came very close to grasping his prey.

The boys made it to Derby, with the hermit on their heels, and shouted for assistance. The quiet little village was alarmed; in its history no such excitement had ever been seen. Kupler continued to demand a sacrifice, even as a dozen of the town's strongest men wrestled him to the ground. Kupler, though short in stature, was as strong as an ox, and it took everything the men had to keep him down. Someone ran off to fetch a rope and, with great difficulty, Fred Kupler was bound at the hands and feet. The authorities hauled him off to the county jail, and a hearing was set by a judge in order to assess the Swiss hermit's level of sanity.

It was evident to the judge that the old hermit was a few sandwiches short of a picnic, so Kupler was sent to the insane asylum, where he lived out the remainder of his days. Since the immigrant had no known relatives, he was laid to rest in a potter's field, forever leaving the story of his tortured past a mystery.

44. The Strange Funeral of Otto Shaffer

On a summer day in 1896, the skies above Butler County grew dark and ominous. Farmers toiling in their fields raised their furrowed brows to the heavens and then calmly headed for shelter. If the storm brought a tornado, it would be just one of many encountered in their lifetimes. But others, who didn't have the good fortune of living in a house with thick walls or a strong foundation, were more frightened and scrambled beneath their beds or dove into their bathtubs. Meanwhile, the poorest of the poor—the itinerant laborers and dirt farmers—fell to their knees in prayer.

A tornado never struck the Walnut River valley that afternoon, but the angry bruise-colored clouds brought forth a horrific thunderstorm. Otto Schaffer, a hermit farmer, sought shelter inside his tiny ramshackle cabin, and just as he was offering up a prayer of protection from the ferocious storm, a bolt of lightning demolished the house and killed the hermit. When neighbors found the body beneath the pile of timbers, poor Otto was still on his knees with his wrinkled, old hands folded.

The coroner was summoned, and the hermit's body was taken away. Otto's relatives and heirs could not be notified, because he didn't have a friend or a family member left in the world. For thirty years Otto had been living the life of a recluse, and nobody seemed to know much about the life of the queer, little fellow who lived in the crooked, wooden shack on the outskirts of the village of El Dorado. Unlike most hermits, Otto didn't have a tangled beard or long, matted hair; he preferred to be clean-shaven and favored hair that was cut short. But, like many folks who gravitate toward the life of a hermit, Otto refused to speak of his past or hold conversation with the locals. He made his own clothing and grew his own food and was self-sufficient in every possible way. Otto owned a considerable amount of land, so the reason why he preferred to live such a spartan and miserly life was a mystery to everyone in Butler County.

As the hermit's body was being prepared for burial, it was learned that Otto had been living off his meager government pension, which he earned by being a soldier in the Grand Army of the Republic. Further investigation revealed that Otto had fought at nearly every major battle of the war, and had fought with bravery and valor. The local authorities arranged for the hermit to have a proper soldier's burial. Meanwhile, the coroner who was tasked with the chore of preparing the hermit's body made his own startling discovery—Otto Schaffer was a woman.

In spite of this unusual development, it was agreed that Otto still deserved a soldier's burial due to her bravery on the battlefields of Dixie, and the veterans of the Grand Army of the Republic turned out in great numbers to give the dead hermit a proper send-off, even though the weather was still rainy and dismal. However, Otto's burial would prove to be just as bizarre as her mysterious life. During a lull in the rain, the veterans raised their rifles one by one and fired off a salute. The veteran who fired the last salute accidentally shot a dove that was in mid-flight over the old country graveyard, and the snow-white bird fell from the sky and landed in Otto's grave, right on top of the hermit's rain-soaked coffin. The veterans decided that the bird should be left there, and both hermit and dove were covered with the damp Kansas soil.

MINNESOTA

45. The Hermit of Swan Lake

Shunning the society of man and content with a life of solitude, a man named John Walters adopted the life of a recluse in the years following the Civil War, making his home inside a tiny cave on a lonely island in Swan Lake. The life of this remarkable man may have escaped the notice of history were it not for a businessman from Nicollet who discovered the hermit and related his sad story to the public.

Walters arrived at Swan Lake shortly after the end of the war. He came unannounced, and his arrival was not witnessed. One summer morning a farmer was rowing a boat across the lake when he saw a repulsive-looking man emerge from the island cave. The startled farmer, when he returned to shore, spread the word about the mysterious man on the island. Such a sighting created a stir among the rural farmers, and before long a delegation of locals decided to take a trip to the island in the middle of Swan Lake to investigate the matter.

The men successfully managed to locate the hermit, but, like most hermits, Walters wasn't particularly in the mood to converse or answer questions. The farmers found the hermit to be sullen and reserved, and the more questions they asked the more silent Walters became. Walters refused to give the men his name, and when asked about his future intentions, the ugly hermit with the repulsive face flatly refused to speak. The only thing the hermit said was that he had no intentions of leaving the island.

Their mission a failure, the delegation of farmers returned to their homes and decided that it was best to leave the sullen recluse to his own devices. Of course, this didn't prevent rumors from circulating throughout the countryside. Some folks speculated that Walters was a fugitive hiding from the law, while others believed he had been scorned or jilted by a lover. After all, he did have a disfigured face, which might explain his decision to remove himself from society. One thing the locals could all agree upon, however, was that the inhabitant of the island in Swan Lake was a very peculiar and ornery fellow.

The years passed, and on rare occasions the hermit would leave the island and go to New Ulm for provisions, trading in pelts and furs for ammunition and gunpowder. Hunting and trapping allowed Walters to eke out an income sufficient for his simple needs. But whenever he went to town, he refused to converse with the villagers. Somewhere along the line it was learned that the mysterious man had a name after all, and that it was John Walters.

At some point "Old Walters," as he became known, became convinced that an attempt was being made to wrest his island away from him. During this time he grew suspicious of anyone attempting to land on the island, and would greet intruders with a wave of his shotgun and a stern warning. Eventually, his suspicions ceased, and Walters had no further troubles with the boaters and sportsmen who descended upon the island each fall to hunt for ducks. The hunters knew all about the island's strange occupant and, respecting the hermit's desire for privacy, tried their best not to be a bother.

Years later, a businessman from Nicollet made a trip east to visit friends in a small hamlet in Upstate New York. In the village he overheard someone talking about a fellow named John Walters and wondered if it could be the same man he had heard about living on the lake. The odds were astronomical, naturally, since there were probably hundreds of people with the same name, but the businessman knew that if he didn't ask around, his curiosity would've eaten him alive.

The man the villagers from New York knew as John Walters had been orphaned at an early age. The boy pluckily worked his way through school and upon graduating obtained a position as a cashier at the bank. In 1861, when President Lincoln called for volunteers, the bank teller was among the first of the town's residents to enlist, and helped to raise a company of soldiers. During one battle in the South the young man was struck down by an exploding shell. So grave were his injuries that he was reported dead.

The few friends he had in New York mourned for the fallen soldier, but time stands still for no man, and eventually John Walters faded from memory. Nothing was heard of him until the end of the war, when the veteran returned to his old hometown, ragged and unkempt. He had been so mutilated by his wounds that people did not recognize him at first. The horrors of war had warped his mind to such an extent that his neighbors whispered to each other that the man with the mutilated face was stark raving mad. His ghastly appearance prevented him for obtaining work, and for a few months he was supported by charity. But Walters was too proud a man to be a charity case and suddenly he disappeared, never to be seen in New York again, leaving behind no indication of where he had gone.

IOWA

46. William Knight

In April of 1869, near the village of Rockingham, a hermit named William Knight drew his last breath. His death, at the age of seventy-five, made all the local papers, and eastern Iowa was abuzz with the news. The reason why the death of a recluse should arouse such interest was likely due to Knight's colorful and mysterious past, when he was a wealthy and famous lawyer in England.

Thirty years earlier, Knight decided to leave England without a word to his friends or relatives. When he arrived in Iowa, he decided to resume his career as an attorney and quickly became one of the most esteemed lawyers in Davenport. Meanwhile, across the Atlantic, a frantic search was still taking place for the missing barrister. His old friends took out newspaper ads offering rewards to anyone who had any information about Knight's disappearance. Year after year, their efforts were fruitless.

His friends in England remembered that William owned a gold watch, remarkable in its size and of peculiar construction. There was no other watch like it in the world. His friends in England sent out descriptions of this watch all over Great Britain and, deciding to leave no stone unturned in the search for their missing friend, even sent this description to the leading watch dealers in America. It was a long shot, they knew, but if Knight's watch were to be discovered, then the whereabouts of its owner might be discovered as well.

As luck would have it, William's gold watch stopped working one day, and he sent it to Philadelphia to an establishment in which a description of the unusual timepiece had been posted. The watch dealer immediately wrote to London, informing the lawyer's friends that the watch belonged to a man in Iowa. The Londoners wasted no time in traveling to America and trekking westward to Davenport, where they were reunited with their lost friend.

Much to their disappointment, Knight expressed no desire to leave Iowa and return home. Numerous attempts at changing the lawyer's mind were made, but Knight was adamant. So great grew their frustration, that the Londoners resorted to underhanded tactics and strategies. An attempt was even made to secure his arrest for some fictitious offense, so he might be sent back to England as a prisoner. These attempts to persuade Knight to return to England left a foul taste in his mouth, and the lawyer grew agitated. After his friends had exhausted their supply of ideas, they had no choice but to go back to England in defeat. From this time forward, until his death, William Knight was a changed man.

The lawyer gave up his practice and bought a small farm near Rockingham on a heavily wooded tract of land, and there he erected a primitive shanty in the forest. He lived alone, with no companions except for his pipe and his books. Knight loved to read. He received newspapers from England regularly, subscribed to many periodicals, and always managed to keep himself apprised of current events. The hermit cooked his own food, washed his own clothes, and chopped his own wood. Not many years earlier, when he was a powerful man in London, he had a multitude of servants to do these menial tasks.

As the years rolled by, Knight was seen less and less by the villagers and neighbor farmers. He invited no one to his shanty and had no reason to return to town after teaching himself the basics of agriculture. And thus, he lived the remainder of his days as a hermit, never once regretting his decision to turn his back on his wealthy friends and luxurious manor and flee to the rugged American frontier.

Though he rarely left his shack, occasionally the hermit would be seized with the urge to write letters. These letters, conversational in tone, were often addressed to his peers in the legal profession. In one of these letters, William Knight alluded to the true reason for leaving England so many years earlier, admitting that he had been hopelessly disappointed by love. He wooed, won, and then lost a lovely English girl. She had preferred a "belted knight" who lived in a castle to a young, handsome barrister who had to beat his own path to fortune and fame. William Knight decided to take a different path altogether; one that would lead him

away from fame and fortune to a secluded shack in the
Iowa woods.

47. Captain Stubbs

Today, the city of Davenport is a bustling center of
trade and commerce and one of the fastest-growing cities
in the Midwest. However, back in 1822, it was a small
settlement along the Mississippi River known as Stubbs'
Ferry. The settlement was named after Captain Stubbs, a
West Point graduate, eccentric genius, and one of the most
colorful hermits in the history of the Midwest.

Stubbs fell in love with the region after spending four
years stationed with the army at Rock Island, Illinois. In
1827, after his stint at Rock Island came to an end, Stubbs
went east to work for the Postal Service under his brother-
in-law, Judge McLean. From there, he went on to work for
the post office in Cincinnati, which suited him for a little
while, but he always dreamed of returning to his old
stomping grounds. He returned to Rock Island in 1833, but
he was a changed man; he seemed to have lost his vigor
and zest for life. Deep melancholy brooded over him. Some
suspected that he had been hurt in love, but no one ever
knew for sure because Captain Stubbs refused to talk
about it.

Stubbs became withdrawn from the world and found a
secluded spot in East Davenport where he dug a hole into
the ground. From his man-made burrow on the hill he
could gaze out upon the languid Mississippi, and it is in
this cave he lived for eight years with his two companions
—a cat and a pig. Captain Stubbs was known to converse
with his companions, and his cat and pig received many a
lecture from their eccentric master.

A lawyer named A. C. Fulton met the hermit in the
summer of 1842 while wandering along the banks of the
river during an afternoon stroll. Fulton wanted to get a
better view of the scenery, so he ascended the hill,
unaware that a man was living beneath his very feet. Once
atop the mound he caught the sound of a human voice,
but could not determine where it was coming from. The
volume of the voice increased, and the lawyer was able to

discern a few colorful words. Fulton studied every inch of the mound until he discovered that the angry voice was coming from a small pipe that served as the hermit's chimney. The alarmed attorney shouted into the pipe, "Hallo! What are you doing down there?" His query was immediately answered with, "What are *you* doing up there? Get off my house, good sir!"

This was the first meeting between the two men, but it wouldn't be the last. Fulton and Stubbs became friends, and it was a friendship that would last until the end of the hermit's life. According to A. C. Fulton, the reason why Captain Stubbs had been cursing up a blue streak on the day of that first visit was because his pet pig had commenced eating dinner before the captain had given the order. Stubbs was a strict disciplinarian and ran his household with an iron fist, so he was quite perturbed when he placed a fresh-baked loaf of cornbread onto the table and the pig forgot his tableside manners. This experience wasn't typical, however, since the pig was rather well-behaved most of the time. In fact, whenever Captain Stubbs went out for his daily stroll along the Mississippi, his cat and pig marched behind their master with military precision.

Captain Stubbs was a surveyor by trade and was responsible for drawing up most of the deeds and contracts between the earliest settlers of Davenport. Though he was a peculiar fellow, he was respected throughout the county for his shrewdness, intelligence, honesty, and education. In spite of his ragged appearance, he was a man of refinement and integrity. In 1846 he was finally persuaded to leave his cave and rejoin society in Davenport. He had such a respectable reputation, in fact, that he was elected justice of the peace, an office he held until his death in May of 1848.

48. The Nun and the One-Eyed Hermit

In 1906 a bizarre string of events occurred near Dubuque involving a Catholic nun, a one-eyed hermit with a mysterious twin, and a $50,000 inheritance. It is a story that would make for a terrific mystery novel, except for the fact that the publisher would have rejected the manuscript as being wholly unbelievable. If the author of this far-fetched tale had written a short synopsis of the novel, it might have read as follows:

On the evening of obtaining the estate of her late brother, Sister Mary Carlos discovers that the one-eyed sibling she had not seen in forty years either has a doppelganger living in Ottumwa, or that the man she believed to be her brother was an imposter all along.

The most interesting part of the story? It is not a work of fiction at all.

A recluse named Michael Carlos had died three months earlier in Dallas Center, a small town not far from Des Moines. He left behind a farm valued at $50,000, and the executors of his will searched far and wide for Michael's next of kin. One day, a man showed up at a convent near Dubuque bearing a photograph, which was shown to a nun by the name of Sister Mary Carlos. She immediately recognized the man in the photograph as the brother she had not seen in forty years—a brother named Michael who had lost an eye and part of his jaw during the Civil War. After the identification had been made, Sister Mary Carlos requested that the estate be sold and the proceeds sent to the head of the Catholic order Sisters of Charity.

The story took a bizarre twist a few days later, however, when the nun received a letter and a photograph from a second man, also named Michael Carlos. The man was a dead ringer for the nun's estranged brother, right down to the deformed jaw and missing eye. What are the odds, you ask? Some with an inclination toward mathematics might be tempted to calculate the probability of such an event, but it is doubtful that the average high school graduate possesses the level of mathematical education needed to come up with an accurate answer to the puzzle. It just may require a professor armed with a bucket of chalk and the longest blackboard known to the world of academia.

The man claiming to be Michael Carlos wrote that he was the brother of Mary, whom he had not seen since he left the family home in Zanesville, Ohio, at the close of the war. As further proof of his identity, he described the particulars of his departure. He had been betrothed to a

HAIRY MEN IN CAVES

girl of high social standing in Zanesville. While in battle, he had lost an eye and part of his chin, courtesy of an exploding Confederate shell. Michael's beloved, horrified at her beau's facial disfigurement, broke off the engagement. This so humiliated the young soldier that he left home without a word, roaming the Midwest until he took up the life of a hermit farmer. He also included a photograph of Mary with his letter.

Several experts compared the photograph of the hermit from Ottumwa to the photograph of the dead man from Dallas Center. They all arrived at the same conclusion—the man in both images was Michael Carlos. But how could this be?

The bewildered nun traveled to Dallas Center as well as Ottumwa in an attempt to clear up the mystery, but her travels were in vain. Both stories seemed to check out, although the Michael Carlos from Ottumwa speculated that the Dallas Center hermit was an imposter. The $50,000 estate, however, was not a part of a nefarious scheme. A judge determined that the estate would be held until the matter was resolved.

The truth always comes out in the wash, so the saying goes, and the true relatives of Michael Carlos were eventually found. The hermit's brother, a man from Omaha named John McCaffrey, came forward and cleared up the mystery. McCaffrey's claim was corroborated by a sister in California named Celia, and another brother in Seattle named Charles Carlos. McCaffrey stated that the deceased hermit had come from Ireland as a young boy and lived in Zanesville. Michael Carlos has been enrolled in law school, but enlisted in the army when the war broke out. He suffered his disfigurement at the Battle of Antietam, and was rejected by his lover when he returned. He fled to Dallas Center, Iowa, and lived the life of a hermit, hiding his disfigured face behind a gauzy veil held in place by his ragged Union slouch hat. As for the Michael Carlos of Ottumwa, he appears to have been the creation of one mentally unstable nun—at least, for the most part.

There *is* a Civil War veteran named Michael Carlos buried in Ottumwa. He was also born in Ireland, but never set foot in Ohio. He died in 1910 and his headstone indicates he served in Company F of the Third Iowa Cavalry. But this Michael Carlos was never disfigured and rejected by a lover; he returned from the war unscathed, married a Miss Prather, and raised a son. He didn't have a sister named Mary. He didn't have a sister at all.

In the summer of 1905 a nun by the name of Sister Mary Carlos was sent to Michigan after serving four years as the superioress of the Immaculate Conception School in Denver, a school founded by the Sisters of Charity. She had been sent to Michigan by her superiors in order to recover from a nervous breakdown. While recovering from her mental illness, she became familiar with the story of the one-eyed hermit, as the details of his life had been printed in numerous newspapers. The disturbed nun must have written, in her own hand, the letter from her fictitious "long-lost brother," and enclosed a photograph of herself as a young girl in order to lend her claim a touch of credibility.

INDIANA

49. The Hardshell Harpers

Some of the first settlers of Franklin County were followers of Elder William Tyner, a Primitive Baptist preacher who left Virginia in 1797 and migrated to Indiana. The Primitive Baptists flourished in the rugged and uncultivated wilderness of eastern Indiana, where they were known as "Hardshells" by others who soon settled in the Whitewater River Valley.

The Primitive Baptists were given the "Hardshell" name because of their strict religious beliefs. They draw all of their beliefs directly from the 1611 King James Version of the Bible; they do not use musical instruments in church services, and they do not permit their members to own any pictures or likenesses of Jesus, believing that such images are "idols." But the one tradition for which the Hardshells are best known is the ritual of foot washing, in which the sexes are separated and one person physically washes the feet of another. To outsiders, many beliefs of the Primitive

Baptists are strange, so it's perhaps no surprise that one family of hermit Hardshells living in Franklin County were the topic of much curiosity in the latter part of the nineteenth century.

Lizzie and Mary Ann Harper were born in the heart of Hardshell country, in a small and simple home on Snow Hill, a mile and a half west of the village of New Trenton. Though the sisters lived to a ripe old age, they never left the dilapidated, wooden shanty in which they were born— not even after their roof caved in.

Mary Ann was the oldest of the curious pair, Lizzie was two years younger. Even when they were children, the rustic shack they called home was in a state of disrepair, and only got worse over time. By the time the women reached the age of sixty, the ancient abode had fallen into a serious state of decay. Years earlier, the clapboard roof had collapsed, and the spinster sisters made no attempt to repair it beyond nailing a few rough boards over the holes in order to keep out the rain. A few years later, the collapsed roof finally caved in completely. Fortunately for the eccentric occupants, it found support on the high bed posts and remained precariously perched just inches over their heads for several more years. As luck would have it, had the Harper family chosen a different style of bed frame, Lizzie and Mary Ann surely would've been crushed when the cave-in occurred. Though they had no interest in home renovation or interior design, it would be entirely fair to say that the Harper sisters had unwittingly been the inventors of the "dropped ceiling."

Even though the sagging shanty was a den of squalor, the strange sisters seemed satisfied with their sanctuary. At one time the family had owned a considerable amount of land and livestock, but the cattle perished from neglect, and the property grew thick with weeds. The neighbors attempted, in vain, to induce the old maids to change their neglectful ways, but every neighbor's plea was met with cold rebuffs. Eventually, the neighbors came to the realization that the Harper sisters would never change, and the two hermitesses were left to their own devices.

However, as Lizzie and Mary Ann grew wrinkled with age, the villagers once again grew concerned; this time not because the Harper homestead was a horrid eyesore, but because they feared for the safety of the spinster sisters. From the looks of the shanty, it seemed that a strong wind was all that would be needed to reduce the structure to a pile of debris. The decent God-fearing folks of Franklin County took up a collection and enough money was raised to make repairs to the Harper home. Several workmen donated their talents and a small, but adequate, one-room cottage was built adjoining the woeful, wooden hut.

The sisters did not enter the new addition for quite some time. Lizzie, in particular, vowed that she would never set foot inside the new room, but eventually the sisters made the decision to live in the new residence. Shortly thereafter, in February of 1891, a reporter from the *Cincinnati Enquirer* paid the sisters a visit, as word of the eccentric female hermits had spread across state lines. At the time, Mary Ann was sixty-two years of age; her sister, sixty.

Before visiting the house, many strange facts were related by the neighbors to the man from Cincinnati. He was surprised to learn that Lizzie went to bed like clockwork every November and remained in a state of hibernation until spring, usually awakening sometime in April. This odd conduct had been going on for at least fifteen years, the reporter had been told, and no one had any explanation for it. Upon visiting the Harper sisters, the reporter found Mary Ann hunched over inside the old hut, engaged in cooking over the ancient stove. She received him warmly, and seemed excited to have a visitor. It was likely the man from Cincinnati was the first visitor the sisters had in several years. The other sister was in bed in a corner of the room, it being February, and she in a state of hibernation. Much to the visitor's astonishment, Lizzie couldn't be roused from her slumber no matter how hard Mary Ann tried.

The elder sister reported that she liked the new house very much, but preferred the old one because she had been born there and because her parents had lived there many years before the sisters were born. The reporter included these details in his article, which appeared in the *Cincinnati Enquirer*, along with this description of the sisters, beginning with Mary Ann:

"The strange woman has a homely but interesting face. She is above the medium height and slender and wiry. She knows nothing about what is going on in the outside world, and pays little attention to the ordinary affairs of life. She hasn't even that common feminine failing, a love for gossip. Lizzie, although two years younger, looks much older, and her vacant look indicates that her mind is nearly gone . . . It is probable that the demented Lizzie will not survive the winter, although the people in the neighborhood say she is liable to live twenty years longer. Her remarkable habit of imitating the groundhog in retiring to winter quarters, which she has done for at least a score of years, leads every one to doubt that she is any more ill than she has been in half a century."

50. Diana of the Dunes

On the shores of Lake Michigan, amid high sand dunes and pine forests, lived a remarkable woman named Alice Gray. Born to wealthy parents in Chicago in 1881, Alice Mable Gray established herself as a dazzling intellect; at the age of sixteen she enrolled at the University of Chicago, where she studied mathematics, astronomy, Greek, and Latin. She was named a Phi Beta Kappa honor society member. Upon graduating, Alice continued her studies in Germany at the University of Gottinger, where she was introduced to a movement called Wandervogel, or "Birds of Passing." It was a counterculture embraced by many young people in Germany, who adopted the hermit life by giving up their material possessions and living off the bounty of the land.

When Alice returned to Chicago, she obtained employment at an astronomy magazine; however, in spite of her excellent education, her position was that of a stenographer. Alice compared this work to slavery and grew frustrated with the lack of job opportunities for educated women. Even in a bustling city like Chicago, Alice found nothing but low-paying, menial jobs. To Alice, it wasn't about money, but purpose. She didn't crave fame or fortune, but she hungered for a cause, something she could fight for and devote her life to. This hunger for purpose is what brought her to the Indiana dunes in 1915, where she would live in solitude for the next seven years in a tiny hut.

Alice had a deep love for the dunes and devoted much of her time studying and writing about the area's native wildlife. She believed that the dunes were in danger of extinction because of land development, and she grew nearly militant in her zeal to protect them from the ever-encroaching hand of man. She believed that the Indiana Dunes should be a national park, and during her years of self-imposed exile she wrote hundreds of letters to men and women of influence hoping to make her dream a reality.

Although she preferred to live her life in quiet seclusion, Alice became something of a media celebrity shortly after arriving at the dunes. She had cut her hair boyishly short, and her lithe, tanned physique was concealed only by a single scrap of cloth. This, of course, caught the attention of the local fishermen, who abandoned their duties to catch a glimpse of the nymph-like creature. Word of her beauty spread far and wide, with newspaper reports of the day referring to her as a bronze goddess who roamed the dunes in a state of undress. The press had dubbed her "Diana of the Dunes," a reference to the chaste huntress of Roman mythology. The nearby city of Chesterton even held an annual beauty pageant in her honor.

In reality, Alice Gray's reputation as the "Water Nymph of Lake Michigan" was a creation of the press, which took great liberties in describing the physical attributes of the hermitess: "If you were lucky some night when the moon was up and bathing the dune crests in its soft greenish glow, you could see Diana. She would stand there, beautiful in the moonlight, arms outstretched . . . breasts firm, thighs gently curving, like a statue of Galatea . . ."

Alice Mable Gray, "Diana of the Dunes."

"Of course, it's all right to call her a beautiful nymph and tell of the gleam of her white glistening skin as she bathes like Venus in the waters and all that," reads a more honest description given in 1916 by a Valparaiso writer named Bob Harrison, "but the fact remains that she's 40 and brown as a berry and tolerably husky."

Alice's life took an unfortunate turn in 1921, when she became romantically involved with a furniture maker named Paul Wilson, whom she later married. Wilson was, to put it quite bluntly, a hot-tempered lout. Some accounts imply that he was a giant of a man, standing about 6'6", and that he had an extensive criminal background. The two moved into a shack, which they had named "Wren's Nest" on the western end of Ogden Dunes. Alice and Paul were accused of a series of break-ins at neighboring cottages, though the accusations were never proven. Then, in June of 1922, a dead body was discovered near Wren's Nest. Paul Wilson was believed to be the murderer, but he was later acquitted of the charges.

Paul Wilson had a jealous streak, and he was known to verbally and physically assault reporters who traveled to the dunes to interview Alice. Just days after the body was found near their home, Wilson got into an altercation with a fellow named Eugene Frank, who made his living by bringing Chicago tourists to the dunes. Though details of this fight are sketchy, it is believed that Wilson attacked the tour guide in a jealous rage, before turning his anger on Alice Gray. On June 15, 1922, newspapers around the country ran the following: "Diana of the Dunes is lying in a Gary hospital, with a skull injury, and her husband giant, Paul Wilson, was shot in the right foot, in a fight which occurred near their shanty, east of Miller beach, Tuesday night. Eugene Frank, boatman, is under arrest."

Alice was never the same after her skull injury. Knowing that her time was growing short, she made it known that she wanted to be buried in Chicago, next to her family members. Alice Gray, the "Diana of the Dunes," died on February 11, 1925, but her final wish was never granted. Paul Wilson had her buried at Oak Lawn Cemetery in Gary, Indiana. And thanks to Paul Wilson, even Alice Gray's funeral took a bizarre turn. The February 19, 1925, edition of the *Chesterton Tribune* reported that Wilson drew a pistol in the middle of the funeral services and threatened to kill two men. He was taken to the police station and missed the remainder of the service. The following year, Wilson reportedly married another woman and was later shot dead during another burglary attempt.

One year after her death, Alice's dreams were partially realized with the establishment of the Indiana Dunes State Park in 1926. The twenty-five-mile stretch of shoreline would become the Indiana Dunes National Lakeshore in 1966. In all likelihood, this unique landscape would not have escaped extinction if not for the efforts of one unforgettable and remarkable hermitess.

MICHIGAN

51. The Heroic Henry Malone

Most of us know the major details of the life of Jefferson Davis, the former Mississippi senator who infamously became the first and only president of the Confederate States of America. Davis helmed the Confederacy, but was unable to find a way to stop the larger, more-powerful, and better-equipped Union Army. After General Lee's surrender, Davis planned to flee to the safety of Havana, Cuba, but was captured on May 10, 1865, and charged with treason. According to a popular legend, one that still persists to this day, Jefferson Davis had attempted to avoid capture by dressing up as a woman.

After two years of imprisonment, Jefferson Davis was released on bail, and the charge of treason was later dropped. He kept a low profile in his later years, writing his memoirs and serving as the president of the Carolina Life Insurance Company in Memphis. When he died in 1889, at the age of eighty-one, his funeral was one of the largest and most spectacular affairs the South had ever seen. While Jefferson Davis remains an iconic and legendary figure in the South even to this day, one detail of Jeff Davis's saga, which is scarcely known, even to the most ardent student of American history, is that his capture may not have taken place if not for a hermit named Henry Malone.

When Henry Malone died in Bay City, Michigan, in the March of 1902, the nation lost not only an unsung war hero, but one of its most colorful and unique hermits. Malone lived most of his adult life in a crudely-constructed shanty on the marshy prairie alongside the Saginaw River. The shanty, which was nothing more than a nine-foot-long pile of scrap wood and brush, was a windowless structure that could only be entered by climbing a pile of wood chips and descending into an opening. Malone put some boards over this hole in the winter months, but anyone familiar with the Saginaw Bay winters of Michigan can imagine the bitter torture the old hermit must have endured shortly after the autumn faded away like the morning mist over Lake Huron.

Unlike many hermits, Henry was known to make friendly conversation with the locals and, in turn, the locals tried not to interfere with his peculiar lifestyle. During extreme cold spells, the neighboring citizens would check on the hermit, but old Henry would always appear to be as snug as a bug in a rug, even when the thermometer dropped well below zero. Henry Malone also had family who attempted to convince him to leave his dreary surroundings; his brother John, a prosperous farmer, once convinced Henry to live with him at his home in Taymouth. The old hermit decided to give it a try, but after a few days Henry grew homesick for his shack along the Saginaw.

One evening in November, just a few months before Henry died from pneumonia, one local resident struck up a friendship with the old hermit and learned of his military career, which included serving in Michigan's Fourth Cavalry—the unit responsible for the capture of Jefferson Davis.

"I was one of Lieutenant-Colonel Pritchard's company of the Michigan Fourth Cavalry that ketched Jess Davis. I was right thar," bragged the hermit to his visitor.

"How did it happen?" the visitor asked, humoring the old man.

"He was campin' in a tent, and we came upon him. That's about all there was to it."

The visitor wanted to know about the legend, which stated that Jefferson Davis had attempted to elude escape by dressing as a woman. The hermit snorted and shook his head dismissively. "Thar's no truth to it at all," he answered. "The man that says that is tellin' something he don't know nothin' 'bout."

"What was the real truth of the capture?" asked the visitor, who knew a fair deal about Civil War history himself. He was curious to find out if he could catch the old recluse in a lie. Henry Malone, his mind as clear as a mountain stream, told the story of Davis's capture as if it had happened only days earlier.

"Wal, 'twas just like this: Davis was no coward, not at all. He was brave enough, but he didn't have the strength some of us had and couldn't keep out of our way. He had to rest and he rested once too often." It seemed strange to the visitor that Henry would know about Davis's ill health, since it was something the Confederate president kept to himself, for fear that it might jeopardize his political career. Jefferson Davis had contracted malaria as a young man and had never fully regained his strength and vitality.

"He had pitched his tent near Irwinsville, in Georgia. Colonel Pritchard—we used to call him captain—had been followin' with us men on hossback and we struck Jeff's campin' spot jest about daylight. We made our advances in the night so as to not be suspicioned. Jeff knowed thar was somethin' up when our hosses halted and we dismounted. He peeked through a rip in the canvas and knowed his jig was up

"'Ha, Federals!' he shouted to the people in the tent with him. There was his wife, her brother and sister, two children, Miss Howell, and some others there. Things was so excitin' I couldn't see everything, but I heerd Miss Davis say, kind of excited like, 'Then you are captured,' but he put on a bold front and run his hand over his head, wonderin.'

"Mrs. Davis was smart and quick-witted, Jeff slept in a loose wrapper, somethin' like after the Mother Hubbards the women wear nowadays," said the hermit. A Mother Hubbard was a long, loose-fitting gown worn by women of the era. The garment was originally invented by missionaries, who gave the gowns to naked Polynesian savages in order to "civilize" them. "She ketched an idea quick," continued Malone. "She tied the wrapper about his waist, and standin' still you couldn't see his feet, but if he was walkin' his boots stuck out. Her idea was to pass him off fer a woman and Miss Howell was goin' to help her. Miss Howell threw a shawl over his head and told him to bend over so as to look like an old woman.

"When we was comin' to the door of the tent and was walkin' in, we nearly runned into Jeff. We had orders to stop every person who tried to escape. There was an old darky woman with Jeff. They had buckets in their hands and when they was stopped Mrs. Davis says, she says, 'Let poor old women go.' But we didn't let the poor old women go because we saw Jeff's boots, and snatched the shawl off his head too quick. Now, that's all there is to it. Jeff never had any woman's dress on, no hoops, nor nothin' they tell about."

"Do you think he would've escaped had he not been stopped as he came out?" asked the curious visitor. The old hermit paused to consider the question, searching through his mental filing cabinet containing eight decades of memories. He nodded.

"Sartin', sar. He was headed for his hosses and arms, which were near the spring, and if he got there, he'd been away instanter."

"Did he offer any resistance?"

"Never a bit," replied Malone. "'Twas no use. Strange, but Jeff didn't have a sign of a firearm in his tent. If he had, there might'a been some blood spilled."

"Is it true that Jeff offered you money if you would let him escape?" asked the visitor. The hermit replied that Jefferson Davis made no such offer. "No, not that way," he explained. "Mrs. Davis's brother offered us $2,000 in gold if we'd let him get away. They said they had a chest full of it."

The November chill rattled the bones of the visitor, and as he took his leave he wasn't sure whether or not to believe the old hermit's story. After all, very few people would mistake an eighty-year-old man who lived in a pile of brush and timber as a reliable source of information. Nonetheless, after Henry Malone died, the unnamed visitor told the story to the local papers, which printed the account of Jefferson Davis's capture with a grain of salt. Very few people believed the hermit's tale until 1906, when Jefferson Davis's slave and personal valet, the "darky" who had been with Davis at the time of his capture, gave an interview to the *Washington Herald* and corroborated the story told years earlier by Henry Malone, even describing in detail the shawl that the valet had placed over Davis's head.

52. The Man Who Turned Pebbles to Gold

One summer evening in 1909, a car driven by Harris Eberhart stalled on the railroad tracks near Munster, Indiana. A speeding freight train smashed into the rear of the automobile, throwing Eberhart fifty feet from the vehicle and instantly killing Richard Flagg, a friend who was sleeping in the passenger seat at the time. Eberhart was taken to a nearby hospital with life-threatening injuries and died a few hours later. His family discovered a journal belonging to the young man that was found at the scene, and Harris Eberhart's diary contained detailed plans for the building of a youth camp along the shores of Corey Lake in Michigan. In memory of their deceased son, the Eberhart family donated a large sum of money to the YMCA for the construction of the camp, which is still known as Camp Eberhart to this day.

Two years later, a group of boys from the summer camp were digging a hole for a flag pole on the grounds of Camp Eberhart when they unearthed a rusty, large, iron box containing pistols, books, time-worn documents, and several other interesting objects that had been buried for half a century. The box contained more than just a few antiques, however; it contained the life story of an eccentric, but forgotten, hermit named Hesikia Thomas.

By the time the metal box was lifted out of the ground, word of the discovery had spread throughout every corner of the camp. Dozens of curious onlookers gathered around, their minds reeling with thoughts of what may rest inside.

There was a large lock on the iron chest, but every attempt to open the lock failed. The bottom of the chest had to be broken. Found inside were two rusted pistols of an ancient design, a plain gold ring, and a silver pocket watch. Two hunting knives were also found in the box, along with several leather-bound books, the oldest dating back to 1767. The books were of a religious nature and included a Bible, a few hymnals, and some schoolbooks. The box also contained a cache of pennies, minted between 1781 and 1854. The strange collection also featured an assortment of smooth pebbles, arrowheads, and a deed to property in Connecticut, dated 1739.

As interesting as these rusted relics and trinkets may have been, they weren't as interesting as the faded and yellowed letters that were also found inside the box. These letters painted a colorful portrait of the long-forgotten man who buried the box near the shoreline of Corey Lake. One of the letters read:

"This chest is the property of Hesikia Thomas, formerly of New England, later of the Michigan wilderness, a spiritualist of God, believing my spirit still roams over the lakes in the full moon seasons, guarding all my valuable deposited possessions, for they are many and varied. God gave me many wonderful secrets, but because of the great sin He took them all away but one—the least of them—the turning of sable stones into gold.

"I have buried this secret by the body of old Duckwing in the big swamp. God rest my soul. God has filled the Earth with gold. Devils do not believe it, but has He not promised 'seek and find'? The blue heron is wise and the night owl, but man is an ass, for he walketh not in the ways of the Most High."

The name Hesikia Thomas didn't resonate with any of the campers, but it was a name remembered by George Knevels, who lived near the camp in a house that had been originally built by the hermit. Knevels said that as a boy, he remembered finding carefully hidden piles of pebbles throughout the family home. Nobody in the family could think of any logical reason why the previous tenant had hidden the pebbles, and it wasn't until the hermit's note was found that it made sense to Mr. Knevels: The kooky, old hermit actually believed that he had the ability to turn pebbles into gold!

When Hesikia's "treasure" was unearthed in 1911, some of the older residents who lived near the lake or in the nearby city of Three Rivers still had vivid recollections of the old hermit. It was said that Hesikia's wife had deserted him for unknown reasons, giving him back the simple gold ring that had been pledged as a symbol of never-ending love. It was around this time the New Englander became unhinged and was seen on many occasions conversing with animals and cursing at trees. The older citizens of the region remember the hermit's claim that he had talked to God and had been given the secret for transmuting ordinary stones into precious metals.

Hesikia sold his home and took up residence on an island in the lake, Coop's Island, which he referred to in another one of his letters as the "abode of the seven devils." The hermit stated that he had hidden two other chests, one of which was supposedly buried on the island. For weeks, the entire neighborhood descended upon the island in the lake, in the hopes of finding more of the hermit's treasure. To this day, the remaining two chests have never been found. The hermit described the perils of the island in one of his letters: "The island is doomed forever as it is the abiding place of the seven devils. Beware; fish die, birds drops as they pass, and man disappears in the cavernous depths of the cave."

Hesikia Thomas didn't die on the isle of the seven devils, however. The older citizens of Three Rivers recalled that his body had been found in the woods, not long after he had sold his house. It was determined that he had frozen to death, and he was later buried in a pauper's grave, its location now forgotten.

53. The Robinson Crusoe of Lake Huron
Benjamin S. Kellogg was a boy of twelve when he and his father left the Vermont village of Wells and headed west in search of a better life. Ben's mother died shortly after he

had been born, leaving the young boy and his father to face each bleak and empty day alone. The Kelloggs were poor and honest, but honesty couldn't put food on the table. In the spring of 1835, Mr. Kellogg made the decision to head for the land of promise.

After reaching Lake Erie, the Kelloggs boarded a vessel bound for Lake Superior. A violent storm arose, and the ship was lost; young Benjamin found himself clinging for life to a piece of wood in the choppy, gray waters near the upper end of Lake Huron. The boy was washed ashore, and from that day forward he never learned of the fate of his father or the rest of the ship's crew. Even at the tender age of twelve, he knew how dangerous and foolish false hope could be, so he decided it was best to assume that all hands were lost. The exhausted youth laid upon the rocky shoreline and wept until he fell asleep.

In the morning, hunger made him forget about fear, and the ravished lad decided to forage for food. After eating a meager breakfast, he followed the shoreline in search of civilization but wandered until nightfall without spotting a sign of human habitation. The following day he changed course and wandered until he was hopelessly lost. Weak from hunger and exhausted from exertion, Benjamin dropped into a deep sleep. He was awakened during the night and found himself surrounded by a small band of Indians, but he was not afraid. The only thing he could think about was food. Through the use of hand signals the boy communicated with the natives. They brought him meat and drink and signaled that he should follow them.

For several months he lived among the natives, all the while penetrating deeper into the strange, dark wilderness. Near Lake Gogebic, in the far western end of the Upper Peninsula, Benjamin left the Indians and started to retrace his steps. He had no fear of the wilderness; the natives had taught him how to hunt and fend for himself. Although he was confident in his survival skills, he was unable to find his way back to the lakeshore. In the Porcupine Mountains near Lake Superior he built himself a shack where he would spend the next seventy years of his life, completely isolated from mankind.

The years rolled on, and Benjamin came to enjoy the solitude. He trapped game and made the occasional journey south to a small village where he traded his pelts for tobacco and the bare necessities of life. The village was nothing more than a half dozen cabins, so Benjamin knew nothing of the world beyond the forests. The Civil War came and went, presidents were elected, assassinated, impeached, and re-elected, and men like Edison and Ford and Tesla made great contributions to mankind, none of which Benjamin S. Kellogg was aware. Of the steady, onward march of progress, Benjamin knew little and cared even less.

As his hair turned gray and his body grew frail by the unrelenting thievery of time, Benjamin began to fear his inevitable death. He desired to return to society and staved off this desire until he could resist it no more. In 1907 Benjamin Kellogg finally made his return to civilization at the age of eighty-four. He visited his hometown of Wells, Vermont, and then proceeded to Massachusetts, where he visited a man whose father had known Benjamin's father. After spending a week in Massachusetts, he once again returned to Wells, prepared to live out his remaining days in the town of his birth.

Benjamin saw his first automobile in Wisconsin and remarked that he almost wished that he had never left his shack in the Michigan wilderness, preferring to die naturally instead of being scared to death. He feared electricity, and was skeptical of any man who could harness bolts of lightning from the sky and use the magical energy to suit his own whims. There was much about the world he didn't understand, from the way the women dressed to the way the men talked. Everyone seemed to be in such a hurry, he noticed. What was the rush?

Nevertheless, his fear of progress was only surpassed by his delight at once more being among people of his kind, strange as they may be, and everything he saw proved to be a source of jaw-dropping wonder. Lightbulbs! Automobiles! Flying machines! What will they think of next? As Benjamin Kellogg took to his sickbed and prepared himself for the final journey into the great unknown, the old hermit took comfort in the knowledge that he had already made that voyage twice before and had come out stronger and wiser on the other side. He smiled and closed his eyes one final time, eager to find out what new adventures were waiting for him.

54. Edgar Donne

The star of twenty-eight movies, Greta Garbo was one of the few Hollywood icons whose success spanned both the silent era and the "Golden Age" of film. Garbo, who was born Greta Lovisa Gustafsson in Stockholm in 1905, retired from acting at the age of thirty-five. Although she was offered starring roles in many films, Garbo refused to make a comeback, and she spent the rest of her life avoiding the spotlight. She never married, never had any children, and preferred a life of quiet seclusion. As a result, she was often referred to as a recluse. Perhaps, then, it's no surprise that Greta Garbo had a bizarre link to a hermit from Michigan named Edgar Donne.

Outside of the tiny village of Dorr, near the city of Allegan, Edgar Donne lived alone in a shabby, wooden hut at the edge of a neglected and barren farm. Donne was born in England in 1876 and became an American citizen in 1922. Edgar and his brother, Duncan, were raised by a very strict father, and the two young men, long deprived of life's pleasures and adventures, made the decision to leave England and see the world. While Duncan later returned to Britain, his brother continued his life of adventure and worked a variety of different jobs. He spent a few years at sea aboard a Canadian ship and when the seafaring life had grown stale Edgar became a rolling stone, finding employment as a waiter, dishwasher, bellhop, farm hand, and bus driver.

Shortly after arriving in Michigan he became a naturalized citizen and made his home inside the tiny, one-room shack in Dorr Township. Aside from trips to England in 1936 and 1937, Edgar never left his hut until old age, when he made an appearance in town to buy some new clothes before embarking on a mysterious trip to Hollywood. Upon his return, Edgar's neighbors insisted upon hearing the details, since it's not every day a resident of Allegan County (or a hermit, for that matter) takes a trip to Tinseltown. The old recluse refused to discuss his trip, just as he had refused to discuss so many other details of his life since arriving in Michigan a quarter of a century earlier.

Edgar Donne died in September of 1946 at the age of seventy, a hermit to the very end. Inside his tiny hut authorities found a tattered letter, yellowed with age, amid Edgar's few possessions. It was a letter he had written to Greta Garbo during one of his trips to England. The envelope had been stamped with the word "refused" by the post office. The local authorities found the letter to be interesting, but not very important, and the hermit soon faded from memory—at least for a few weeks.

In February of 1947, the judge of the county's probate court, Judge Irving Taylor, received word from England that Edgar H. Donne had bequeathed $20,000 to Greta Garbo. Judge Taylor must have thought he was the victim of a prank and probably refused to believe a word of the news. How could a penniless hermit possibly have amassed such a sizeable fortune? And why would he leave his entire estate to a famous movie star? Surely somebody wanted to make the judge a victim of a practical joke. Then Judge Taylor remembered the letter found inside the shack and recalled the hermit's mysterious trip to Hollywood. Could it be possible that Allegan County's shack-dwelling recluse had once known the legendary Swedish film star?

A copy of Edgar's will was sent to Michigan. The will, written in England on September 12, 1936, stated: "I hereby give my estate to Greta Lovisa Gustafsson, whose stage name is Greta Garbo, to her and no other. If Greta Garbo becomes my wife, then it goes to Greta Lovisa Donne."

State Public Administrator Archie Frazer intervened in the case, arguing that Edgar Donne wasn't mentally competent at the time he made his will, and that the estate should revert to the State of Michigan. Then Duncan Donne, the hermit's brother, appeared in the picture, and Frazer decided that he would step aside and let the Englishman battle it out with Miss Garbo, who had since learned of the hermit's will and intended to claim Edgar's estate for herself. The hermit's estate included $15,000 in British securities and jewelry deposited in a London bank, $900 in American currency and war bonds, and more than 160 acres of property, much of it on oil-rich land. How Edgar amassed his fortune was never known, although the residents of Allegan County suspected that it may have had something to do with his infrequent trips to England.

In April of 1947, two months after the reading of the will, Greta Garbo finally broke her Sphinx-like silence and addressed the topic that had all of Hollywood in a frenzy. Garbo stated that she had never met Edgar Donne. Evidently, the old hermit had an infatuation with the husky-voiced Swedish bombshell. This infatuation was confirmed by the hermit's cousin, Sissy Donne, who gave a statement to the London press. She told reporters that "Edgar was head over heels in love with Garbo from the day he first saw her in films. He amazed us by stalking around in oilskins and a sou'wester like the ones Greta had worn in *Anna Christie*." She added, "It was frightening every time he greeted us. Despite our ridicule he always said, 'She'll be my wife soon.'" Another resident of Dorr spoke to reporters and claimed that Edgar actually believed that his letter to Garbo had been returned as the result of a nefarious plot concocted by the postmasters in Dorr and Hollywood, and intimated that this had been the real reason behind his mysterious trip to Tinseltown. Garbo addressed the matter of the letter, saying, "I think my secretary handled it as a piece of routine business." She then hinted that she may be interested in becoming heiress to the Donne estate.

Garbo did make the trip to England in order to claim the hermit's estate. She later remarked, "I do not know Mr. Donne. I vaguely recall that he once sent me a letter some years ago which was returned to him. I don't recall anything he said in it . . . I'm told that he once made a trip to Los Angeles to see me. I didn't see him, nor did I ever talk to him." Why the film star decided to accept the hermit's estate is just one of the many mysteries surrounding the life of Greta Garbo. She certainly didn't need the money. Perhaps she felt that old Edgar was a kindred spirit who, like herself, preferred to live in seclusion. Perhaps she felt a strange obligation to honor the hermit's final request. Perhaps there's more to the story than anyone knows.

Whatever her reasons for accepting the hermit's fortune, Garbo didn't see one penny of her inheritance. Most of Edgar's fortune had been consumed by inheritance taxes and assorted fees after the probate process in both the United States and Great Britain. The remainder of Edgar's assets could not legally be taken out of England, so Garbo decided that it would just be easier to donate the rest of the hermit's fortune to charity.

MISSOURI

55. The Man Who Lived in a Cage

Mark Twain is credited with being the first to state that truth is stranger than fiction. The great American storyteller from Missouri very well may have been thinking about an eccentric genius from St. Louis when he made that famous statement. That eccentric genius was a man who lived during Twain's time, a Swiss hermit named Joseph Custer.

Joseph Custer, an immigrant shoemaker, lived at 1009 North Fourteenth Street in the city of St. Louis, but the home at this address was made of neither brick nor stone. Joseph Custer lived in a cage. To be more accurate, the dwelling had once been a wagon shed, but had since fallen into a state of disrepair, neglected by the owner of the property until all that was left was a wire skeleton. Custer made this cage his home and improved its condition somewhat by affixing all sorts of old window sashes to the framework. Though these renovations did little to improve the home's "curb appeal," the window sashes at least offered a slight measure of protection against the elements.

The inside of this cage was more than just a home to Custer, it was also his workshop. Scattered about the room were various machines used to manufacture shoes, most of which had been disassembled by the hermit, giving the room the appearance of a junk shop. Custer studied these machines with an eye toward improvement and innovation. His first success as an inventor came in 1877, when he created a shoe-patching machine with a universal foot. Though this invention may mean little to those of us who aren't in the shoemaking business, it was a tremendous leap forward in footwear technology, and for decades Custer's machine was used by virtually every shoe manufacturer in the world. Sadly, Custer never saw a dime from his invention, and this would not be the last time such a misfortune would happen to him.

At the time, Custer didn't mind the fact that others were getting rich from his shoe-patching machine. He was getting by just fine, or so he thought. There were always shoes to mend in the Kerry Patch neighborhood, and he had a reputation for performing quality work at a fair price. Things were about to take an ugly turn, however.

Kerry Patch was a rough neighborhood filled with street gangs and petty criminals. The leader of the meanest neighborhood gang was "Bad Jack" Williams, whose sidekick was a young ruffian named Jimmie Powers. For reasons unknown to the Swiss shoemaker, Bad Jack and Jimmie turned their attentions to the hermit, and Custer was harassed and attacked by the gang for several years. In 1900 the cobbler's patience wore thin after Jimmie Powers ransacked his home. Jimmie was just about to beat up the cobbler when Custer pulled out a pistol and fired at the rowdy, young punk, shooting him in the thigh. The cobbler was arrested and left to languish in a jail cell for two months before being acquitted of the charges.

After his release from jail, Custer gathered up his belongings and relocated his "cage" to a lot on 23rd Street. Though he had only spent a few weeks in jail, the experience changed him, and he shifted his focus from inventing shoemaking machines to inventing implements of warfare. "I just studied an' studied, and experimented an' experimented. But I never got anything for it," Custer told a reporter from the *Sunday Republic* when asked about his newest invention. "It took me seven years to perfect the new rifle tube, which is now used by the Government, and which increases the pressure for every inch from 25,000 to 57,000. I applied for patents in 1888 for a number of improvements and inventions for firearms. The Board of Fortifications, under General Schofield, examined my inventions and dragged along a decision for several months.

"During that time they wrote to me repeatedly for clearer specifications, which I sent to them to explain my drawings. Finally, after waiting several years, I received a letter from the Board of Fortifications through the Interior Department, saying that the specifications were too complicated for military service.

"Yet, in August, 1889, two months after they had written me that letter, the Government had the Diamond Drill Company of Pennsylvania make a rifle tube exactly in accordance with my specifications, and the records of the Patent Office do not show that anybody else ever filed such an application." At this point in the story, Custer stopped to show the newspaper reporter a large bundle of correspondence between himself and the Patent Office in Washington. He went on to explain that he fought to get back the $25 fee that he had sent to Washington along with his patent applications. The money was later returned to him by Governor Francis, who was serving as the secretary of the interior at the time.

"Why didn't you hire a patent lawyer?" Custer was asked.

"Well, you see," he answered, "I had no money, and the money of my partner, who helped me out at first, was also gone, and he had lost his patience. Anyhow, the different occurrences in life bring a fellow to different conclusions."

The hermit dismissed the hope of ever seeing a penny from his seven years of labor, implying that such was the fate of the majority of inventive geniuses. The shoe-patching machine and the rifle tube were just two of Custer's inventions that had been stolen from him. He had reams upon reams of drawings for all kinds of machines, most of them having to do with warfare. Custer also spent his time making his own household tools and utensils, including a coal-burning stove with a temperature control that got hot enough to cook on, but could also be used to sit on in order to keep warm in the winter—without fear of being caught on fire. While it seems commonplace today to have a stove with knobs for controlling the temperature, it was a bizarre contraption at the time. The Swiss hermit never sought to patent this invention, however, since it was, more or less, a novelty item. How many American housewives needed a stove they could sit upon in order to warm up their hindquarters?

A year after completing his stove, the hermit found himself threatened with eviction after falling behind on his rent. For two days, deputy constables attempted to evict Custer, which was no easy feat, because the hermit had chained all of his belongings to the sidewalk. He had also threatened bodily harm to the officers if they dared to enter his home. The old cobbler vigilantly remained at his post while the constables set about dismantling the cage. When they succeeded in making their way into the hermit's abode, Custer's spirits fell and he surrendered his fort to the enemy. The hermit chuckled at the officers, however, as they toiled to unfasten his belongings from the ground.

The most difficult item to remove was the stove. Though the appliance was small in size, Custer had it bolted and chained to the floor. The stovepipe, which reached to the second story of the adjacent building, had also been bolted. It took nearly four hours just to unfasten the stovepipe. Also difficult to remove was the hermit's bed, which had been suspended from the ceiling of the cage by chains. It was a marvelous contraption; once tucked into his bed, Custer devised a system of pulleys that would raise the bed to the ceiling, keeping him safe from burglars and other unwelcome visitors.

The siege of Fort Custer, which ended on March 21, 1903, resulted in the Swiss cobbler being forced to live on the streets, but as the mad inventor wandered the dark alleys of St. Louis in search of a new place to call home, he undoubtedly derived some strange sense of satisfaction knowing that the city had gone through great trouble and considerable expense in the process evicting a harmless hermit who was only $4 behind in his rent payments.

SOUTH DAKOTA

56. Patrick Welsh

In August of 1888, a lonely hermit living in the remote wilderness of South Dakota drew his final breath. Patrick Welsh was his name, and his story is nothing short of remarkable. It is a story that not only begins in Ireland and ends half a world away, but it is also a story filled with romance and adventure—and a string of bad decisions that transformed a promising, young man into a wretched recluse.

The story began sixty years earlier in Kilkenny, Ireland. Thomas Welsh was a successful farmer who owned eighty acres of land, which he tilled and plowed with the help of his two sons, Patrick and Michael. On the neighboring property lived Rose McCarthy, the flower of Kilkenny, whose coal-black eyes, ivory skin, and rosebud lips made her famous throughout the county. She had the sweetest smile and a kind disposition, but she was well aware of the charms she possessed and, as a result, every lad's effort to woo her proved unsuccessful.

On a wickedly cold night in the terrible winter of 1829, Rose became lost on the bleak and barren moor after she had been sent on an errand by her family. Every able-bodied man in Kilkenny joined in the search for the missing beauty but, as the early gray of morning dawned blustery and bitter, they had no choice but to return home, fearing for the worst. The only ones who refused to abandon the search were Patrick and Michael Welsh. They pressed on, in spite of the howling winds and sleet that relentlessly pelted their skin until it was raw. Around nine o'clock Patrick found the missing girl, who was frozen badly but would later recover.

Rose was so impressed by Patrick's heroic actions that she agreed to marry him, much to the chagrin of his brother. Before that day, the two brothers had been the best of friends and were inseparable, but a coldness suddenly sprang up between them. Michael also had eyes for Rose McCarthy and was smitten with jealousy. Things only got worse a few months later when Thomas Welsh died and bequeathed the bulk of the estate to Patrick. Rose was sixteen at the time, and a wedding date was set for three years down the road, but Michael announced that he would not be in attendance; he said that he was going to America.

On the eve of his brother's departure, Patrick found himself in a quarrel with a constable. The confrontation turned physical and ended with Patrick injuring the lawman severely with a club. A hearing was held the following morning, and Patrick Welsh was sentenced to ten years in prison. On his way to prison, he somehow managed to escape and made his way to America, hoping to be reunited with his brother and hoping to someday be reunited with his love, Rose McCarthy.

Welsh arrived at Castle Clinton, which served as America's first immigration station before Ellis Island. Between 1855 and 1890 more than eight million immigrants passed through the gates of the sandstone fortress in Battery Park, at the southernmost tip of Manhattan. Welsh found a boarding house on Cherry Street, where he stayed for the night. The owner succeeded in getting the young man drunk before robbing him of all the money he had in the world. Around this time, Patrick learned that his brother Michael never made good on his vow to set sail for America. Patrick Welsh found himself a stranger in a strange land, without a roof over his head or a penny to his name. He wandered the streets of New York for a few days before finding temporary employment as a laborer. A kind-hearted Catholic priest took pity on the young man and provided him with a place to stay until he got back on his feet.

The priest grew fond of Patrick and encouraged him to go to a college in Baltimore in order to study for the priesthood. Patrick, who viewed the kindly, old priest as a father figure, decided that it would be a good idea and eventually succeeded in becoming an ordained priest himself after years of study. He was then assigned to a church in Cambridge, Maryland, where he soon found himself involved in a scandalous relationship with the wife of a prominent member of his congregation. Patrick was run out of town.

From this time until 1849, Welsh became a drifter. At different times he was employed as a teacher, a literary agent, and a snakeoil salesman. While drifting through California he was bitten by the gold bug and became a prospector. In this new El Dorado, Welsh thrived and soon amassed a sizeable fortune. Once satisfied that he had earned enough, he returned to Ireland, only to find that Rose had given him up for dead. In his absence she married his brother, Michael, and was mother to a large and happy family. How strange, thought Patrick. He was supposed to have been the one to marry Rose and remain in Ireland, while Michael was the one who was supposed to make a name for himself in America. With a broken heart Patrick returned to America and resumed his life of wandering, ending up in the remote vastness of the Dakota Territory. He made his home about eighteen miles north of Elk Point.

Welsh's home was nothing more than a hole dug into the side of a bluff, in front of which was attached a simple porch. There was only one piece of furniture inside the cave, and that was a black coffin, which Patrick used as a bed for seventeen years. From above the coffin glowed a number of candles that had been fastened to the wall, along with several silver crucifixes. Patrick's only companion, except for the cattle that he raised, was a wolf he had nurtured ever since it was an abandoned pup. He kept the wolf tied to the coffin with a length of rope.

Late in the summer of 1888, neighbors passing by the hermit's property noticed that his cattle appeared to be starving, and they ascended the cliff to see if the old hermit was sick. They found Patrick Welsh dead, stretched out in his coffin with a silver crucifix in his cold hands.

WISCONSIN

57. The Angry Englishman
Anger is, without a doubt, the most powerful of human emotions. When harnessed properly, righteous indignation

can inspire the meek to greatness; when bottled up and suppressed, it can gnaw away at our insides and cut short the days of our lives. When it is not controlled, anger can lead even a priest to the penitentiary or a grandmother to the gallows. It can even lead a brilliant university professor from the marble halls and manicured lawns of academia to a hermit's shack in a wretched, mosquito-infested swamp.

In September of 1899 a skeleton of an unidentified man was found at the edge of a swamp four miles north of the village of Armstrong Creek. Though there were no clues found at the scene to indicate the identity of the deceased, it was instantly assumed that the skeleton belonged to the old hermit who had recently been discovered living in a nearby shack.

Eight months earlier a group of woodsmen representing the Murphy Lumber Company arrived at a long-abandoned lumber camp with the intention of making it their headquarters while they surveyed the surrounding wilderness. The men were approaching the main structure when they saw an odd-looking man dash out the back door and disappear into the underbrush. The man's back was bent by old age, and he was clad in garments made of animal skins. A tangled mess of gray hair hung down his back, while a matted, gray beard, two full feet in length, appeared to conceal the entire front of the wild man's body.

The curious woodcutters entered the shanty from which the wild man had darted and were surprised to discover that the walls and floors were covered from top to bottom with animal pelts. In the middle of the two-room shack was a table made of rough boards, while a crude chair, fashioned from the hollowed-out trunk of a tree, stood near the table. On one side of the room was a bookcase constructed of rough pine planks, and this case contained nearly three hundred books written in a variety of languages. The covers of the leather-bound volumes were worn from constant usage and had evidently belonged to a man of superior education. There was only one novel among the many volumes, and, judging by the well-worn pages, it was the hermit's favorite—*Robinson Crusoe*. The woodsmen rummaged through all of the books, even those written in Latin and Greek and French, in the hopes of finding a clue that would reveal the wild man's identity. Some of the books were inscribed "Kings College, Cambridge," while two of the oldest books were inscribed with the name John Holden.

The workers soon left the logging camp and returned to their homes, and some of the men made inquiries about John Holden, but the name failed to ignite a spark of recognition from anyone in the area. Several weeks later the men from the lumber company returned to the old logging camp and found everything in the shack exactly as they had left it. The frightened hermit had never returned after dashing off into the brush.

Meanwhile, word of the wild man had spread throughout Forest and Florence Counties, and even folks as far away as Menominee were eager to learn more about the mysterious John Holden. Someone even went so far as to address a letter to the chief of police who, in turn, sent a letter to Cambridge asking for more information about John Holden. Three months passed without a response, but then came a reply that put the mystery to rest.

According to the letter, John Holden had been a respected and esteemed tutor at Cambridge in 1862. In his charge was the son of an English aristocrat, whose name was not disclosed in the letter. Though Holden was a brilliant man, he was also a man of ungovernable temper, stated the Cambridge authorities. One evening in the spring of 1863 Holden and his pupil had a disagreement. Angered by a comment the tutor deemed as disrespectful, Holden flew into a rage. He grabbed a heavy, wooden cane and felled the disrespectful student with a blow to the temple. A group of students, attracted by the noise, raced to the side of the fallen boy and pronounced him dead. Holden grew scared. He hastily gathered a few of his belongings and fled from the scene, never to be seen again.

The young man was not dead, however, but merely unconscious, and he soon recovered from the effects of the blow. John Holden had no way of knowing this, since he had already hopped a ship bound for America. He chose the life of a recluse, because he feared that he would be arrested and charged with murder, and thus lived in continual fear for the rest of his tormented days. Rather than facing the consequences of his anger, he chose to run away, and instead of being dealt a sentence of perhaps a few months in jail for his assault on the young pupil, he condemned himself to thirty-six years of solitary confinement. Because he failed to face the consequences of his actions, he exchanged a short period of time in a jail cell with a cot and three meals a day for a lifetime in a shack on the edge of a swamp, feasting upon frogs and squirrels, shivering beneath his pelts in winter, and constantly looking over his shoulder in fear. As brilliant as John Holden may have been, he never realized that he had been his own judge, jury, and executioner.

After the skeleton had been fished from the murky bog, a coroner's inquest was held. Although it may never be proven, in all probability John Holden had been frightened by the men from the Murphy Lumber Company and fled from the shack, convinced that the woodsmen were men of the law coming to hold him accountable for striking down a student in England over three decades earlier. Gripped with mortal fear, the hermit ran blindly through the forest and into the swamp, where he became trapped in the soft, stinky mud and perished after being unable to extricate himself from the murky bog.

OHIO

58. The Treetop Hermit

In 1914 Orrin Sternbarger was a fifty-seven-year-old art professor at Ohio's Wittenburg College when he received devastating news from his doctor. The art teacher, who had been diagnosed with a severe case of tuberculosis, only had a few weeks to live. Sternbarger said farewell to his friends, gathered his belongings, and set out on foot to the wooded hills along the Mad River.

His wanderings among the hills and forests led him to Tiffin where, a mile or two outside of town, he built a crude treehouse up in the branches of an old elm tree. Sternbarger had decided that he would either cure his illness by surrounding himself with fresh air, or spend his final days in the peaceful embrace of Mother Nature. Orrin Sternbarger managed to accomplish both of these things.

After a few years living in the branches of the elm tree, every vestige of Sternbarger's illness was gone. Even though he had been pronounced cured by physicians, Sternbarger had become so fond of his lofty perch that he continued to live in his treehouse for nearly three more decades. When the fierce winds of winter lashed his treehouse, he covered his home with a canvas sheet, and in summer he turned his home into a convertible by removing the top and living on the wooden platform.

Neighboring farmers thought that Sternbarger was odd, but they never gave him any trouble. To them he was merely the "Hermit of Mad River," and respected his desire to be left alone, with birds and squirrels as his only companions. The hermit rarely needed to venture into town for supplies, and most of his wants he supplied himself. He constructed his own fishing rod as well as his own bow and arrows, and devoted his time to becoming an expert hunter and angler, while using only the most primitive equipment. Once he managed to obtain his food, he would hoist himself up into the tree by means of a rope and pulley.

One day, in 1921, Sternbarger's rope broke. Though he was no longer sick, he had grown too old and frail to climb the stately elm, so he made his home at the foot of the tree instead of choosing to return to civilization. It was the first time in seven years the hermit had slept on the ground. A few years later he was found by Amandus Grossman, the former sheriff of Seneca County, who happened to be passing by with a friend. The friend introduced Grossman to the hermit and, after a long and friendly conversation, the hermit implored the men to bring him a new rope in order to replace the one that had snapped two years before. Grossman, who felt sorry for the old hermit, immediately left for Tiffin and returned a short while later with the rope.

The three men were then confronted with a problem: how to get the rope up to the treetop platform. None of them were young or nimble enough to climb the one hundred-foot elm. Sternbarger asked for a spool of thread and a ball of twine. He attached the thread to the end of one of his arrows and then drew his bow. To the amazement of the former sheriff and his friend, Sternbarger's shot went up and over the limb near his platform. Onto the thread he attached the twine, and he proceeded to draw it over the limb until all of the thread was returned to the ground. Then he tied one end of the rope to the twine and repeated the process until he managed to get the rope placed over the tree limb. With graceful ease the seventy-five-year-old hermit scampered up the rope, passed it through the pulley, and attached the counterweights. Once again, the Hermit of Mad River was able to ascend and descend from the tree by himself, and once again all was right with the world.

Orrin Sternbarger, "The Treetop Hermit." From The Winnipeg Tribune, Oct. 15, 1932.

59. Charles Allenton Comes Home

At the foothills of the Appalachians lies the county of Guernsey, which, according to some historians, was settled by a fugitive named Thomas Ogier. Ogier lived in Les Duvaux on the island of Guernsey during the Napoleonic Wars, when six thousand Russian troops were garrisoned on the island. The residents of Guernsey despised the

Russians, because the poorly rationed soldiers often resorted to theft in order to feed themselves. Ogier was working his fields one day when he caught a Russian soldier stealing apples from his orchard. He fired a shot at the fleeing soldier and later found out that before the soldier died, he had reported Ogier to his commander. Fearing for his life, Ogier fled to France, where he immediately boarded a ship to America. When Ogier reached Ohio in 1808 he wrote home to Guernsey, encouraging others to come to the Appalachian foothills. While Ogier is remembered as one of the earliest settlers of the county, he wasn't the first to settle there. The region was home to another early inhabitant who also ran away from his past.

Nearly a decade earlier, when the region was a howling wilderness, Charles Allenton's parents were among the first white settlers to call present-day Guernsey County home. The father built himself a log cabin, and it was inside this cabin where his eldest son, Charles, was born in 1818. Charles was a bright lad with a good head on his shoulders, and grew up to become a fine young man. At the age of twenty-four he became engaged to the daughter of another pioneer family. The night before the wedding the girl fell ill; by the morning she was dead. Charles couldn't bear the shock, and he soon came down with a terrible fever. His parents feared that the young man would soon follow his betrothed to the grave, but Charles pulled through and recovered from his mysterious sickness after several weeks.

Although Charles recovered from his illness, he never recovered from the loss of his beloved. He was never quite the same after that, and he soon grew restless. He could not bear to stay at home, where everything seemed to remind him of his lover, and so he decided to leave. His departure was sudden and unannounced, and for many years his family searched high and low for the young man, but no trace of him could be found. They wrote letters to territorial governors and faraway sheriffs and pioneer politicians, but no one seemed to know the whereabouts of Charles Allenton. His parents finally had to accept the possibility that their oldest child was dead.

With the California gold rush of 1849 came news that Charles Allenton was living out West; however, by this time, no one back in Guernsey County remembered who he was or why he had left in the first place. Nonetheless, Charles no longer had the desire to live the life of a tumbleweed and yearned to return to the place of his birth, where he hoped to put down some roots and reconnect with the family that had given him up for dead years earlier.

Sadly, his parents weren't there to welcome him home. Charles returned to Ohio only to discover that his brothers and sisters had all moved away and his mother and father were dead. The only trace of his former life was the old log cabin, long-abandoned and overgrown with weeds and vines. Charles decided to move into the wooden shack, which his father had built with his own hands. Until his death, which occurred sometime in the late nineteenth century, he lived the life of a hermit inside the very same cabin in which he had been born.

The sad tale of Charles Allenton proves that not all homecomings are celebrated with cheerful parties and festive parades down Main Street; the vast majority of homecomings are never celebrated at all. The life of this lonesome hermit, now moldering in an unknown, unmarked grave, also brings to mind the famous words of Thomas Wolfe, who wrote that "you can't go home again." However, Charles Allenton, like countless individuals who attempted to shed their former lives like the skin of a snake, discovered that you *can* go home again—but you may be forced to confront the stark reality that there will be no one there to welcome you back once you get there.

ILLINOIS

60. Gottlieb Leitsof

During the 1880s, the Fifth Illinois District was represented in Washington by Congressman Robert R. Hitt, who also served as chairman for the House Committee on Foreign Affairs. Hitt, who was a close personal friend of Abraham Lincoln, was enormously well-liked by his peers and constituents alike. A man of superior education and intellect, he spent his twilight years as regent of the Smithsonian Institution in Washington. As a congressman, Hitt was proud to represent the citizens of northwestern Illinois—even an eccentric hermit from Jo Daviess County who often sent letters to Congressman Hitt, imploring the politician to push ridiculous legislation of one type or another.

The hermit's name was Gottlieb Leitsof, a Prussian-born farmer who made his home for thirty years on a chunk of Jo Daviess County, which had become separated from the mainland by a slough, which the currents of the Mississippi River had carved through the soil. Leitsof resided on this island entirely alone, away from the sights and sounds of society. His simple hut, concealed behind a network of willow brush and wild grapevines, could only be reached by a boat expertly guided by someone who knew his way through the maze of sloughs and channels that snake through thousands of acres of lowlands. Every ten years or so, floodwaters would wipe away the hermit's shack and drown his crops, forcing the old hermit to rebuild his home from scratch. The thought of abandoning his island for higher ground was a ridiculous notion to Leitsof. Instead, he wrote letter after letter to his congressman, urging him to induce Uncle Sam to build a dam across the Mississippi in order to protect his tiny farm.

Gottlieb Leitsof was born in the province of Pomerania in 1826, and he owed his spunk to his ancestors. He came from a family of warriors and fathered two sons, who became distinguished military men themselves. One son fought valiantly in the war with Austria in 1866, and his other son fought in the Franco-Prussian conflict of 1870. In addition to his letters to Congressman Hitt about building a dam, the old hermit also wrote letters stating that if any help was needed to whip the French, he would emerge from his island hut and lend a willing hand. It is unclear whether or not Congressman Hitt ever wrote back to inform the hermit that France and the United States had been on good terms since 1798.

When he wasn't crusading for a dam in the wilderness or offering to take up arms against America's allies, Leitsof spent much of his time raising his chickens, tending to his cow, or conversing with his two cats. The hermit prepared his meals and ate and slept in his hut, which boasted ten square feet of interior space. He farmed his land without the aid of any beasts of burden, pulling a plough-like contraption, which he designed and built himself. The machine was constructed from the forked branch of a tree, with the forks serving as the handles. At the end of the branch he affixed a rusted iron ploughshare and built a harness that fit over his back and around his waist. By strapping the bizarre contraption to himself and walking backwards, he was able to plough his field.

In spite of his peculiarities, Leitsof was a model citizen. His taxes were always promptly paid, and he never gave a hard time to any of the hunters or fishermen who trespassed on his beloved island. He bore no hostility toward anyone; he was merely a rugged individualist who loved peaceful seclusion. Ironically, not long after his death in the early days of the twentieth century, politicians made a push to build a series of dams on the Upper Mississippi in order to facilitate barge transportation. The U.S. Army Corps of Engineers began building these dams and locks in the early 1900s, and by 1940 there were twenty-nine locks and dams on the Upper Mississippi. While most hermits live their rustic lives clinging to the simple ways of the past, it could be argued that old Gottlieb Leitsof, probably the first man to advise the federal government to dam the Upper Mississippi, was years ahead of his time.

PART IV
HERMITS OF THE WEST

OKLAHOMA

61. John Stink

Pawhuska, named for a nineteenth century Osage chief, has been the capital city of the Osage Nation since 1872. The city of Pawhuska has the distinction of being the unofficial birthplace of the Boy Scouts of America; the first scout troop in the United States was organized in Pawhuska in 1909 by an English priest named John F. Mitchell. The city of Pawhuska also has the distinction of being the birthplace of one of the most memorable individuals who ever lived on Indian territory.

John Stink, whose Indian name was *Ho-tah-moie* ("Rolling Thunder") lived in a primitive tent on the outskirts of town with his pack of beloved hounds. Shunned by the whites and the Indians alike, he lived the lonesome life of a hermit and refused to set foot in the city of Pawhuska. He distrusted the white man, while simultaneously being the object of distrust by his own race. As a result, John Stink was a man without a country, and that seemed to suit the old hermit just fine.

John's exploits were known throughout Oklahoma and, according to local legend, he had once been a mighty chieftain who led his brave warriors into battle with the Creeks. John was wounded and knocked unconscious during the battle, and his companions, thinking he was dead, buried him beneath a pile of rocks. When John regained consciousness he burrowed out of his rocky grave and returned to the tribe, but the tribe refused to admit John to the camp because its members believed that he was a spirit. Shunned by his own people, he sought fellowship with the white men, but the white men said, "Hey, wait a minute. Didn't you try to kill us once?" and so John Stink had no choice but to live in isolation, with his beloved dogs as his only companions.

John was said to be mentally deficient and as stubborn as a mule, charges that were substantiated by L. J. Miles, who was appointed Indian agent to the Osage tribe in 1887 by President Rutherford B. Hayes. The agent also dispelled

*John Stink, "The Osage Hermit." Courtesy of the Ursuline
Sisters of Mount Saint Joseph Archives.*

the rumors about Ho-tah-moie's legendary return from the
grave. Here is Miles's recollection of John Stink:

"John Stink's Indian name is Ho-tah-moie. He was the
only child of his parents, who were members of the Big Hill
band of Osages living on Salt Creek, 20 miles south of
Pawhuska. I knew John Stink as a boy and remember that
he was short mentally, and was an outcast among his
fellows. In 1889 the government made it a requirement for
all Indian children from the ages of 8 to 21 to attend school

here. John, who was about 17 years of age at that time, was reluctant to go to school and his parents were not particularly in favor of it, but as it was required by the government, I put him in school where he remained for two or three months.

"John was so decidedly deficient mentally that he could not comprehend anything, so he was taken out of school and never attended again. About a year afterward John's mother died, and six months later his father died. This left John quite alone in the world with no friends.

"The members of his tribe thought that he had no right to live. In olden times it was an Indian custom to kill those members of the tribe who were half-witted or physically deficient. Fearing the consequences of murder, his tribe did not try to kill him outright, but disowned him, which was nearly the equivalent of murder to poor John. He had no fixed abode and was a pitiable wanderer, half-starved and utterly friendless. Out of compassion, Jim Lawrence of this town cared for him for a while.

"In those days the Osages only drew $40 or $45 per quarter, which was scarcely enough for the barest existence. John was unsuspecting (and) was cheated out of most of these quarterly payments and was continually in debt for something to eat and wear. Later, T. H. McLaughlin of this town took John in hand and acted as his guardian. McLaughlin owns a grocery store here and is a pioneer citizen. John was grateful to him for his kindness and for several years slept in the doorway of the store, guarding it against intrusion at night. Once, the store was accidentally left unlocked and John, observing this, immediately notified his benefactor. John Stink actually made this entrance his boudoir, sharing part of it with his three dogs, for over four years. He was offered a place to sleep inside but refused it, disliking confinement.

"In 1914, the city marshal, out of what he called humor, killed two of John's dogs. The bereavement must have been stinging to John, but he made no other demonstration than to retire to the country, never to return. His quarters now consist of a small tent, which is situated about three and one-half miles southeast of Pawhuska on Bird Creek. His food is sent to him each day by McLaughlin.

"McLaughlin tells an interesting story of John's frugality and how it came to be somewhat moderated. Several years ago, when the Osages drew much less money than now, John was a heavy eater of canned tomatoes. Some time since, however, John's appetite for tomatoes seemed somewhat abated, for he no longer ordered them. McLaughlin, wondering what was wrong, went out to see John one day and asked him why he ordered no more tomatoes. John would not answer for a while, but finally smiled and said: 'Eat tomatoes when poor; now plenty money, no more tomatoes for a while.'"

John Stink was referring to the secret wealth he accumulated as a land owner. Unbeknownst to anyone, he gradually bought up 657 acres of land that was deemed worthless. After the great Osage County oil boom of the 1910s, he sold a portion of it for $30,000, which he kept in a distant bank. In November of 1919, the Tulsa *Daily World* estimated John Stink's net worth to be over $100,000—the equivalent of nearly $1.4 million in today's money. Even though he had been shunned and laughed at for most of his life, it was John Stink—the dim-witted outcast hermit of Pawhuska—who had the last laugh.

62. Pierre the Prophet

Pierre Davis made his home in a small hut on the bank of the Canadian River, near the village of Porum in Oklahoma's Muskogee County. He lived in solitude in this humble abode for thirty years, and during that time he never journeyed more than six miles in any direction, and then only for the most necessary of provisions. Pierre stood six feet tall, was finely built, and had a commanding presence. However, it was neither Pierre's hut nor his imposing physique that made him famous throughout Muskogee County; it was his hobby. Pierre Davis's hobby was prophecy and, from what history records of the hermit, he was pretty darn good at it.

Unlike many prophets, whose predictions are vague and open to interpretation, Pierre had a specialty. His predictions were limited to floods. So accurate were Pierre's predictions that railroad workers from the Midland Valley Railroad consulted with the revered recluse before laying tracks and building bridges. Three times, in the autumn of 1908, he had predicted that floods would come, and each time he was proven correct; the deluge arrived precisely on the date he had named.

Pierre first made his predictions known years earlier, while workmen were completing a new Midland Valley Railroad bridge to replace the one that had been washed away. For a long time he watched the bridge workers in silence, and the workers paid little attention to the queer old man on the river bank. Finally, Pierre spoke to the foreman of the work crew. "You see little water in the river bed now," said the hermit, "but in thirty days the floods will come and the bridge will be carried away." Saying nothing more, the old recluse strode away, amid the laughs and jeers of the workmen. Exactly twenty-nine days later the rains came, and the river flooded. On the thirtieth day, the Canadian River swept away the newly built bridge.

The bridge was yet again rebuilt, and once more the hermit appeared just as the bridge was nearly complete. He warned the foreman that on the twenty-second of November there would be a fourteen-foot rise in the river, and once again the bridge would be swept away by the raging waters. On the prescribed date, the river raged, and the bridge was destroyed.

Four days later, while the workers were repairing the badly bent and battered bridge, Pierre Davis appeared, saying nothing more than, "The following Sunday the bridge will again go out." By this time, no one was surprised when the old man's prophecy came true.

The workers who at first laughed at the hermit began to defend him, as the wealthy railroad executives pushed once again for the rebuilding of the bridge that had collapsed so many times before. Even the prophet's skeptics grew worried when word came that the bridge over the Canadian River must be built yet again; some even speculated that the land was cursed. Were they building on a site held sacred by the Creek people? Whether or not the old hermit was right, one thing seemed certain: Mother Nature did not want a bridge built in that particular location.

Nevertheless, the railroad executives got their way and the bridge was rebuilt once more. On December 13, as the workers waited for the first train to cross the bridge, the elderly hermit made his final prediction. He declared that the first train would not cross the bridge until the fifteenth of December. Even some of the hermit's supporters scoffed at this prophecy, as the first train was already on its way. However, there had been an obstruction on the tracks miles away, and the train that was expected to cross the Canadian River on the twelfth didn't reach the bridge until three days later. Pierre Davis, the "Prophet of Porum" was seen very little after this event, and it was supposed that the old hermit had taken ill and succumbed to the ravages of time, ultimately ending up buried in a potter's field in a pauper's grave, forgotten by all, except for the mystified workmen who had been bedazzled by Pierre's precise prognostications.

63. The Mysterious Adolph Hauserhufen

One summer day in 1912, when a cowboy from Oklahoma rushed into a newspaper office and excitedly announced that he had discovered a dead body in a cave, the paper sent a novice reporter to locate, identify, and recover the body of the deceased. The reporter sought the aid of A. G. Soldani, who owned three thousand acres of prairie. There was a cave located on Soldani's land, and it was theorized that the dead body discovered by the cowboy might be an old hermit who had once made his home in Soldani's cave. The reporter rushed to the stables and immediately embarked on his quest to locate the cave, armed with directions given to him by Charley Lessart, an inveterate cowboy who knew every nook, cranny, and cowpath in the area. According to Lessart and Soldani, the cave was located in one of the most remote and dreary spots in all of Oklahoma, some twenty miles southwest of Hominy Post.

Just going to the secluded spot was a perilous endeavor, the intrepid reporter soon discovered. Numerous small streams wound their serpentine course through the virtually impassable jungle of stunted trees and thorny brush, through which the sun's rays could hardly penetrate. Treacherous ravines cut up the land into small desolate chunks unfit for agriculture, unfit for human habitation, and unfit for any other practical purpose. The soggy ground presented the reporter with a damp, malarious miasma. It was the most miserable place on Earth, thought the reporter.

This place near the Osage Hills, long ago, was rumored to be the haven of outlaws, horse thieves, and booze peddlers. Visions of these dangerous rogues undoubtedly flooded the mind of the reporter as he neared the vicinity of the cave sometime around midnight. After fumbling through the darkness and poking his nose into hidden holes, the reporter finally located the cave that Charley Lessart had told him about. Inside, he found the body of an aged recluse, who appeared to have died from either thirst or starvation.

The reporter explored the tiny cave and found several tin cans and wooden cigar boxes, each filled with gold and silver coins, paper currency, and handwritten notes and letters. By lamplight, the reporter was able to make out the name on one of the envelopes: Adolph Hauserhufen. The letters had been directed to Hominy Post and bore the postmark of March 10, 1908.

Most of the letters and notes were faded and impossible to read, but the reporter was able to decipher part of one document, which seemed to read "my commission expires July 4, 1908." These words didn't make any sense to the inquisitive reporter, so he rummaged through the hermit's home for more clues. On the back of a business card, the hermit appeared to have written something. Upon closer examination, the reporter discovered that the scribbling referred to a romantic tragedy, one which must have deeply affected the mysterious tenant who had occupied the dreary cave. The hermit had written, "Strife and worry may fade the bloom of youth, but love's first dream remains in the heart forever."

The coroner took possession of the corpse, and every effort was made to locate the family of Adolph Hauserhufen. Sadly, the investigation bore no fruit, and the details surrounding the deceased cave-dweller's strange life and inexplicable treasure were never discovered, forever leaving cowboys a mystery with which to occupy their minds while riding the lonesome Oklahoma plains.

64. A Sad Story of What Might Have Been

While razing an abandoned shack on the farm of Levi Weston in 1914, workmen found a time-worn diary. Its faded and yellowed pages contained the story of Henry Martin, an elderly recluse who was found dead inside the small shack several months earlier. Henry had arrived in the village of Haywood fourteen years before his demise, and when the aged hermit passed away, the older citizens of the village nostalgically recalled the peculiar fellow and his strange habits.

Day after day, old Henry hobbled to the train station in town, where he would watch the passengers boarding and departing. After all the passengers had alighted, Henry would then hobble back to his cabin, which was located in a clearing about a mile outside of the village. During these daily excursions the residents of Haywood would endeavor to engage the old-timer in conversation, but all attempts to become acquainted with Henry proved futile. He might remark about the weather or ask the farmers about their harvests, but any time someone asked him about his past, Henry would become aloof and silent and stare at the railroad tracks with a faraway look in his eyes.

Once a month, like clockwork, Henry ambled into town to visit the general store, where he purchased household necessities for the coming month. The old man always seemed to have a ready supply of cash, though he had no occupation, and this led to the usual front-porch gossip throughout the lazy streets of Haywood. Those with more active imaginations supposed that Henry Martin had been a cattle thief or a bank robber, possibly running with the likes of Billy the Kid and Jesse James in his youth. Others put forward the theory that he had come from somewhere "Back East," and had fled to Oklahoma after embezzling vast sums of money from a business partner. Those with more rational imaginations suggested that old Henry had probably been a soldier during the Civil War, and had served long enough to be eligible for a government pension. The mail carrier refuted this theory, however, since he didn't recall ever delivering any mail to Henry's homestead.

The source of Henry's money will always remain a mystery, but the diary that was recovered from the old recluse's shack after his death told a remarkable story nonetheless. It was a story that could've been published under the title of *What Might Have Been*, and while it didn't solve the mystery of the hermit's income, it put to rest the mystery of how he had come to live in his simple shack and why he made his journey to the train station every day and stared at the passengers with a faraway look in his eyes.

The first page of the hermit's diary begins with the following lines: "Nell will leave tomorrow and in a few hours we will be together forever. The little rose covered cottage of which we have dreamed so long is waiting for her, and I know that she will be pleased."

The next entry in the hermit's journal reads, "Waiting for the train that was to bring her to me, the message came that Nell was dead. Killed in a wreck while only a few miles from me. There is nothing now for which to live. The past is a blank, the future holds nothing for me. I am going to seek where I can live alone, where I can forget, if that is possible."

The rest of the diary tells of his coming to Oklahoma and settling in the clearing outside of Haywood, where he lived until his death. The hermit's diary also speaks of his daily walks to the station, where he would stand and wait until the end of time, if necessary, just in case the news of Nell's death had been in error.

"I must go to the store today, I am almost out of food," reads the final line of Henry Martin's diary. It was thus presumed that Henry had either succumbed to an illness or had simply run out of money and starved to death. He was found lying upon his bed, holding a faded photograph of a beautiful girl in his lifeless hands. Even in death, his final thoughts had not been of himself, but of the sweetheart whose train had never arrived at the station.

IDAHO

65. The Tragic Fate of William Hamley

In January of 1898, a horrible murder took place in Washington State, near the farming town of Tekoa, not far from the Idaho state line. An old bachelor farmer named Dan Calland had been murdered inside his home, and his body thrown into his hog pen in the hopes that the hungry swine would devour the evidence. Two boys from nearby Farmington had gone to visit Calland and discovered blood splattered on the walls of the farmer's home, proving that a terrible struggle had taken place. The boys raced home and fetched a few neighbors, who searched the property and located Calland's body. The home had been evidently ransacked, and locals knew that Calland was a successful wheat farmer who kept thousands of dollars in the Farmington bank. Constable Sparks and the county coroner arrived on the scene and they, too, agreed that the bachelor farmer must have been killed for his money.

The police had very little to go on and only a precious few leads. Calland's farm was tucked away in a remote location, half a mile from the railroad tracks, and the nearest neighbors lived too far away to have seen or heard anything that would help crack the case. In mid-February the Whitman County commissioners authorized Sheriff Sims to spend up to $500 to catch and bring the murderer of Dan Calland to justice—a considerable sum of money at the time. The commissioners urged Sims to take any steps necessary to catch the killer.

Meanwhile, across the border in Idaho lived a man by the name of William Hamley. Hamley was known around the Palouse region for being eccentric and quite possibly demented. He had been born into a respectable family from the town of Kendrick but didn't amount to much and failed to live up to the Hamley name. Nonetheless, he was considered harmless and was permitted to roam the woods and mountains at his leisure.

William Hamley became a hermit, it was said, because he had a fear of the insane asylum. Perhaps this was proof that he was not crazy at all, since only a person who wasn't demented would have no fear of life inside the walls of a nineteenth century mental hospital, where bizarre and barbaric devices would be used to torment the unfortunate patients in the name of science and medicine. Medical literature of the era listed a variety of brow-raising conditions for which institutionalization was recommended: business trouble, being kicked in the head by a horse, asthma, egotism, and excessive reading of novels—just to name a few.

Figuring that failure to live up to the family name and the expectations of his father were reasons enough for institutionalization, William took to the hills. His wanderings made him something of a local celebrity of sorts. Hamley was a bit strange, but those who knew him agreed that he was a harmless and kind fellow, who kept to himself and lived off the land. He was a skilled hunter, though his weapon of choice was a derringer pistol. The tiny gun was not the best choice for shooting game, of course, but it was an effective tool for self-protection that wasn't a hindrance to a nomad who roamed the wilds of Idaho.

Hamley became so well-known throughout the Palouse that it wasn't long before the hermit was brought to the attention of Sheriff Sims. When the sheriff learned of the strange man in the mountains across the state line, he presumed that he might have been the one who murdered Dan Calland and cast his body to the swine. Sheriff Sims, armed to the teeth and carrying the order that authorized him to catch the killer by any means necessary, immediately set out to find the hermit.

The hermit eluded the sheriff and Sims, stymied by the rugged terrain, returned empty-handed to Whitman County in Washington, but not before turning over the search to his deputy. The deputy, alone in the rugged wilds of Idaho, convinced a local resident to help him locate and apprehend William Hamley. The local told the deputy that he knew the precise location of the hermit's hut, located in the Hoodoo Mountains.

When the two men approached the hut, the skittish and frightened hermit ran away, and the two men chased after him, calling for Hamley to halt. The deputy, who assumed that the hermit's actions were a sure indication of guilt, shouted, "Stop, or I'll shoot!" The hermit, who had very few enemies and was unaccustomed to being chased by armed thugs, must've been scared out of his wits, so he continued to run. He must've thought the world had gone mad, for he had lived in peace and solitude for years without being harassed by anyone; yet now he was running for his life. Perhaps he believed that the authorities had finally come to take him away to the insane asylum.

One of the men fired a shot at Hamley, breaking the hermit's leg and putting an end to the chase. Fearing what would happen next, the harmless hermit decided that he would not wait for his pursuers to reach him. He put the derringer to his head and pulled the trigger, taking his own life because his fear of being put into an institution was so great.

The deputy returned to Washington and reported that William Hamley had fired at him first. This was later proven not to be the case, however. The hermit was found with a double-barrel derringer, and only one barrel had been discharged. The only shot the hermit had fired was the shot that had taken his own life. Sheriff Sims and the deputy were disgraced and publicly humiliated in newspapers across the country. Their zealousness had resulted in the death of a harmless man, and the murder of the bachelor farmer from Tekoa remains unsolved to this day. Most shameful of all, the lawmen had knowingly crossed state lines without a warrant in order to catch the murderer of Dan Calland—becoming murderers themselves in the process.

66. An Ogre's Ship Comes In

Every one of life's hardships and pleasures seemed to have been etched into the face of Edwin Hurd, a seventy-year-old hermit who was occupying the hills of the Lemhi River valley when his ship finally came in, in February of 1905. Five decades earlier he had run away from his home in New York. He was the only son of well-to-do parents and longed for a life of adventure. He would not be disappointed.

After a few years of sowing his wild oats, Edwin grew remorseful over his abrupt departure from home, and within him grew a strong desire to rekindle his relationship with his parents. By working a series of odd jobs, Edwin managed to gradually find his way from the wilderness of the western frontier to his old hometown in New York, but any hopes for a happy reunion were dashed to pieces; during his absence, the Hurds had sold the family home and moved away. Edwin asked every soul in town where his family had gone, but nobody seemed to have any idea. The prodigal son spent months trying to track down his family, but eventually had no choice but to abandon his search.

Unbeknownst to the young wayfarer at the time, Edwin's parents had been untiringly seeking some trace of their missing son. When Edwin was in the East looking for them, his father was in the West looking for Edwin. While Edwin traipsed through the swamps of the South in search of his parents, his parents ventured to the windswept coastlines of the Northwest in the hopes of finding their son. Sadly, their paths never crossed. Years fell by the wayside, and Edwin's father eventually died, bequeathing $70,000 in cash and securities to Edwin, wherever he may be.

Edwin never forgave himself for leaving home, and so he settled into the life of a recluse. He built a tiny cabin in the Lemhi River valley and shunned society for the next fifty years, in part because of his physical appearance. His face was said to have been so repugnant that the villagers referred to him as the "Ogre of Idaho." Mothers wishing to scare straight a troublesome child often mentioned the hermit's name, threatening to send little Johnny or Suzie to his shack in the hills. As Edwin grew old, whatever remnants of physical desirability he once possessed departed. Even on the frontier nobody wanted to hire an aging ogre, so Edwin had to steal food in order to survive.

He found himself in many a courtroom, defending himself against charges of stealing a chicken here, a bushel of corn there, and a basket of eggs somewhere in between. Records indicate that he served a brief term in the county jail.

At the age of seventy, Edwin decided that he could no longer bear to be alone, so he got in touch with one of the marriage agencies that advertised in frontier newspapers of the era. These agencies specialized in finding brides for lonesome prospectors and lovelorn cowboys, so Edwin figured they'd also be able to help out a poor, old hermit. Through the agency Edwin signed a marriage contract, and a bride was dispatched to the hills of Idaho. The bride was so excited to meet her new husband that she missed her coach, and marched on foot for three miles through mud and snow to reach the cabin. She opened the door, saw the ugly mug of her new husband, and made up her mind to run away whenever the opportunity first presented itself. She bit her tongue and endured the hermit's company for about a week, when she decided to sneak away during the night.

Edwin, quite understandably, was heartbroken when he woke up the next morning and found that his wife had abandoned him. But the heartbreak would not last for long. A few days later, an attorney in charge of the Hurd family estate managed to finally track down the missing son and informed him that he was the sole heir to the $70,000, which had been bequeathed decades earlier. Day after day, month after month, and year after year, the Hurd family fortune had collected interest, and the father's stocks and bonds and other investments had grown into a bundle that would make even Andrew Carnegie drool. After Edwin's ship came in, newspapers across the country jumped on his rags-to-riches story. Marriage proposals poured in from every corner of the country. History fails to record the reaction of his runaway bride, but Edwin must've relished the thought of her kicking herself in the shins once she realized that she would've been the heiress to an enormous fortune, if only she hadn't been so eager to escape.

When it comes to the life stories of hermits, many of us delight in a sad and tragic ending. The jilted lover forced to live in a cave and eat bugs for thirty years, only to freeze to death with a photograph of a childhood sweetheart in his hands. A fugitive from the law living out the remainder of his days in self-imposed exile, forever doing penance for a misdeed that would've netted but a few years in jail. The handsome young man whose bride-to-be contracted a rare disease and expired en route to the wedding ceremony. But the story of Edwin Hurd, though it has a happy ending, is worth remembering, because it brings to mind the old adage about every dog having his day. The story of Edwin Hurd also proves that the old adage applies not only to dogs, but to ogres as well.

COLORADO

67. Anton Glasmann

In 1863 Jim and John Reynolds assembled a band of daring young men and marched through Texas, en route to Colorado, carrying the flag of the Confederacy, intent on claiming Colorado for their cause. Their attempt to wrest Colorado away from the Union was a failure, but the band of marauders was successful in inflicting casualties and leaving a trail of blood in their wake. The "Reynolds Gang," as they came to be known, believed that they could provide much-needed financial aid to the Confederacy by robbing everything from stagecoaches to gold mines. By 1864 the gang had managed to amass over $100,000 and may have gone on to have an important impact on the outcome of the war had it not been for Colonel Chivington, whose troops chased down the gang and captured most of its members. The captives were taken to Fort Lyon to await trial, but two of the gang members escaped to New Mexico.

Shortly before their capture, members of the gang buried the treasure in Elk Creek country, marking the location by sticking the blade of a bowie knife into a pine tree and breaking off the handle. The blade pointed to the mouth of a cave, where the treasure had been hidden. Moments later, Chivington's troops caught up with the outlaws. The soldiers bound the hands of the criminals behind their backs, lined up the outlaws with their backs to the cliff, and shot them down, one by one. In turn, each body tumbled down into the stony abyss. The last man to be shot, however, fell not over the cliff, but off to the side. The soldiers, thinking him dead, left the scene. The surviving gang member was John Reynolds, the leader of the group.

Although Reynolds had survived the ordeal, his wounds were life threatening. Determined to pass on his secret before he died, he dragged himself over the rocky terrain and managed to crawl to a miner's cabin in the valley. Before he died, Reynolds drew out a map of the scene of the hidden treasure, in the hopes that one of the miners might be a Confederate sympathizer willing to pick up where the Reynolds Gang left off.

Early in the 1870s, Anton Glasmann took up a mining claim near the headwaters of Elk Creek and built himself a cabin. What Glasmann lacked in mining experience, he made up for in pluck, and day after day he dug holes on the northern side of his home in search of gold. The fact that he was never successful in finding any didn't stop the miner; he had the gold fever, and, as any prospector will admit, it's one malady for which there is no cure. Glasmann married twice, but the miner's incurable disease made victims of both women; his first wife died of loneliness, and the second, unable to bear the burdensome existence, took her life by drinking poison.

Undeterred, Glasmann continued his pursuit of gold. He grew thin and wrinkled and frail and eventually abandoned the cabin and moved into a cave that was located on his property. Whenever he left the cave to prospect, he concealed the entrance with piles of brush and leaves. One day, years later in 1901, the old hermit ambled into the village of Pine Grove in a highly excited state. He displayed gold coins of great value, explaining to the villagers that he had found the long-lost treasure of the Reynolds Gang.

Normally, such a revelation would've caused a great deal of jealousy and bitter envy among the local miners, but since they all knew that old Anton was a sad figure, they didn't begrudge him his good fortune. They knew how many years he had suffered in his futile search for all that glimmers, losing two wives and the best years of his life along the way. The shaggy hermit with the bent back, gnarled hands, and wax-like skin had finally discovered something big in the bottom of the eternally empty gold pan that was his life. Who could resent the old coot after all he had been through?

One of the locals, looking out for the hermit's best interests, advised him to catch the train for Denver so that he could hire an attorney and protect his newfound treasure. He left Pine Grove that evening and early the next morning found himself wandering the city streets in search of a notary office. What a sight old Anton Glasmann must've presented to the city dwellers; his frail and bent form shuffling down the wide boulevards of Denver, his weak and tiny eyes peering cautiously from beneath a large, battered sombrero. A Good Samaritan pointed old Anton in the direction of an attorney's office.

Once inside, the tired miner sank into a chair. Though he was exhausted, he excitedly told the lawyer about the treasure he had discovered. He babbled incoherently, and the confused lawyer wasn't quite sure what to make of the curious old man in the tattered sombrero sitting before him. Then there came a pause, a quick convulsion followed by a gasp, and the helpless lawyer watched the hermit's bearded, gray head sink forward upon a tired breast. His lifelong quest for treasure was over, and old Anton Glasmann died without ever divulging the whereabouts of the famous Reynolds Gang treasure.

68. The Ballad of Beatrice and John

A one-hundred-gun salute echoed through Monument Canyon on the Fourth of July in the summer of 1911, rending the air with the reverberations of patriotic splendor. This was not a patriotic event, however, but a wedding celebration between two of the most eccentric souls who ever trod the steep canyon trails in the high desert of the Colorado Plateau.

The groom was John Otto, the colorful hermit whose name would later be recorded in history as the man responsible for the creation of the Colorado National

Monument and its inclusion in the National Park Service. The bride, an artist and sculptor from New England, was Beatrice Farnham, who gave up a palatial home in Massachusetts in order to live in a mountain cave with her lover.

The marriage, unfortunately, would only last a few short years.

The life of John Otto began forty-one years earlier, in the sleepy Missouri town of Marthasville, where the body of Daniel Boone was originally laid to rest before its infamous and bizarre posthumous journey to Kentucky, where some believe he was finally buried. How strange that two expert frontiersmen would have roots in the same tiny village, yet embark on two completely divergent paths, with one man ending up in the Virginia General Assembly and the other ending up in a cave. Remarkably, the bodies of both men would eventually come to rest in unmarked graves on opposite ends of the country.

John Otto arrived in Grand Junction, Colorado, in 1906, after a failed attempt to enter the ministry in Iowa. Preaching just wasn't in John's blood, and so he ran off to Colorado, where he fell in love with the scenery of the high desert and decided never to leave. After months of wandering the canyons and exploring the rugged wilderness, John wrote, "I came here last year and found these canyons, and they felt like the heart of the world to me. I'm going to stay and promote this place, because it should be a national park." John found a cave, ten thousand feet above sea level, and made it his home.

Miss Beatrice Farnham was born in South Weymouth, Massachusetts, in a house that had sheltered her wealthy family since the days of the Revolutionary War. When she was a young girl she had made up her mind that she would someday study art in San Francisco. Beatrice followed through on her plans and became a distinguished sculptor. She traveled often, and her quest for adventure led her to the mountains of Colorado. At the end of one day's hike, she came upon the cave of John Otto. Unfazed by the hermit's appearance, she unrolled her sleeping bag and introduced herself.

After a one-year courtship, the pair decided to get married. During this time, the hermit had become an unofficial spokesman for the Colorado Plateau. Newspapers and magazines eventually took notice of John's efforts to preserve and promote his beloved canyons. It was he who carved the steep stairway into the stone of Independence Monument, which has become the most recognizable natural feature of the national park. Horace Albright, the famed conservationist and second director of the National Park Service, once remarked, "Otto was a marvelous guide and knew every inch of his monument, which he tended like a personal kingdom."

On the day of the wedding, which was the social event of the season, the couple stood before an altar, carved from stone by the hands of the bride herself at the summit of Independence Monument; he, dressed in leather breeches and a cutaway jacket, and she in white satin. An Episcopal minister performed the service and, at the proper moment, all of the guests in attendance fired a salvo from the revolvers at their sides. Straddling the hermit's burrows, Foxie and Cookie, the newlyweds, rode off into the sun.

"I like John because he is so unconventional," the bride wrote home to her mother shortly after the ceremony. "There's no nonsense about him. He is all man."

As many hermits have discovered, married life isn't all that it is cut out to be, and just one month after the wedding the free-spirited artist returned to Massachusetts. Beatrice told her hermit husband that she was going back to settle her estate, and that she would return in six weeks. She never came back. Three years later, Judge Sullivan granted a divorce to John Otto. Shortly after the divorce, Beatrice Farnham met and fell in love with a rancher and trick rider named Dallas Benson. They were married in March of 1915.

Only weeks before John Otto married Beatrice Farnham, the National Park Service—thanks to the efforts of one hermit—designated the area as a national park, known officially as Colorado National Monument. John Otto was hired as the park's first ranger and custodian, a position that he held until the mid-1930s. He was paid a token salary of one dollar per month, as he had requested.

Beatrice Farnham lived to the age of 103 and died in Virginia on February 19, 1979. John Otto eventually left the canyon that he had once loved so dearly and headed to California, in pursuit of gold, at the age of sixty-one. A hermit to the very end, John lived in seclusion on a mining claim along the Klamath River near Yreka. He died on June 19, 1952, and was buried in a pauper's grave at Yreka's Evergreen Cemetery. In 2002, fifty years after his death, the Colorado National Monument Association erected a marker over his grave at Evergreen Cemetery in the shape of Independence Monument.

ARIZONA

69. Old Man Reavis

The Superstition Mountains of Arizona have been a source of folklore for thousands of years, even long before the Apaches believed that a hole leading to the underworld could be found somewhere within the Peralta Canyon. The fabled mountains are also home to the Lost Dutchman's Mine, said to contain wealth beyond imagination. Scores of miners and treasure seekers have flocked to the Super-stitions in search of this mother lode since 1891, when a German immigrant revealed clues to the gold mine's location on his deathbed. Many of these adventurers exhausted their life savings searching for the mine, returning home broke. Many others never returned at all, leaving their bones to bleach beneath the hot Arizona sun.

Jacob Waltz was the German immigrant who claimed to have discovered the mother lode known today as the Lost Dutchman's Mine. There's a very good chance he might have personally known a strange fellow named Elisha Marcus Reavis, who is still remembered today as "The Hermit of the Superstition Mountains."

Reavis was born in Beardstown, Illinois, in 1827. He was college educated and, for a short time, taught school in California. It is there he developed a case of gold fever and gave up teaching in order to become a prospector. He

Elisha Reavis, "The Hermit of the Superstition Mountains."

worked a claim along the San Gabriel River, said to be teeming with gold, but was unsuccessful.

He traveled to the Arizona Territory in 1863, returning to San Gabriel a few years later to marry a girl named Mary Sexton. The gold bug once again got the better of Reavis, and after Mary gave birth to a daughter, Louisa Marie, the prospector abandoned them both and returned to Arizona with an uncle. Reavis's uncle, Isham Reavis, had just been appointed to the territory's Supreme Court, and Elisha found work at a horse ranch on the Verde River, breaking in and training pack animals for the army at Fort McDowell. During one of his excursions with the army, he toured the idyllic Salt River Valley and decided to make his home on the mountain, which today bears his name, in 1872.

For twenty years Reavis farmed the valley, growing food for the many mining camps in the region. He was a renowned marksman with his Winchester rifle, and his shooting skills were so well-known throughout the valley that the Apache gave him a wide berth and avoided straying onto his property. It was during this time Reavis's reputation began to grow, fanned by the rare visitor he would entertain at his mountain retreat. He possessed one of the finest libraries ever seen in the Arizona Territory; certainly the finest ever kept in the Superstition Mountains. In spite of his education and keen intelligence, Elisha Reavis never shaved, bathed, or cut his hair.

In the fall of 1895 the old hermit fell ill, but the friends who visited him were surprised to find that the seventy-year-old man still made his regular trips throughout the valley, selling his vegetables to the miners. They marveled at his ability to maintain his fifteen-acre ranch in his old age and ill health; for the chores around the farm were enough to wear down men half his age. Alone, Reavis cared for the land and its feathered and hooved tenants. He kept chickens and turkeys and swine, and also cared for two horses and a pack of dogs.

A neighboring rancher, James Dalabaugh, often visited the aged hermit to see how he was doing. By the following spring, Reavis's health had declined further, and Dalabaugh knew that the Hermit of the Superstition Mountains didn't have much time left. The hermit, on the other hand, was much more optimistic. During one visit in April, Dalabaugh stopped by the ranch, and Reavis explained that he was preparing to take a trip to Mesa to buy seed potatoes. On May 6, 1896, Dalabaugh was surprised to learn that the old hermit hadn't put in an appearance since his trip to Mesa and decided to look for him. Along the dusty trail, outside of Roger's Canyon, Dalabaugh discovered the remains of his old friend under a large juniper tree. Half of the old man's body had been eaten by the wolves.

The body of Old Man Reavis was laid to rest in a grave on Indian burial ground, which presented the only soil suitable for digging. A simple stone marker denoted the site for many years, inscribed with the hermit's name, his date of birth, and date of death. Sadly, sometime in the 1980s, vandals stole the marker. Though the gravestone may be gone, the hermit's legacy can still be observed throughout the Superstition Mountains through a variety of landmarks that still bear his name. On maps, Reavis Mountain, Reavis Valley, Reavis Trail Canyon, Reavis Gap, Reavis Creek, Reavis Saddle, and Reavis Falls can be found.

On one of the hermit's final journeys he went to Phoenix, where a tourist took a snap shot of the curious-looking fellow with a Kodak camera. The photographer finished the photograph, had it enlarged, and had it displayed at the Chicago World's Fair in 1893. Also known as the Columbian Exposition, this event featured several historic firsts; it displayed the original Ferris wheel built by George Ferris, the first version of the clothing fastener, which would later become known as the "zipper," and the exposition also introduced the world to brands like Cracker Jack, Cream of Wheat, and Juicy Fruit gum. The photograph of Old Man Reavis was recognized by one of the fair's visitors—a woman from California who identified the hermit as her long-lost brother. The woman sent letter after letter to Reavis in the hopes of a happy reunion, but the hermit had no desire to reconnect with his shaded past. The only thing that really resulted from the exhibition of the photograph was a threat sent through the valley by Reavis, who swore up and down that if he ever met the man who had taken his picture, he would send a bullet through his brain.

70. Lord Neville of the Garbage Dump

Few journeys through life have been as strange as the one taken by Philip E. Neville, whose bizarre journey carried the Baron of Latimer from the castle walls of old England to a garbage dump in Arizona. While most men muddle through life engaged in a continuous struggle to attain power and wealth, Philip Neville spent his later years repudiating the title bestowed upon him at birth, and willingly became a penniless hermit in a foreign land.

Neville never disclosed the reason for abandoning his life of ease and grandeur in his homeland, other than to say that it was the result of family troubles, but he maintained a friendship with an aunt, whose letters were always addressed to "Lord Neville." The aunt continually pleaded with Neville to return to England, but he was determined to remain in the Arizona desert until the end of his days.

Neville's strange journey might never have come to light if a church in Phoenix hadn't discovered a $250 bundle of bills in its collection plate one Sunday morning. The package had been wrapped in paper so that the amount of the contribution could not be seen. The hermit's anonymous act of charity on that summer morning in 1904 is what ultimately led to his discovery. It was the only time the hermit had made an appearance in the church, and the other members of the congregation correctly assumed that the mysterious stranger had been the one who made the contribution.

The shocked but well-intentioned parishioners believed that the mysterious donor had inadvertently placed the wrong package in the basket. They sought and found Neville in order to return his money. The hermit insisted that his gift had not been given in error. He claimed that he had recently inherited a large sum of money and could afford the generous contribution. However, such an incident could not remain a secret, and dozens of curious locals hungered to learn more about the stranger and the source of his extraordinary wealth.

It was discovered that Neville lived in a shanty on the garbage dump in the dry riverbed below the city, and that his only discernible source of income was salvaging scrap metal that had been tossed into the dump. Neville became something of a local celebrity, much to his displeasure. He was angry that a prying world should interfere in his affairs and spread wild rumors about the source of his wealth. Finally, Neville decided that he would "come clean" and tell the local papers about his former life in merry old England. Neville hoped that if he could satisfy the curiosity of the local population, he might be allowed to resume his monastic life of solitude.

Neville told the snooping reporters that he was no longer the Baron of Latimer, at least not in his own mind, but, as the lineal descendant, he couldn't exactly resign from his position, since it was his birthright. The money he had given to the church was part of the $8,000 his aunt had sent to him against his wishes. He showed the curious locals these letters as proof, letters of a sweet and affectionate nature from an elderly aunt who pleaded with Lord Neville to return to Brancepeth Castle. This, he vowed to the curious citizens gathered around his dump, was something that he would never do. He was determined to spend the remainder of his days as a hermit.

Neville's admission didn't achieve the desired result, and, much to his chagrin, the story of "Lord Neville of the Garbage Dump" spread to every corner of the United States. The hermit had to abandon his shack in Arizona and headed to California where he hoped to find the seclusion he craved. But everywhere he went, from Los Angeles to Redondo Beach to San Pedro, he was identified as Lord Neville. In 1906 he returned to Arizona and decided to become a businessman, having learned the hard way that the path to hermitry is not always a lonesome wilderness trail, but often a bustling highway thronged with curious crowds.

Philip E. Neville's failed experimentation with hermitry didn't leave him bitter, however. Lord Neville never lost the generous spirit that had led to his discovery in Arizona. In May of 1906 the child of one of Neville's employees was bitten by a rabid dog. Neville immediately visited every physician in Phoenix before deciding that the child should be sent to the Pasteur Institute in Chicago for the best treatment possible. Lord Neville himself paid for the trip to Chicago as well as the child's medical treatment. On June 16 the father of the sick child, Thomas Rain, sent the following letter to Neville from Chicago:

Dear Sir,

Dr. Lagorio pronounces my little girl cured from the bite of that hydrophobia stricken dog. In fact, he has saved her life from one of the most dangerous bites in the face. Thank God for your timely and brave assistance. If it had not been for you, God help us, I don't know what we should have done. Thank God and bless you.

Baby is now down with a very bad cold and I am afraid to start with her as it is cold and raining and a raw wind is blowing. I may be able to start with her between Sunday and Tuesday next. I hope this will find you well.

Your obedient servant,
Thomas Rain

The strange journey of Philip E. Neville should serve as a reminder that some people are called to be hermits, only to be called back to civilization to fulfill a higher purpose at a later time, for reasons known only to the creator. Perhaps a higher power had brought Lord Neville from a castle in England to the sun-parched landscape of Arizona to save the life of an innocent child. If such is the case, it proves the old adage that God—like many hermits—works in mysterious ways.

WYOMING

71. The Green River Hermit

For over seven hundred miles the Green River meanders through the states of Wyoming, Utah, and Colorado. Along its serpentine route, the river cuts through some of the most spectacular canyons in the world. Its headwaters reside in the untamed Teton Wilderness of western Wyoming, equally as picturesque and awe-inspiring as the canyons of the Colorado Plateau. Just south of the Bridger-Teton National Forest, the Green River flows through Sweetwater County. On the right bank of the river, twenty miles from the frontier town of Granger, lived an unusual hermit during the latter half of the nineteenth century.

The hermit's crude dwelling, a dugout in the ground guarded by a heavy oak door, was far less remarkable than the man who lived inside. Opposite the door, in the center of the subterranean chamber, stood a small stove, flanked on one side by a wooden crate and by a simple cupboard on the other. Against one wall was a tiny bed, filled with straw and covered by coarse, wool blankets. This was the extent of the hermit's furniture, but not of his worldly belongings. The well-stocked bunker was strewn with steel traps used for hunting, as well as a great deal of fishing tackle and ammunition. A Winchester rifle was mounted on the wall, perched upon a noble pair of antlers. A black bearskin covered the cold, clay floor.

On the other side of the room stood a large bookcase and this bookcase held the hermit's most prized possessions—a collection of books that would impress any professor of English literature. They say that you can learn a great deal about a man by the books that he reads and, if this is true, then the occupant of the glorified potato cellar was a man of exquisite taste and refinement. The hermit's collection contained works by Shakespeare, Milton, Bacon, and Pope, along with the novels of Thackeray, Hawthorne, and Eliot. It was evident that the hermit was also fascinated by philosophy; James McCosh, Immanuel Kant, and Thomas Hamilton were well-represented in his personal library. In its old, leather cover was an edition of Cicero's *De Senectute*, bearing the inscription: Dartmouth College, 1848.

From the appearance of the hermit, very few people would guess that he was a man of such education and refinement. Grizzled and weather-beaten, his sixty-odd years made him as tough as antelope hide, which he wore as clothing. Yet, in spite of his rough appearance, visitors to the man-made cave would be surprised to discover that the hermit was kind and hospitable. Friends would often visit the old hermit, who would prepare a dinner of venison steak over his simple stove, served with coffee strong enough to put hair on the chest of a newborn. After supper the hermit would sit in front of a fire and smoke from his corncob pipe. At this point in the evening, if you were lucky enough to be considered by the old man as a friend, he would tell you the story of his life.

After graduating from the hallowed halls of Dartmouth College, the young scholar with a promising future became smitten with adventure. After a long journey around the Horn, the Ivy League graduate reached California in the spring of 1850, where he would spend the next seventeen years prospecting for gold. Time had gotten away from him, and before he knew it, he was no longer a young man with a brilliant mind and a limitless future, but a forty-year-old tramp with dirt under his fingernails. The golden treasure was always within sight, but always out of grasp. Finally admitting defeat, the luckless prospector devoted himself to hunting and trapping in the Sierras. His wanderings eventually led him to Wyoming.

The hermit was happy to discuss many aspects of his peculiar life. Was he poor? He would state otherwise; coyote hides, beaver pelts, and bear skins provided him with more than enough income to get by. How did he keep himself entertained alone in the wilds of western Wyoming? He would reply that much of his spare time was spent in writing and rewriting his copious notes on the flora and fauna of the Sierras and Rockies. One thing the hermit would not reveal, however, was his name.

The name of the hermit who lived on the banks of the Green River has been lost to history, but his is not an isolated case. From the Appalachians to the Sierras, the mountains of America are full of misanthropic Thoreaus, men who love nature to such an extent that they are content to be forgotten by society. This brand of hermit did not flee into the wilderness because of personal tragedy or unrequited love, as so many other hermits have done since time immemorial. This rare species of hermit, kindred spirits of men like John Muir and Gifford Pinchot, choose to make their homes in the wilderness because that is where they feel absolute enjoyment. These are not your garden-variety wild men; they are not stubborn and ornery old recluses. Though his exterior may be rugged, inside his chest beats a heart soft and kind. These hermits are masters of their majestic wilderness kingdoms, at peace with the scenery.

72. Upside-Down Mullen

In the sparsely-populated extreme northeast corner of Wyoming resides Crook County, home of the 5,114-foot-high monolith known as Devil's Tower. Immediately to the west of Crook County is Campbell County, which was formed out of parts of Crook and Weston counties in 1911. Since many residents of northeast Wyoming live in utter seclusion miles away from their nearest neighbor, one could argue that many of the region's citizens could be described as hermits. However, when it comes to eccentricity, few of these hermits could hold a candle to Cyrus "Upside-Down" Mullen.

Cyrus Mullen lived alone in a simple log hut about twenty-five miles west of Gillette, back when the frontier boomtown was still part of Crook County. Very little was known of the hermit since he shunned conversation and disliked society, but one thing that was known about Cyrus was that, in his younger days, he had once been an acrobat in the circus. Another well-known fact about the hermit was that he enjoyed spending his free time writing nonsensical letters to newspaper editors throughout Wyoming.

The editors of half a dozen papers published Cyrus's letters, presumably for the sole intention of giving the subscribers something interesting and whimsical to read. The old hermit was a crusader of many causes, most of which were diametrically opposed to common sense, but his most passionate argument revolved around the premise that the human body was designed upside-down.

"The human body was made wrong end up," he once wrote to the editor of the Kelton newspaper. "Why should the feet be on the ground and the head up, when the head is the heavier end? Gravitation calls for the head to be downward, that the resistance forced on the backbone be thus loosened. Walk on the hands at least half your time. Any person can do it with a little practice. I do, and I am one of nature's noblemen—Cyrus Mullen."

Cyrus was such an advocate for walking upside-down that he even dragged politics into the debate. "It is all wrong," he once wrote, in reference to tariffs and taxation. "Too high, and too high on leather. Shoes cost entirely too much. Walk on your hands, people, as I do and as nature decreed you should, and save shoe expense! Blessed be the man who walks on his hands and thus obeys nature."

Even though his critics argued that nature had never issued such a decree, pointing out that no member of the animal kingdom walks on its hands, Cyrus Mullen held firm to his beliefs. The hermit's claim of having been a circus acrobat in his youth was known to most of the residents of Crook County, and anyone who doubted this claim was forced to eat crow when they traveled along the dusty highway to Gillette and spotted the shaggy recluse walking to town on his hands. During these sojourns, Mullen would stop every three hundred yards or so to rest, then he would flip up onto his hands again and away he would go. While walking on his hands, Mullen was known to wave his feet in the air and clap them together, thus making himself the most peculiar detail of the Wyoming landscape next to Devil's Tower.

It was said that it was impossible to approach Upside-Down Mullen from the front; if he encountered anyone walking in his direction, he would take to his feet and dash off across the range like an antelope with its rear end on fire. Anyone wishing to approach the hermit had to do so from behind. Those who followed behind the hermit at a safe distance claimed that Mullen would stop at intersections, where he would whistle a lively tune and excitedly dance on his hands while waving his feet in the air.

These details were about as much as anyone knew about the upside-down hermit. Where he had come from was a mystery. He first appeared at the tiny, one-room cabin one July and made his home there, claiming the dilapidated structure, which had been abandoned decades earlier by another recluse. He was occasionally seen hunting on the grassy range, stalking his prey with his feet in the air, and word around Cook County was that he once succeeded in running down a rabbit while upside-down. A local who witnessed the incident stated that Cyrus Mullen did, in fact, run down the rabbit, but only after he threw a rock at the creature and wounded it. Nonetheless, it was still a memorable feat by a memorable man who lived the better part of his life believing that man was made wrong-end up.

WASHINGTON

73. The Skunk Whisperer

Those who hunger for a life of seclusion would be pleased as punch to call Grant County home. When the first white settlers arrived in the untamed wilderness of central Washington during the time of the Civil War, they found a land so desolate that many of them turned right around and went back home. In 1879 one government official described the place as "a desolation where even the most hopeful can find nothing in its future prospects to cheer." Nevertheless, a few brave souls decided to stay, eking out a meager existence by raising livestock and attempting to farm the drylands. When Grant County was established in 1909, the 2,791 square miles of land within its borders was home to less than nine thousand souls.

It was around this time a hermit named Joe Martin called Grant County home. Though he lived a solitary existence inside of a lonesome cave, Martin was the subject of much curiosity. Rumors had spread throughout central Washington that Martin was extremely wealthy, and these rumors inspired treasure-seekers and ruffians to brave the rugged terrain in an attempt to separate the hermit from his money.

Would-be robbers descended upon the harmless hermit dozens of times over the years, and Martin took every conceivable precaution. He obtained several Russian wolfhounds and attempted to train them as guard dogs. This seemed to work for a while, until robbers discovered that, by tossing the dogs chunks of wolf meat, they could journey to the hermit's cave unmolested. A few years later Martin rigged an elaborate alarm system, which he believed would be impressive enough to make even the guards at

Fort Knox green with envy. He strung the trees and boulders with wires, which were connected to horns and bells. Quite literally, the hermit's electronic alarm system had all the bells and whistles—certainly more bells and whistles than any other alarm system in the Pacific Northwest. Burglars easily bypassed the hermit's alarm system by snipping the wires. In spite of his numerous attempts at home security, Joe Martin's cave was ransacked over and over again. The fact that the robbers never discovered any money did little to discourage rumors of the hermit's wealth from spreading.

If anything, failure to unearth the hermit's treasure only seemed to motivate the robbers even more. Surely there could only be a limited number of places to hide the loot inside of a tiny cave. The robbers believed that with a little perseverance, the treasure would soon be theirs. Eventually, the hermit discovered a solution to his problem: Joe Martin began to collect skunks, stockpiling the stinky creatures by the dozens inside of his cave. After months of painful experiments, the hermit was able to train the animals to "attack" on command.

In the summer of 1917, Joe Martin's army of bodyguards were put to the test. Two suspicious-looking characters were seen prowling around the woods in the vicinity of Martin's cave, and a few hours later they crawled back into town leaving a trail, which even the most inept deputy could follow. The robbers wandered the streets of Jericho, desperately seeking relief.

It wasn't long before the bandits had stunk up the whole town to such an extent that the villagers formed a posse and drove the men beyond the city limits. Prodded by the pitchforks of the townsfolk, the two robbers were driven to the banks of a river where they were forced to strip naked and bury their clothes, before being ordered to bathe in the river. As the two men bathed, some of the villagers returned to town and took up a collection of sorts, asking the women of Jericho to dump the contents of their perfume bottles into a bucket. When the robbers emerged from the river, they were doused from head to toe with the buckets of perfume before being escorted to the county jail.

From that day forward, Joe Martin was never again bothered by treasure seekers and thugs. The trained skunks, who came to view the hermit as their mother, followed at Martin's heels wherever he roamed, and the citizens were always happy to give him a wide berth whenever he came into town for supplies and provisions. After many years of practicing the fine art of hermitry, Joe Martin finally found the peace and seclusion he desired.

OREGON

74. Ike Powell

In 1905 the life of one of the most remarkable residents of Baker County ended in a lonely cabin on the banks of the Snake River. The tragic protagonist of our story is "Ike" Powell, a recluse prospector who, for thirty years, offered his humble shack to any weary traveler in need of a place to rest.

Ike arrived in Oregon in 1864, where he prospected for ten years without any success. Yet, he never lost hope; for mining was in his blood. He had come from the anthracite coal fields of Pennsylvania and descended from generations of miners. His goal was to someday return to his home state with the gold he had found so he could finally provide for the girl to whom he was betrothed.

In 1874 Ike received word that his betrothed had been fatally injured in a horrible mine explosion, which flattened half of the town in which he had grown up. The news broke his heart. Ike was so saddened by this loss that he quit visiting the settlements and mining camps along the Snake River. For five years he was completely lost in the world, wandering aimlessly and uninterested in the companionship of his fellow man. He built himself a cabin in a canyon, which echoed with the tumbling waters of the river, perhaps in the hopes that the cacophonous rumbling of the river would drown out his tortured thoughts.

The day he received the news about his sweetheart, Ike vowed never again to shave or cut his hair, and within months he had acquired the classic visage of a hermit. But civilization gradually encroached upon his lonesome kingdom, much to Ike's displeasure. Brownlee's Ferry was established on Snake River, and a road leading from Pine Valley to the mouth of Pine Creek was opened, bringing a flood of hunters, prospectors, and ranchers.

Ike decided that he would never be able to find an escape from the hand of man, so he did his best to live in peace with the outsiders who passed by his cabin on a daily basis. Ike was a fine gardener, and the hermit's bed of melons, cabbage, and tomatoes became the envy of many a hungry traveler. Ike decided to feed everyone who passed, always refusing money whenever it was offered to him. Right around that time, old Ike's luck began to change. He continued with his prospecting and was delighted to discover gold in the bottom of his pan where none had ever been before. He withdrew a respectable amount of gold dust from the river banks, which he took to town and traded for shoes and clothing.

At one time, Ike had been an excellent violinist and a voracious reader. After the death of his lover, Ike never again touched the strings of an instrument or opened a

book. The only thing that satisfied the old hermit in the twilight years of his life was feeding hungry travelers and giving them a place to rest their heads for the night. Hospitality became his hobby, and throughout the river valley it was a well-established fact that if you went to the hermit's cabin, you would never leave hungry.

As the years rushed by like the waters of the Snake River, Ike began preparing for his inevitable departure from the world. Like many who had made the perilous journey through life's winding pathways, he knew his time was drawing to a close. Soon there would be no more travelers to feed, and the gold he had chased after for so many decades of his life seemed as unimportant and worthless as the sandy gravel that crunched beneath his feet along the water's edge. He found the prospect of death to be bittersweet; he lamented the misspent years of his youth and his fruitless search for wealth but, at the same time, he longed to be reunited with the lover who was lost on the hardscrabble coalfields of Pennsylvania more than half a century earlier. Ike only had one final request: to be buried near his beloved cabin with no stone or monument to mark the spot.

Ike Powell died not long after making his last request, and he was buried along the roadside by his teary-eyed neighbors in August of 1905, in sight of his home. Before boarding up the hermit's cabin, his neighbors searched the interior in the hopes of finding a farewell letter, or some testament left behind by the man who had devoted his final years to feeding the hungry. Ike didn't leave so much as a scrap of paper behind; no will, no deathbed confession, no letter written with the intention of telling his life story.

As the army of time marched on, the hermit's garden grew tangled with weeds and was reclaimed by the forest. The timbers of his old cabin rotted away and returned to the earth, leaving behind no trace that it had ever existed. Even the hermit's unmarked grave disappeared, as the narrow dirt road was widened and paved to make way for future generations of hopeful travelers, who still traverse the river valley seeking a place to rest their weary heads for the night.

75. Sailor Jack Seeks a Bride

Today, Coos Bay has the distinction of being the largest city along the Oregon coast, but in the early twentieth century the bay was nothing more than a spattering of small villages, each consisting of a handful of simple, wooden shacks. A few miles away from the coastal village of Marshfield, tucked away in the redwood-crowned hills, lived a hermit known around the bay as Sailor Jack.

Now, countless hermits have wandered into the desolate wilderness because of love; some to forget it, and others to escape from it. Sailor Jack was the rarest variety of hermit; for he took to the wilderness in order to find love and to seek a bride.

For forty years Sailor Jack lived in seclusion, hidden from society in a pine shack high on the hills overlooking the bay, with his only companions an old rooster and three starving cows. It was a rustic and rugged life, but it never stopped Sailor Jack from dreaming about romance and marriage.

Even at the age of eighty, the hopeful hermit never gave up on his dreams. For nearly half a century he kept a bridal chamber in a perpetual state of readiness and, while the boudoir lacked the feminine touch, it had all of the necessities that the wife of an eremite could ever want. There was a chest of drawers and a bed, both hewn from the majestic firs that stood guard atop the hermit's hill. There was a chair, which Sailor Jack had fashioned from cedar, and a washstand made from redwood. Jack's bride would also be privileged with a spectacular view; from the front window of the cabin, one could gaze down a one thousand-foot-tall cliff. The bride's back yard would be filled with towering redwoods, rising more than two hundred feet into the sky, even older and more majestic than the spires of Christendom's grandest cathedrals.

Sailor Jack was so certain that his bride would come, that every morning he meticulously and carefully wended his way down the perilous path to the logging road at the bottom of the cliff. This road was the hermit's only link to civilization, and he was sure that he would encounter his future bride if he waited long enough. Day after day, oblivious to the weather and the changing of seasons and the perpetual trickling of the rivulets of time, he went down to the road and waited. This was his daily ritual for four decades.

He began this ritual a few years after he had made the regrettable decision to desert a young bride, leaving her humiliated and embarrassed on the steps of the village church. Sailor Jack was young then, and the lure of the sea was too irresistible. He promised his betrothed that he would return after he had a chance to explore the world. A year or two later he returned to the bay and cleared a small patch of land among the towering trees. There he built a four-room cabin, more than large enough for him and his bride. He saw her often, on the sidewalks of Marshfield, in the stores and shops, and he pleaded for forgiveness until his mouth grew dry and his throat grew hoarse. It was never given.

Until the day of his death, Sailor Jack fervently believed that he would find his bride; perhaps the one he left on the steps of the church when he was young and foolish, or perhaps another who would take her place. He paid for his sins with forty years of puritanical penance and abstinent austerity, and even though his jilted lover never forgave him for abandoning her on their wedding day, we can only hope that old Sailor Jack finally found his bride on the other side, after his body returned to the Earth and his soul sailed into the port of Paradise.

TEXAS

76. The Frontier Pharmacist

The city of Boerne, in Kendall County, was established under most unusual circumstances. Boerne, originally known as Tusculum, was established as a utopian settlement by exiles of the March Revolution, which was a series of rebellions in Germany, Austria, Poland, and many other European countries in 1848. Those who protested, known as the "Forty-Eighters," rallied against the autocratic political structure and demanded more liberal political freedoms. The rebels were defeated by the conservative autocrats, and the Forty-Eighters, fearing repercussions from their involvement in the rebellions, immigrated to places such as Canada, Australia, England, and the United States.

Boerne was founded as an offshoot of the Texas Hill Country Free Thinker Latin Settlements. Members of these settlements fancied themselves as free-spirited and open-minded intellectuals. They conversed in Latin and debated such things as philosophy, theology, literature, and music. They believed in utopian ideals and personal freedom, which sounded good on the surface, but these ideals accomplished little in the way of economic progress. Within a year, most of these utopian settlements had fallen into dystopian despair (presumably because the act of paying taxes would be a violation of personal freedom), and the colonies of free-thinking intellectuals dispersed. Boerne was one of the few colonies that managed to survive, becoming incorporated as a town in 1909.

Naturally, any town founded by eccentric intellectuals will contain its share of colorful citizens. One such citizen was a middle-aged recluse named J. J. Bayard. He was born in Delaware in 1824 and was the nephew of Thomas F. Bayard, who served as secretary of state under President Cleveland. The son of a U.S. senator, Bayard was born into a life of ease, comfort, and blue-blooded bliss. He never had to work a day in his life, and his wealthy father spoiled him rotten. After graduating from Yale at the age of twenty-one, J. J. Bayard spent the following ten years of his life living in the lap of luxury on his father's dime.

For reasons known only to himself, Bayard decided to move to Kendall County sometime around 1875, taking with him only a small sum of money. He was regarded as a kind and charitable man, and soon became one of the most popular residents of Boerne. Perhaps in his middle age he had decided to atone for his life of ease; he spent a great deal of his time in Kendall County visiting the sick in local hospitals and helping strangers in need. Dressed always in his long, black coat, prim, white necktie, and highly polished shoes, Bayard stood out in the dusty mountain town like a sore thumb.

He later purchased a few acres of land about nine miles outside of town and became a hermit, devoting himself to religious meditation and manufacturing patent medicine, which he brewed from the herbs he grew outside of his home. As for Bayard's home, it was one of the most unusual domiciles in central Texas. He dug a cave into the side of a hill and then built himself a crude, wooden cabin a short distance away. The cave and the cabin were connected by a subterranean passageway, which he had excavated four feet under the ground.

Bayard brewed his potions inside the cave, which he essentially turned into a frontier pharmacy. In the mouth of the cave he built a counter made of stone and from behind this waist-high wall he would interact with his customers. If they wanted medicine, he would hand them a bottle and write down explicit instructions for its use. He was happy to dispense this medicine with a lecture about proper dosage and a thorough explanation of its strength and side effects. He adamantly refused to accept any money for his medicine, but was happy to converse with his customers about anything and everything under the sun—except for his personal life. If a customer inquired about the hermit's past, he would order him to leave and never come back. At the end of each day, the hermit would close his shop and then crawl back through the tunnel into his cabin.

The once-sociable pharmacist was rarely seen on the streets of Boerne. He made occasional trips to deliver medicine to a customer, but was never seen in any of the town's stores or at the post office. He never sent letters to his relatives in Delaware, and no letters were sent to him in return. Until the day of his death, J. J. Bayard refused to talk about his past or his famous family. When the hermit died in 1890 at the age of sixty-six, the telegraph operator sent several messages to Bayard's surviving family members in Delaware. The Bayards were asked about funeral arrangements and burial instructions and suggestions for the disposal of the hermit's body. The Bayard family never responded.

It was a sad ending to the story of a generous man who devoted the latter half of his life to curing the ill and visiting the sick in sweltering, germ-ridden frontier hospitals; a man who grew tired of the taste of the silver spoon and severed his ties to one of the nation's most prosperous and powerful families, whose privileged members lie side by side in New Castle County beneath impressive marble monuments. Yet, it is doubtful that any of these wealthy senators and congressmen cared more deeply about the suffering of man as the forgotten frontier pharmacist who died without a penny to his name and was buried in a pauper's grave in the hills of central Texas.

NEW MEXICO

77. The Hermit Priest of Old Baldy

Of all the wondrous sights to be seen in the Southwest, few are as awe-inspiring as the Cimmaron Range of the Sangre de Cristo Mountains. One can only imagine the splendor beheld by the eyes of settlers traversing the fabled Santa Fe Trail, after weeks of traveling through Comanche territory, and arriving in an untamed land of majestic

William Pester, "The Hermit of Palm Canyon."
From the Washington Herald, August 4, 1919.

peaks and towering granite hills. Here they saw the ruins of Spanish palaces and the pueblos inhabited by strange cliff-dwellers who tilled the fertile valleys in a most primitive fashion. Here they passed the bones of daring frontier scouts like Kit Carson and long-forgotten Spanish conquistadors.

As the settlers crossed the Cimarrons, they no doubt would've gazed upon the peak they call Old Baldy, the highest in the range, jutting abruptly from the ground and rising to an elevation of 12,441 feet. If the travelers on the Santa Fe Trail looked closely at Old Baldy in the 1860s, they would've spotted several large, wooden crosses dotting the face of the mountain, and perhaps they might have caught a fleeting glimpse of the peculiar hermit who built those crosses, a recluse priest named John Mary Augustiniani.

Augustiniani was a hermit by choice, but a nobleman by birth. He was born into a family of Italian aristocracy in Sizzario, Lombardy, in 1801. One day he was strolling through the gardens of the family's luxurious estate when he saw a gleaming apparition; it was the Virgin Mary, pointing her finger in the direction of lands far away. Young Augustiniani interpreted this as a sign that he should turn his back on wealth and luxury and lead a solitary life in a land far away from home.

After three years of tireless meditation and prayer, the twenty-year-old nobleman set out for Rome on foot. For seven years he dwelt in the caves of Italy, and for five more years he wandered across Europe. He had no idea where he was supposed to go, or what he was supposed to do when he got there, but he had faith that he would be guided by an invisible hand. He felt that he was being called to the shores of a new continent, so he went to Venezuela. From there, he wandered through Brazil, Chile, and Argentina on foot until he eventually reached Mexico, where he settled on the slope of the dangerous volcano, which they called Orizaba. In Mexico he lived among the wildest native tribes and earned a reputation as a healer and a priest.

While preaching in the shadow of Pico de Orizaba, Augustiniani was arrested by the civil authorities and convicted of a trumped-up charge. He was banished to Cuba. From Cuba he boarded a ship and set sail for New York, and wandered until he reached St. Louis in the early 1860s. In Missouri he heard many stories about the Santa Fe Trail, and Augustiniani believed that he had finally discovered his destiny—to preach among the Indians of the American Southwest.

The priest walked to Kansas City and then on to Westport, where he boarded a wagon train and joined a group of settlers headed for the tiny New Mexico settlement of Las Vegas, which was a haven for outlaws and bandits. The priest found a cave west of town in Kearney's Gap and made it his home. However, the hermit found Las Vegas to be too rough and rowdy for his liking, so he wandered until he reached the Cimmaron Range. Today, a well-worn path leads to the summit of Old Baldy, and it is said that this path was made by the feet of John Mary Augustiniani as he walked to and fro in his devout meditations. The hermit priest remained on Old Baldy until his sad and tragic death in the summer of 1867.

During his time on Baldy Mountain, thousands of followers made pilgrimages up the mountain in order to hear the hermit preach. Augustiniani erected fourteen enormous crosses on the mountain for his followers, who would make pilgrimages each May and September. These followers formed a society and called themselves the Brotherhood of the Holy Cross. During the May pilgrimage of 1867, the hermit priest gave a farewell speech that crushed the hearts of his devout followers. Augustiniani stated that he believed that it was time for him to move on and that he planned on returning to Mexico.

Before his departure he visited a friend, Father Baca, in Las Cruces. Father Baca gave the hermit a large sum of gold for his journey to Mexico. In the morning, taking his leave of Father Baca, he said, "Tonight I will be in my cave and will build my last fire on the peak to tell you goodbye. I will pray the rosary and I want you to do likewise with your people on the roofs of your houses. If you do not see the fire, you may know that I am dead and may come tomorrow and get my books and property."

No fire appeared on the peak of Old Baldy that night. A group of the hermit priest's followers climbed the mountain and found John Mary Augustiniani. His body had been pierced through with dozens of Navajo arrows.

The Navajos had long feared the hermit priest, believing that he had supernatural powers. Near the summit of Old Baldy there is a spring that gushes cold and sparkling water, even in the driest of summers. According to Navajo legend, the spring did not exist until the mysterious, white stranger climbed the mountain searching for a place to live. Overcome with unbearable thirst, the hermit smote a rock with his staff, and from that rock sprang the life-sustaining stream of pure water.

While the wooden crosses atop Old Baldy may be long gone, and the grave of the hermit priest forever lost in the rugged Cimarrons, the spring near the summit still flows to this day and serves as a perpetual reminder of the adventurous life of John Mary Augustiniani, an Italian nobleman who gave up his wealth in order to roam the world and preach the word of God.

CALIFORNIA

78. Billy Pester Goes Hollywood

He lived in the Palm Canyon of Coachella Valley, spending his days strumming a guitar, practicing yoga, collecting herbs, and dispensing spiritual advice to those who visited his palm-frond shack in the desert. Billy Pester, with his long hair and bare feet and beaded necklaces, probably would've been labeled as a hippie, but that is a term that wouldn't even enter the American lexicon for another half century. Billy Pester, who came to America in 1906, was the original hippie, and is fondly remembered today as one of the early pioneers who paved the way for the 1960s California Counterculture.

Friedrich Wilhelm Pester was born in the German state of Saxony in 1886, where he became a practitioner of *lebensreform*, a philosophy that embraced alternative medicine, organic food, nudism, and sexual liberation. Lebensreform ("life reform") was a back-to-nature movement that had many notable followers; famed authors Hermann Hesse and Gerhart Hauptmann and renowned painter Karl Wilhelm Diefenbach were among those who considered themselves *naturmensch*.

In the early 1900s several of these "Nature Boys" immigrated to California and brought the *lebensreform* lifestyle with them. This group of hippie forebears included Billy Pester, who fled his native land to avoid military service, Benedict Lust (a pioneer of homeopathic medicine), and Professor Arnold Ehret. Bill Pester was among the first to arrive in America, making his home in Hollywood. Actually, to be more precise, Pester made his home beneath one of the Ls of the famous Hollywood sign. He soon became a local celebrity of sorts, and it has been written that many leading actors and actresses of the era made the pilgrimage to see the German guru, including Rudolph Valentino, who became a close friend.

Pester soon realized that the twinkling lights of Hollywood were a poor substitute for stars, so he withdrew to the Coachella Valley and built a primitive hut at the foot of the San Jacinto Mountains, where he lived a peaceful coexistence with the Cahuilla Indians. Pester spent his days collecting native artifacts and pottery, exploring the canyons, playing slide guitar, and lounging about completely naked beneath the sunny California skies. He eked out a living by making sandals and walking sticks and by selling postcards imprinted with words of *lebensreform* wisdom. In addition, he charged visitors ten cents apiece to gaze through his telescope while offering a lecture on astronomy, which happened to be one of his favorite subjects. The local Cahuilla had such a respect for the bearded Nature Boy that they came to regard him as one of their own; his name appears on the 1920 census as a member of the tribe.

The hermit of Coachella Valley entertained many visitors, including a budding, young songwriter named Eden Ahbez. Ahbez, who was born George Alexander Aberle, was a late convert to the New Age lifestyle and regarded Pester as a mentor. Like his mentor, Ahbez moved to California and also encamped beneath the first L of the Hollywood sign. In 1947 Ahbez penned a song that would later become one of Nat King Cole's greatest hits. The song, appropriately titled "Nature Boy," would later become a pop standard covered by everyone from Marvin Gaye to David Bowie to even (strangely enough) Leonard Nimoy.

While the song is a favorite of millions of people around the world, most would be surprised to discover that the famous tune about a "strange enchanted boy" who wandered very far (over land and sea), only to discover that "the greatest thing you'll ever learn is just to love and be loved in return" was written by Eden Ahbez about his very dear friend, a hermit named Billy Pester.

79. The Hermitess of Santa Anita Canyon

In the spring of 1909 a little, old woman in a ridiculous costume appeared out of nowhere to run against seasoned athletes half her age in a prestigious race demanding endurance, speed, and strength. This alone would have been enough to create a stir, but the fact that she bested some of the most accomplished athletes in Los Angeles County turned an eccentric female hermit into a local legend.

The race was the Mount Wilson Hill Climb, an annual event that dates back to the nineteenth century and is still being run to this day. The Mount Wilson Trail, built in 1864, has been the setting for this grueling 8.6-mile footrace since its inaugural running, which was so long ago that no one is quite sure how or why the hill climb got started in the first place, much less the name of the man who won the race. Even the organizers of the annual event, which now attracts hundreds of runners from across the country, aren't quite sure when the first race was held; photographs of runners lined up and crouched at the starting line date back to the late 1800s. Thousands of runners have entered the race, but few, if any, were as unusual as Marie Riedeselle, known around the San Gabriel Mountains as the Hermitess of Santa Anita Canyon.

Although the 1909 race was won by Ed Dietricht of the Los Angeles Athletic Club, it was Marie Riedeselle whose name appeared in newspaper headlines the following day. After the last of the sixteen men completed the course, the old woman ambled up to the starting line and demanded to run. She was dressed in a ridiculous costume, the likes of which may have been worn by a ballerina from the early Belle Époque period, right down to the leotard, tights, and silk ballet slippers. Paying no attention to the derisive laughter and jeers, the old hermitess once again demanded to compete. She was told that the contest was limited to men only, but Marie argued that since the trail was government property, no one could stop her. After much cajoling, the timers agreed to let her run.

Marie Riedeselle, "The Hermitess of Santa Anita Canyon."
From the Los Angeles Herald, June 19, 1910.

She started with a flash of speed and soon disappeared up the long, rugged trail. She lost steam as she neared the summit, but still managed to finish the race with a time of two hours and twenty-five minutes; not nearly good enough for the victory, but good enough to beat four of the well-trained, young men who made it across the finish line. After the event, many curious residents of Los Angeles clamored to learn more about the peculiar hermitess, and even though she had spent the better part of her life in seclusion, details about Marie Riedeselle's life began to emerge.

Marie was born in Maine and as a girl became renowned for her striking beauty and musical ability (although in one newspaper article, she claimed to have been born in Montreal and educated in a convent in France). She was a piano prodigy and an accomplished equestrienne, and it was only a matter of time before she left the family farm behind and sought her fortune in New York City. She went into business for herself as a masseuse and soon fell in love and got married. Unfortunately, the marriage ended a few short years later when her husband died suddenly. Marie found herself a widow at the age of thirty, and from that time forward the hustle and bustle of the city held no appeal. She moved to Connecticut and tried her hand at farming for a while, but then she surprised everyone in the spring of 1898 by announcing her intentions to go to the Yukon and join the gold rush.

Like the throng of spectators at the Mount Wilson starting line who would scoff and jeer a decade later, those who heard her announcement to go to the Yukon also shook their heads and laughed. Her detractors, however, changed their tune once they saw the serious preparations Marie was making for her excursion to the frozen wilderness. For three months she applied herself to learning the skills that she would need to survive, such as handling dogs, managing a loaded sled, and propelling a boat. Many of her male counterparts who joined the expedition ignored these preparations and paid for it with their lives.

She set sail for the Yukon with a group led by Elias "Lucky" Baldwin, a California businessman who made his fortune investing in silver mines. She went away light-hearted and optimistic, but when she returned she was a bitter woman. Nobody but herself knew what had happened in the frozen wastelands that caused her to change; though many would ask, she vehemently refused to talk about her experiences. When she returned to California, she grew increasingly distant and stopped talking to her friends and relatives. She ventured alone into the Santa Anita Canyon and built a thatched hut with her own hands. Later, she had a piano shipped to her from Los Angeles.

Marie Riedeselle lived in the depths of the canyon with a piano as her only friend. Spooked and mystified hunters would return to the city claiming to have heard the inexplicable tinkling of piano keys echoing through the canyon, wondering if they had experienced something supernatural. But it was only the hermitess, whose rough hands wandered delicately over the piano keys each evening when the sun dipped below the San Gabriel Mountains.

A year after running the Mount Wilson Trail Race, Mrs. Riedeselle had gold fever once again and journeyed to Alaska, never to return to her hut in the canyon. In March of 1910 she made the sixty-mile trip from Innoko to Ophir Creek on foot and returned two days later, to everyone's astonishment. It was thirty below zero with a strong facing wind, but the old woman was as strong as an ox. She attributed her strength and mental clarity to regular bouts of fasting, writing that she had lost twenty-five pounds by eating nothing but oranges. She also attributed her strength and endurance to the cold climate, writing, "It is wonderful how everything keeps here without decaying, and I believe that it preserves people in the same way. Now I feel cold all the time, but 'tis not debilitating but invigorating; and from being used to it and knowing that it does me more good than harm I really enjoy it."

The trail of Marie Riedeselle seems to end somewhere in the wilds of Alaska, as nothing more appears to have been written about her. Whether she succumbed to the elements or to the greedy hands of man remains a mystery, along with the details of her life after her return to the gold fields. However, the particulars of her final days are of little importance; for it is not her life that matters, but the manner in which she chose to live it—on her own terms and abiding by her own rules.

Perhaps the finest tribute to the hermitess can be found in the words written by Otto Carque, of the *Los Angeles Herald*, whose article about Marie Riedeselle's return to the gold rush might very well have been the last time her name appeared in print:

"This little unassuming woman is a shining example of what will power, strength of character and right living can do in overcoming almost insurmountable obstacles from which even brave men would shrink. Her experiences in Alaska would fill a big volume and we hope it will be written some day to show the world that woman is man's equal, and often his superior in many ways."

MONTANA

80. Roscoe Overhardt

The hardy mountaineers who lived in the sparsely-populated shadows of the Bitterroot Range thought they knew Roscoe Overhardt, the timid, old hermit who lived in a dilapidated miner's shack on the mountainside. Roscoe had lived a life of seclusion in the Twin Bridges region for twenty years and had been known to speak on only a few rare occasions, and then only in response to a persistent questioner. On the rare occasions when he did speak, he never raised his eyes or looked the other person in the face. He never even went into the village for supplies, unlike the other reclusive miners who dwelled in the Bitterroot Mountains. But when Roscoe died, in the summer of 1906, the letters and journals found inside his ramshackle hut painted the shy recluse in a completely different light.

The discoverers found Roscoe sprawled across his bed, wearing a costume of tattered rags that made his shabby and crude furniture seem as though it had come from Buckingham Palace by comparison. An old mutt, the hermit's only friend in the world, guarded the corpse like a soldier guarding the gold at Fort Knox. The reticent recluse had fallen ill a few weeks earlier, and it was evident to the discoverers that he had not left his bed since coming down with his illness. A careful search of the dead man's cabin produced a rusty, tin box containing a few gold coins and a bundle of yellowed letters and mildewed documents. From these faded papers the citizens of Twin Bridges were able to piece together the mysterious life of Roscoe Overhardt.

Overhardt had been born in Germany and was the son of a prosperous merchant from Berlin. At the age of eighteen, Roscoe enrolled at a prestigious university where he studied for a career in medicine. While attending university he met and fell in love with a pretty girl named Katherine Meller, and, after a few years of courtship, she agreed to marry him. Before she met Roscoe, Katherine had been courted by another suitor named Matthew Schoenfeldt. Schoenfeldt was the product of a dignified and powerful family from Frankfort, and he flew into a jealous rage when he learned of Katherine's engagement to Overhardt.

One evening shortly thereafter, Schoenfeldt sought out the man who had stolen his lover away from him. A quarrel ensued, and in a desperate bid to save his own life, Roscoe Overhardt stabbed the aggressor with a knife. Schoenfeldt died from his injuries, but not before he had managed to reveal the identity of his killer to the authorities. Roscoe, crazed with fear after learning he had killed a member of one of Germany's most powerful families, immediately went to Katherine and told her what he had done. Miss Meller implored her betrothed to flee to America, promising that she would join him there once she completed her education. Roscoe became a wanted man and, realizing that there was no safe place to hide in Germany, fled to Paris. He remained there for a week to collect his bearings and then went to London, where he immediately boarded a ship and set sail for America.

After arriving in New York, Roscoe obtained a menial job working under an assumed name. After a few weeks he grew convinced that he might be found out, so he saved up his money until he had enough to head west. His first stop was Cincinnati, where there was a large German population. He worked a string of odd jobs until he had enough money to continue his journey. His next stop was Louisville, and then St. Louis. From St. Louis he traveled up to Milwaukee, where he remained for six months.

Roscoe had been writing letters to Katherine all throughout his wanderings. He promised that he would send for her as soon as he found a place to settle and found a profession that would allow him to support her in the manner she deserved. He ended up in Montana, convinced that none of his pursuers would ever find him there. Roscoe began prospecting for gold and within a year had managed to strike a rich vein. He then penned a letter to Katherine telling her of his good fortune, stating that he would be able to provide her with a life of ease and comfort for the remainder of their lives.

Katherine wrote back, stating that she couldn't leave because her mother had become seriously ill. A few weeks passed and Katherine sent another letter. She wrote that her mother had recovered from her illness, but couldn't leave Germany because of another ailing family member. Every few weeks new letters arrived from Germany; each one containing a different excuse. Then the frequency of the letters dropped off until Katherine Meller was nothing more to Roscoe Overhardt than a painful memory of a life once lived.

When a year passed without word from Katherine, Roscoe sold his gold mine and journeyed deeper into the Montana wilderness, where he built his cabin on the mountainside. What became of the fortune that the old hermit obtained from the sale of his gold mine remains a mystery.

BIBLIOGRAPHY

1. Old Shep (New York)
"Old Shep." *West Seneca Bee* (NY), September 22, 2011.
Pace, James. *West Seneca*. Arcadia Publishing, 2011.

2. The Prodigal Father (New York)
"As From the Dead; Hermit of Ceres was the Missing Henry Smith."
Anaconda Standard (MT) August 27, 1894, 7.

3. The Hermit of West 16th Street (New York)
"Buried Alive in Heart of a Great City More Than Eleven Years."
Washington Times (Washington, D.C.) March 9, 1902, 19.
"Hermit in Great Metropolis." *Saint Paul Globe*, May 4, 1902, 12.

4. The Hermit of Broadway (New York)
"Broadway Hermit Dying of Old Age." *Allentown Democrat*, (PA) June
6, 1911, 12.
"Hermit Left $167,228. New Yorker Remained in Hotel Room 30
Years." *Ottawa Daily Republic*, (KS) May 3, 1912, 8.
"James Fisk Murdered." *New York Times*, January 7, 1872, 1.
"Lived Secluded in Bustling City." *Salt Lake Tribune*, July 31, 1911, 2.
Schumach, Murray. "Broadway Central Hotel Collapses." *New York
Times*, August 4, 1973.

5. Amos Wilson (Pennsylvania)
Cope, Gilbert and John S. Futhey. *History of Chester County,
Pennsylvania, with Genealogical and Biographical Sketches*.
Philadelphia: L.H. Everts, 1881.
"Indian Echo Cave to Be Opened on May 4." *Evening News*,
(Harrisburg, PA) March 1, 1929, 8.
"Indian Echo Cave Mecca of Interest For Tourists." *Harrisburg
Telegraph*, (PA) August 12, 1937, 26.
"Pennsylvania's Hermits." *Harrisburg Telegraph*, (PA) October 15,
1938, 24.
"Pardon Came Too Late to Stay Execution of Lebanon Girl." *Lebanon
Daily News*, (PA) April 4, 1928, 19.
Wilson, Amos. *The Pennsylvania Hermit: A Narrative of the
Extraordinary Life of Amos Wilson*. Philadelphia: Smith &
Carpenter, 1839.

6. "She Was Too Cruel" (Pennsylvania)
"Found in a Cave." *Iron County Register*, (MO) August 5, 1886, 7.

"She Was Too Cruel." *Evening Star*, (Washington, D.C.) July 7, 1886, 6.

7. The Hermit of Buckingham Mountain (Pennsylvania)
"A Hermit on Buckingham Mountain." *The Jeffersonian*, (Stroudsburg, PA) April 29, 1858, 2.

"A Hermit of Bucks; The Wolf Rocks Recluse Has Become Quite a Fad Nowadays." *Allentown Leader*, (PA) August 13, 1895, 1.

"Bucks County's 'High Hills' Rich in Historic Splendor." *Bristol Daily Courier*, (PA) January 28, 1963, 5.

"Hermit in Bucks County." *Lewistown Gazette*, (PA) April 22, 1858, 3.

8. The Hermit of Blue Hill (Pennsylvania)
Arter, Theodore and E. E. Lewis. "What Do You Know About Pennsylvania?" *Altoona Tribune*, (PA) August 28, 1933, 4.

Godcharles, Frederic A. "Today's Story in Pennsylvania History." *Scranton Republican*, (PA) April 22, 1924, 5.

9. Arthur Carey (Massachusetts)
"Cave Hermit Dies Without Revealing 40-Year Fire Secret." *New-York Tribune*, December 7, 1919, 8.

Coolidge, Amos Hill. *A Brief History of Leicester, Massachusetts.* Philadelphia: J. W. Lewis & Co., 1889.

"Mystery of Massachusetts Hermit Is Not Elucidated." *Paris Morning News*, (TX) January 22, 1920, 7.

10. The Hermit of Melrose (Massachusetts)
"Classmate of King, Brilliant Englishman Dies a Pauper Near Boston." *Colfax Chronicle*, (LA) February 29, 1908, 3.

"Fellow Student of King Dies in a Car." *Pittsburgh Post-Gazette*, December 28, 1907, 2.

Goss, Elbridge Henry. *The History of Melrose, County of Middlesex, Massachusetts.* City of Melrose, 1902.

"Hermit's Career Is Revealed by Death." *Wilkes-Barre Record*, (PA) December 28, 1907, 4.

"Hermit Was at College With King." *Vancouver Daily World*, (Vancouver, B.C.) December 31, 1907, 3.

"King's Classmate Found Among Swine; Blow His Downfall." *Washington Times*, (Washington, D.C.) December 29, 1907, 10.

"King's Classmate in Pigpen." *Times and Democrat*, (Orangeburg, SC) January 17, 1908.

11. Old Gold Toes (Vermont)
"Eccentric Hermit Traced to Cavern." *Butte Inter Mountain*, (MT) July 3, 1903, 2.

"'Gold Toes,' Hermit, Found in a Cavern." *Washington Times*, (Washington, D.C) June 23, 1903, 4.

Killington Mountain Resort & Ski Area website,
    http://www.killington.com/site/mountain/mountain-info/
    mountain_stats/index.html.
"Ski Resorts in Summer." *Yankee Magazine*, June, 2008.

12. The Hermit of Hoot Owl Pond (Vermont)
"A Vermont Hermit." *York Daily*, (PA) March 19, 1886, 3.
"Grevy's Uncle." *Wichita Eagle*, January 23, 1889, 5.
"The Hermit of Hootowl Pond." *Daily Commonwealth*, (Topeka, KS)
    March 4, 1886, 6.

13. Jeff Bryant (Vermont)
"Richmond's Hermit." *Burlington Weekly Free Press*, (VT) February 1,
    1906, 13.

14. The Hermit of Avalon (New Jersey)
Penrose, Robert L. *Avalon on the Seven Mile Beach: A History of the
    Geographical Borough, Including Related Developments on the
    Seven Mile Beach.* Avalon: Robert L. Penrose, 2006.
Raymond, Alexis. "Stone Harbor and Avalon, NJ." *Baltimore Sun*,
    August 25, 2003.
"The Hermit of Avalon, Whose Healing Powers Created a Now Buried
    Town." *Kansas City Journal*, (MO) March 21, 1895, 7.

15. The Tramp of West Hoboken (New Jersey)
"His Home Was in a Cave; Police of Hoboken Puzzled Over a German
    Tramp." *Evening Times*, (Washington, D.C.) September 24, 1896, 8.
"Hoboken's Wild Man." *Hocking Sentinel*, (OH) April 1, 1897, 3.
"Jersey's Cliff Dweller." *The Sun*, (New York, NY) September 14, 1896,
    4.

16. Kneeling Francis (New Jersey)
"A Hermit's Romance: His Bride Was Stricken Dead at the Marriage
    Altar." *Altoona Tribune*, (PA) October 16, 1900, 7.
Brown, Elizabeth Stowe. *The History of Nutley, Essex County, New
    Jersey.* Nutley Township: Woman's Public School Auxiliary, 1907.
"Old Hermit Has a Romance." *Daily Notes*, (Canonsburg, PA)
    November 28, 1900, 3.
"History of Nutley," from the Township of Nutley, NJ website,
    http://www.nutleynj.org/content/history.html

17. The Killer Mosquitoes of the Hackensack (New Jersey)
"Catch a 'Wild Man' Who Wears Corset." *Lima News*, (OH) July 16,
    1908, 2.
"Wild Man Captured." *Evening Star*, (Washington D.C) July 14, 1908, 8.

"Wild Cave Man Wears Corset as Shield Against Mosquitoes."
  Washington Times, (Washington, D.C.) July 14, 1908, 9.
"Wild Man Wears Corset." *Bamberg Herald*, (SC) July 23, 1908, 1.
Wright, Kevin W. *The Indigenous Population of Bergen County*. Bergen
  County Historical Society.
  http://www.bergencountyhistory.org/Pages/indians.html

18. The Highwire Hermit (Connecticut)
Banks, George Linnaeus. *Blondin: His Life and Performances*.
  London: Routledge, Warne, and Routledge, 1862.
"Blondin at Niagara." *Bismarck Tribune*, April 11, 1907, 7.
"Blondin Still Alive; Famous Tight-Wire Walker Said to Be in
  Connecticut." *Oshkosh Daily Northwestern*, (WI) August 26,
  1907, 9.
"Blondin, Famous Wire Walker, Is Still Alive." *The Indianapolis News*,
  August 26, 1907, 1.
"Blondin Not Dead." *Washington Herald*, (Washington, D.C.) August
  27, 1907, 1.
"Blondin Living as Hermit." *The Daily Free Press*, (Carbondale, IL)
  August 28, 1907, 1.
"Blondin Is a Hermit." *Houston Post*, August 28, 1907, 4.
"Once Famous Blondin Now Hermit." *Altoona Tribune*, (PA) August
  27, 1907, 9.
The Carolina Mountaineer, (Morganton, NC) August 6, 1884, 4.

19. English Jack (New Hampshire)
"Dead to the World: English Jack, the Hermit of the White
  Mountains." *Topeka Daily Capital*, October 15, 1893, 10.
"English Jack: Sad Romance of the Hermit of the White Mountains."
  Saint Paul Globe, March 28, 1895, 4.
"English Jack: The Hermit of Crawford Notch," from White Mountain
  History
  (http://www.whitemountainhistory.org/English_Jack.html)
"English Jack Near Death." *Altoona Tribune*, (PA) January 26, 1910, 6.
"English Jack Is Dying." *Winston-Salem Journal*, January 26, 1910, 2.
"Famous Hermit Is Ill." *The Inter Ocean*, (Chicago, IL) January 29,
  1910, 6.
Findagrave.com http://www.findagrave.com/cgi-bin/fg.cgi?page=
  gr&GRid=93829500.
"The Ended Romance of English Jack." *The Spanish American*, (Mora
  County, NM) June 15, 1912, 7.

20. Edward Young: The Socialist Hermit (Maine)
"A Piscataquis Hermit." *Wichita Daily Eagle*, February 21, 1898, 2.
"Teacher Turned Hermit." *The Sun*, (New York, NY) January 19,
  1896, 2.

21. Wild Man of the Chattahoochee (Georgia)
"Chattahoochee River," New Georgia Encyclopedia.
   http://www.georgiaencyclopedia.org/articles/geography-
   environment/chattahoochee-river
"Wild Man of Georgia Speaks Unknown Tongue." *The Broad Ax*, (Salt
   Lake City, UT) August 25, 1917, 3.

22. An Inventive Hermit (Georgia)
"An Inventive Hermit." *Marshall County Independent*, (Plymouth, IN)
   January 12, 1900, 3.
"Death of an Old Hermit." *Atlanta Constitution*, October 9, 1899, 3.

23. Mason Evans (Tennessee)
"A Queer Creature Dead." *The Dalles Daily Chronicle*, (OR) March 26,
   1892, 4.
"A Wild Man Dies of the Grip." *The Sun and Erie County Independent*
   (NY), January 22, 1892, 1.
"His Sweetheart Said No." *Caldwell Tribune*, (ID) February 27, 1892,
   2.
Milan Exchange (TN), January 30, 1886, 5.
"Wild Man Captured." *Fort Scott Daily Monitor*, (KS) May 1, 1890, 1.
"Wild Man Evans." *Arizona Silver Belt*, (Globe, AZ) May 10, 1890, 4.
"The Wild Hermit: Mason Evans, the Wild Man of Chilhowie
   Mountains, Captured and Released Again." *The Courier-Journal*,
   (Louisville, KY) April 30, 1890, 1.
"The Wild Man Loose." *Atlanta Constitution*, May 1, 1890, 3.
"The Tennessee Wild Man." *Princeton Union*, (MN) April 7, 1892, 6.

24. The Tree Dweller (Tennessee)
"Death of a Tennessee Hermit." *Richmond Dispatch*, (VA) October 12,
   1860, 1.
"The Tennessee Hermit." *Wellsboro Gazette*, (PA) February 20, 1861,
   1.

25. From the White House to the Wilderness (Tennessee)
"Andrew J. Stover Was Tired of It." *Fort Wayne Daily News*, (IN)
   November 21, 1905, 1.
"Death of Andy Johnson, Jr." *Parsons Weekly Sun*, (KS) April 12,
   1879, 6.
"Grandson of President Johnson is Tired of Being Pointed Out and
   Becomes a Hermit in the Mountains".*Cincinnati Enquirer*,
   November 21, 1905, Page 1.
"Guardian of President's Grandson, Andrew Johnson Stover a Hermit
   for Thirty Years in Tennessee Mountains." *New-York Tribune*,
   July 7, 1908, 4.
 "Grandson of President Andrew Johnson Dies." *Asheville Citizen*,
   (NC) January 29, 1923, 1.

"Hermit Was Once White House Baby." *Lebanon Daily News*, (PA) April 7, 1914, 10.

"Once Lived in White House; Guardian Appointed for Nephew of President Johnson." *Washington Herald*, (Washington, D.C.) July 8, 1908, 3.

"President's Grandson Is Now Tennessee Mountain Recluse." *Oregon Daily Journal*, (Portland, OR) November 26, 1911, 65.

"President Johnson's Grandson." *New-York Tribune*, June 28, 1908, 47.

"The Mistress of the White House." *Titusville Herald*, (PA) February 20, 1869, 1.

"Washington Life, Official and Otherwise." *Washington Herald*, (Washington, D.C.) July 12, 1908, 10.

26. Mum the Meat-Eater (Kentucky)

"A Kentucky Wild Man." *The Intelligencer*, (Anderson, SC) March 29, 1883, 1.

"Barnum's Wild Man." *Decatur Daily Republican*, (IL) April 11, 1883, 1.

"Man or Beast?" *Dallas Daily Herald*, March 30, 1883, 7.

27. Thirteen Years in Darkness (Kentucky)

"Thirteen Years Under the Ground." *Hartford Herald*, (KY) April 21, 1880, 1.

28. Pig Jack (Kentucky)

"A Kentucky Hermit: A Cave Dweller Who Preferred Animals to Men." *San Francisco Chronicle*, December 22, 1886, 6.

"Smoking Out a Moonshiner." *Saint Paul Globe*, December 27, 1886, 3.

29. Polly of the Pines (Kentucky)

"Lives in a Forest: Romance of a Woman Hermit's Life." *The Eagle*, (Bryan, TX) November 28, 1896, 2.

"Polly Blake and Her Cabin." *Kansas City Journal*, (MO) November 7, 1897, 16.

"Why She is a Hermit: Melodramatic Story of the Life of a Kentucky Woman." *Daily Herald*, (Delphos, OH) March 31, 1898, 6.

"Woman Hermit of Kentucky." *The Times*, (Philadelphia, PA) October 11, 1896, 20.

30. Basil Hayden (Kentucky)

"A Hermit for 34 Years." *New York Times*, October 4, 1897, 1.

"A Kentucky Hermit." *Washington Bee*, (Washington, D.C.) August 10, 1901, 5.

"Basil Hayden's Thirty-Year Sulk." *Carlina Mascot*, (Statesville, NC) March 23, 1899, 1.

"Death of a Hermit." *Times and Democrat*, (Orangeburg, SC) September 11, 1909, 1.

"Hayden's Strange Vow." *The World*, (New York, NY) October 17, 1897, 28.

"Has Never Left His House: A Farmer Who Has Been a Hermit for Over Thirty Years." *San Francisco Chronicle*, November 22, 1897, 5.

"He Has Kept His Vow: Basil Hayden, of Kentucky, Has Not Set Foot on Mother Earth for Thirty Years." *Kansas City Journal*, (MO) June 4, 1899, 13.

"Hermit's Queer Oath." *Nashua Reporter*, (IA) May 11, 1899, 7.

"How He Has Kept a Vow." *The Intelligencer*, (Anderson, SC) May 31, 1899, 3.

"Recluse for Thirty-Six Years Dies; Death of Girl Caused Retirement." *Monroe News-Star*, (LA) August 20, 1909, 1.

31. The Hunchback of Chulafinnee Mountain (Alabama)

"A Hermit 40 Years." *Pittsburgh Dispatch*, September 20, 1890, 7.

32. A Lesson in Karma (North Carolina)

"A Southern Hermit." *Anderson Intelligencer*, (SC) July 29, 1886, 1.

"A Strange Romance." Wilmington Messenger, (NC) June 16, 1893, 4.

33. Robert Harrill (North Carolina)

"Fort Fisher Hermit Dies in Seclusion." *Daily Times-News*, (Burlington, NC) June 6, 1972, 19.

"Hermit Found Dead In Concrete Bunker." *Playground Daily News*, (Fort Walton Beach, FL) June 6, 1972, 9.

Rowe, Geri. "Chasing the Gentle Spirit of a Hermit." *News-Record*, (Greensboro, NC) May 10, 2007.

"The Fort Fisher Hermit: The Life & Death of Robert E. Harrill." Rob Hill/Common Sense Films, 2004.

34. The Coward of Blacksburg (South Carolina)

"A Cowardly Hermit." *Pittsburgh Daily Post*, July 18, 1897, 4.

"A Hermit Because He Likes It." *The Daily Review*, (Decatur, IL) July 8, 1897, 1.

"Hermit Dies in a Forest." *Monroe News-Star*, (LA) June 15, 1911, 1.

"Hermit Passes Away." *The Times and Democrat*, (Orangeburg, SC) June 15, 1911, 1.

"John Starnes, a South Carolina Hermit." *Atlanta Constitution*, August 4, 1901, 27.

"Man Who Shot Jackson Dead." *Pittston Gazette*, (PA) June 15, 1911, 4.

"Mysterious Hermit Is No More." *Mount Airy News*, (NC) June 22, 1911, 1.

"Why Starnes Is Hermit." *Topeka Daily Capital*, July 17, 1897, 7.

"The Passing Away of Wild John Starnes." *Gaffney Ledger*, (SC) June 13, 1911, 1.

"Wild Man Dead." *The Courier*, (Ashboro, NC) June 22, 1911, 1.

"Wild John Starnes." *Gaffney Ledger*, (SC) September 23, 1930, 4.

35. Cole Carrington (West Virginia)

"Twenty Years' Hermit." *Atlanta Constitution*, December 14, 1885, 1.

36. Miss Jennie Senkhart (Mississippi)

"Death Reveals Masquerade of Aged Austrian." *Kingsport Times*, (TN) March 19, 1953, 20.

"Death Reveals She Was a He." *Holland Evening Sentinel*, (MI) March 18, 1953, 1.

"He, or She, Was or Was Not a Red, They Think." *Panama City News-Herald*, (FL) March 18, 1953, 1.

"Long Masquerade is Bared; Shack Yields Red Literature." *Tucson Daily Citizen*, March 18, 1953, 64.

"Mrs. Senkhart Was a Man, it is Discovered." *Delta Democrat-Times*, (Greenville, MS) March 18, 1953, 9.

"Officers Study Papers of Late Shemale Recluse." *Odessa American*, (TX) March 19, 1953, 4.

37. The Storm King (Florida)

"A Florida Hermit: The Very Strange Romance that Comes from Lake Eustis." *Fairfield News and Herald*, (Winnsboro, SC) October 13, 1886, 1.

"A Strange Florida Hermit." *Omaha Daily Bee*, October 12, 1886, 5.

"Florida: The March of Progress." Florida Department of Agriculture. (date unknown) from *Exploring Florida: Social Studies Resources for Students and Teachers*: http://fcit.usf.edu/Florida/docs/c/centrfl2.htm.

Publications of the Florida Historical Society. vols.1-2. Jacksonville: Florida Historical Society, 1908, 32.

38. Silas Dent (Florida)

"All Around Our Town." *The News-Palladium*, (Benton Harbor, MI) October 11, 1941, 3.

Atkins, Holly. "Wonders of Florida: Florida's Famous and Infamous." *St. Petersburg Times*, May 13, 2002.

Boyle, Hal. "Cabbage Key, Off West Coast of Gulf in Honeymoon Idyll." *Dothan Eagle*, (AL) March 1, 1949, 1.

Boyle, Hal. "Domesticated Hermit." *Logan Daily News*, (OH) March 1, 1949, 4.

Boyle, Hal. "Fall in Bathtub Convinces Hermit Civilization is Too Dangerous." *Iola Register*, (KS) February 16, 1952, 1.

Boyle, Hal. "Hal Boyle's Americana." *The Progress*, (Clearfield, PA) February 21, 1952, 4.

Boyle, Hal. "Hermit 'Ain't Been Blue' Since 1912." *Southern Illinoisan*, (Carbondale, IL) February 28, 1952, 7.

Boyle, Hal. "Hermit Dent Splits Hairs When Restless." *Decatur Daily Review*, (IL) February 16, 1952, 1.

Boyle, Hal. "Hermit Splits Hairs to While Away Long Hours." *Janesville Daily Gazette*, (WI) February 28, 1949, 6.

Boyle, Hal. "Old Silas Dent, 71, Feels Hermit Can Be Happy Man." *Wilmington News-Journal*, (OH) February 18, 1952, 10.

"Silas Dent Dies." *Kingston Daily Freeman*, (NY) December 24, 1952, 10.

39. From Riches to Rags (District of Columbia)

"Scholar, Soldier, Linguist, Hermit." *Washington Times*, (Washington, D.C) January 21, 1906, 5.

40. Aunt Nancy (District of Columbia)

Bryan, Wilhelmus Bogart. *A History of the National Capital from Its Foundation Through the Period of the Adoption of the Organic Act (Volume 2)*. Washington: Macmillan, 1916.

"Old Aunt Nancy is Dead." *The Evening Times*, (Washington, D.C.) July 29, 1896, 5.

"Voodoo Doctors and Their Many Dupes." *Washington Times*, (Washington, D.C.) May 12, 1895, 8.

41. Hugh Cameron (Kansas)

Cutler, William G. *History of the State of Kansas*. Chicago: A.T. Andreas, 1883.

"General Cameron at Albuquerque." *Cimarron News and Press*, (NM) March 21, 1907, 3.

"General Hugh Cameron Brings Message to Ross." *Albuquerque Evening Citizen*, March 11, 1907, 5.

"General Hugh Cameron, 'Golden Rule' Hermit." *St. Louis Republic*, January 11, 1903.

"Gen. Hugh Cameron Has Reached Kansas Capital." *Albuquerque Evening Citizen*, February 26, 1907. 5.

"Hermit is Gone." *Topeka State Journal*, December 10, 1908, 5.

"He is on the Move." *Kansas City Journal*, (MO) September 8, 1898, 3.

"Kansas Hermit Has Beard Reaching His Knees." *Albuquerque Evening Citizen*, March 1, 1907, 5.

"Kansas Hermit Got Fat." *Albuquerque Morning Journal*, April 9, 1907, 5.

"Real Kansas Crank." *Phillipsburg Herald*, (KS) October 1, 1896, 3.

"The Kansas Hermit Dead." *Barton County Democrat*, (Great Bend, KS) December 18, 1908, 6.

"The Kansas Hermit is a Candidate for Legislature Against W.R. Stubbs." *Topeka Daily Capital*, October 21, 1906, 17.

"The Kansas Hermit." *Lawrence Daily World*, (Lawrence, KS) December 11, 1908, 2.

42. Rudolph Myers (Kansas)

Fry, Steve. "Memorial for TSH Cemetery Needs Funding." *Topeka Capital-Journal*, September 30, 2001.

Hall, Mike. "Topeka State Leaves Mixed Legacy." *Topeka Capital-Journal*, January 17, 2000.

"Jetmore Man Gaining Fame." *The Tiller and Toiler*, (Larned, KS) April 1, 1910, 1.

"Kansas' One Man Railway Slowly Pushing Westward." *Hutchinson News*, (Hutchinson, KS) August 10, 1920, 9.

"Kansas Has a One-Man Railroad." *Chanute Daily Tribune*, (Chanute, KS) August 13, 1920, 4.

"Kansas Hermit Building Railroad All by Himself." *Altoona Tribune*, (Altoona, PA) October 22, 1920, 3.

"Lone Man Builds Railroad Silently." *Los Angeles Herald*, January 1, 1910, 2.

New Castle Herald (New Castle, PA), September 17, 1920, Page 14.

"One Man Railroad Gets More Right of Way." *Topeka Daily Capital*, December 19, 1911, 4.

"One-Man Railway Pushes On." *Chanute Daily Tribune*, (Chanute, KS) September 22, 1913.

"One Man Road Ambitious." *Wichita Beacon*, September 19, 1914, 4.

"One Man With Team of Mules Builds Whole Railroad." *Seattle Star*, September 17, 1920, 13.

"Railroad Being Built by One Man." *The Evening Review*, (East Liverpool, OH) January 31, 1912, 4.

"This One-Man Company Fears No Labor Strike." *Leavenworth Times*, (Leavenworth, KS) August 21, 1920, 8.

43. Fred Kupler (Kansas)

Arkansas City Daily Traveler, (KS) March 26, 1892, 5.

Barton County Democrat, (Great Bend, KS) March 31, 1892, 2.

"Wanted a Sacrifice." *Wichita Daily Eagle*, March 22, 1892.

44. The Odd Funeral of Otto Shaffer (Kansas)

"Death Revealed Her Sex." *Allentown Leader*, (Allentown, PA) July 9, 1896, 4.

45. The Hermit of Swan Lake (Minnesota)

"Story Sounds Like Quane." *New Ulm Review*, (New Ulm, MN) December 20, 1905, 7.

"Swan Lake's Hermit." *Staunton Spectator and Vindicator*, (Staunton, VA) June 22, 1906, 1.

46. William Knight (Iowa)
"A Singular Hermit Dead." *Elk County Advocate*, (Ridgway, PA) April 16, 1869, 2.
"Death of a Hermit." *Fairfield Herald*, (Winnsboro, SC) April 28, 1869, 1.

47. Captain Stubbs (Iowa)
Downer, Harry E. *History of Davenport and Scott County, Iowa (Vol. 1)*. Chicago: S.J. Clarke, 1910.
"Recollections of Pioneer." *Rock Island Argus*, (IL) November 8, 1902, 2.
"Strange Stubbs." *Davenport Democrat and Leader*, October 4, 1955, 40.

48. The Nun and the One-Eyed Hermit (Iowa)
"Buried With Military Honors, Michael Carlos Laid to Rest This Morning in Ottumwa Cemetery." *Ottumwa Tri-Weekly Courier*, (IA) November 24, 1910, 7.
"Claims Riches Left By Hermit Soldier." *Minneapolis Journal*, February 14, 1906, 1.
"Dubuque Nun's Brother Has Double." *Guthrie Daily Leader*, (Guthrie, OK) April 19, 1906, 6.
Marble Rock Journal, (IA) March 1, 1906, 2.
"Omaha Woman One of Heirs." *Omaha Daily Bee*, February 15, 1906, 5.
The Intermountain Catholic, (Salt Lake City, UT) June 24, 1905, 6.
"Veiled Hermit Dies Keeping Sacred Vow." *Albuquerque Evening Citizen*, March 15, 1906, 6.

49. The Hardshell Harpers (Indiana)
"About Franklin County," from the Franklin County, IN website, http://www.franklincounty.in.gov/info-center/about-franklin-county/.
"Female Hermits." *Wichita Beacon*, March 25, 1891, 3.
"Old Maid Hermits." *Omaha Daily Bee,* February 2, 1891, 4.
"Two Women Hermits." *Galveston Daily News*, February 11, 1891, 19.
"Women as Hermits." *Saint Paul Globe*, February 20, 1891, 6.

50. Diana of the Dunes (Indiana)
"Diana of the Dunes Flees From World of Men and Tells Mystery of Weird Life to Star." *Seattle Star*, August 4, 1916, 6.
"Diana of the Dunes Has Lived in Solitude Nearly a Year." *Harrisburg Telegraph*, (PA) September 18, 1916, 6.

"Diana of the Dunes Weeps Over a Giant Friend." *The Tomahawk*, (White Earth, MN) January 16, 1919, 5.
"Diana of the Dunes Said to be Near Death." *Rock Island Argus*, (IL) June 14, 1922, 1.
"Diana in the Hospital." *The Morning Tulsa Daily World*, June 15, 1922, 9.
"Diana of the Dunes Murder Mystery." *The Daily Ardmoreite*, (Ardmore, OK) June 15, 1922, 6.
"Find Girl Robinson Crusoe: University Graduate Lives Life of a Nymph." *Tacoma Times*, August 3, 1916, 1.
"Lives Alone on Shore of Lake." *Hartford Republican*, August 11, 1916, 6.

51. The Heroic Henry Malone (Michigan)
"Prairie Hermit: Henry Malone Dies in Hospital at Last." *Washington Globe*, (Washington, D.C.) March 23, 1902, 6.
The National Tribune, (Washington, D.C.) February 10, 1887, 4.

52. The Man Who Turned Pebbles to Gold (Michigan)
"An Awful Tragedy, Two Young Lives Sacrificed,When Train and Auto Clash: Harris Eberhart and Friend the Victims." *The Mishawaka Enterprise*, (IN) July 30, 1909, 1.
"Boys Dig Up Relics Buried by Old Hermit." *Ottumwa Tri-Weekly Courier*, (IA) July 8, 1911, 2.
"Campers Dig Up an Old Romance." *Rock Island Argus*, (IL) July 6, 1911, 5.
"Find Box of Junk, Campers Dig a Rusty Iron Chest in Michigan." *Topeka State Journal*, July 6, 1911, 6.
"The Making of a Camp: The Story of Camp Eberhart," YMCA Camp Eberhard website, http://campeb.org/history/moac/chap1.html.
"Voice From the Grave." *Evening Standard*, (Ogden, UT) July 6, 1911, 1.

53. The Robinson Crusoe of Lake Huron (Michigan)
"Lived Alone in Woods 72 Years." *Opelousas Courier*, (LA) February 1, 1908.

54. Edgar Donne (Michigan)
"English Charity Gets Garbo's Inheritance." *Decatur Herald*, (Decatur, IL) August 17, 1947, 6.
"Garbo's Secret Fan Leaves Her $20,000." *Cumberland Evening Times*, (Cumberland, MD) February 18, 1947, 1.
"Garbo to Give $16,000 Bequest to British Charity." *Winona Republican-Herald*, (Winona, MN) August 16, 1947, 1.
"Garbo in England to Return Bequest." *Council Bluffs Nonpareil*, (Council Bluffs, IA) August 17, 1947, 12.

"Garbo's Allegan Stake Melts Away in Courts." *The Holland Evening Sentinel*, (Holland, MI) October 6, 1948, 1.

"Garbo's Former Property Might Be Oil Boom Scene." *Cumberland Evening Times*, (Cumberland, MD) December 27, 1955, 8.

"Hermit Admirer's $20,000 Accepted by Greta Garbo." *Nevada State Journal*, (Reno, NV) July 6, 1947, 1.

55. The Man Who Lived in a Cage (Missouri)

"Dweller in Hallway Chains Effects to Floor in Vain Attempt to Prevent His Eviction." *St. Louis Republic*, March 22, 1903, 2.

"Inventor's Idea for Wholesale Destruction." *The Eagle*, (Bryan, TX) December 30, 1896, 2.

"Joseph Custer, Interesting Hermit, in the Heart of a Great City." *St. Louis Republic*, April 6, 1902, 2.

"The Ideas of a Mad Inventor." *Johnstown Weekly Democrat*, (PA) April 18, 1890, 4.

"Trials of an Inventor." *Kansas City Gazette*, (KS) October 26, 1896, 4.

56. Patrick Welsh (South Dakota)

"He Died a Hermit." *St. Paul Daily Globe*, September 1, 1888, 9.

57. The Angry Englishman (Wisconsin)

"A Hermit in Wisconsin: Possible Fate of a Former Tudor of Cambridge, England." *New York Sun*, September 10, 1889. 5.

"A Hermit in Wisconsin." *The Sunday Inter Ocean*, (Chicago, IL) September 17, 1899. 27.

"Hermit in Wisconsin." *Saint Paul Globe*, September 24, 1899, 12.

Sedalia Democrat, (Sedalia, MO) November 23, 1899, 7.

58. The Treetop Hermit (Ohio)

"18 Years a Crusoe, He Cheats Death." *Manitowoc Herald-Times* (WI), October 3, 1932, 9.

"75-Year-Old Tarzan Returns to Treetop Home." *Freeport Journal-Standard*, (IL) October 31, 1932, 11.

Harrisburg Sunday Courier, (PA) October 9, 1932, 10.

Oshkosh Daily Northwestern, (WI) October 1, 1932, 16.

"Spends 18 Years in Tree Top Home." *La Plata Home Press*, (MO) February 2, 1933, 6.

59. Charles Allenton Comes Home (Ohio)

"A Guernsey Hermit." *Coshocton Daily Age*, (OH) June 9, 1883, 4.

"An Old Hermit." *Belmont Chronicle*, (St. Clairsville, OH) July 5, 1883, 4.

"An Ohio Hermit: Why Charles Allenton Lives in a Lonely Hut." *Western Sentinel*, (Winston-Salem, NC) July 12, 1884, 1.

Sarchet, Cyrus Parkinson Beatty. *History of Guernsey County, Ohio, Volume 2.* Indianapolis: B.F. Bowen & Company, 1911.

Tristram Riley-Smith, "Les Duvaux, 29 May 2010." *The Cracked Bell.* http://www.thecrackedbell.com/les-duvaux-29-may-201/.

60. Gottlieb Leitsof (Illinois)

"Biographical Directory of the United States Congress," http://bioguide.congress.gov.

"Hermit and Horse." *Vermont Phoenix,* (Brattleboro, VT) April 22, 1898, 10.

"Hermit and Patriot." *Garnett Journal,* (KS) May 20, 1898, 2.

61. John Stink (Oklahoma)

"A Real Hermit, Wealthy Osage Indian is a Friendless Outcast." *Topeka State Journal,* December 4, 1914, 14.

"Back From Grave." *Springfield Leader,* (MO) August 11, 1927, 4.

"Bottle of White Mule Transforms Indian Into 'Ghost'; Is an Outcast." *Rhinelander Daily News,* (WI) January 23, 1926, 1.

"Bury John Stink, Indian; Wonder If He'll Stay Put." *Vidette-Messenger,* (Valparaiso, IN) September 19, 1938, 1.

"'Dead' Indian is Raising Beans." *Weekly Republican-Traveler,* (Arkansas City, KS) June 6, 1907, 7.

Daily Notes, (Canonsburg, PA) May 12, 1925, 5.

"Evil Spirit Scares Osage Indians Away." *Ironwood Daily Globe,* (MI) February 27, 1926, 3.

"Going Back to Tribe, Indian Has Been Outcast for Many Years." *The Evening Star,* (Independence, KS) October 3, 1907, 4.

"Indian Who Hated White Man, Dead." *Hutchinson News,* (KS) September 17, 1938, 3.

"Indian Hater of White Man Dies at Age of Eighty." *The Bee,* (Danville, VA) September 17, 1938, 10.

"Indian Gets Bad Treatment." *Columbus Weekly Advocate,* (KS) January 31, 1907, 3.

"John Stink is Sure Enough Dead." *Hartford Herald,* (KY) October 31, 1906, 1.

Kane Republican, (PA) May 11, 1925, 2.

"Mellowing with Age, John Stink Begins to Forget Animosity Against White Man." *Daily Capital News,* (Jefferson City, MO) December 4, 1936.

"Old John Stink, Wealthy Osage Indian Who Preferred His Dogs to Fellow Tribesman, Will Be Put in a Grave for Second Time." *Corpus Christi Caller-Times,* September 19, 1938, 1.

"Old John Stink, 'Indian Who Died.'" *Wichita Daily Eagle,* June 26, 1919, 10.

"One Poor Osage." *Daily Ardmorite,* (OK) February 3, 1905, 4.

"Philip Nolan of the Osages." *Humboldt Republican,* (IA) February 1, 1935, 3.

"Stink is Dead Indian." *Guthrie Daily Leader,* (OK) July 20, 1906, 2.

"The Injun Who Wouldn't Stay Dead." *The Sun,* (Chanute, KS) December 12, 1906, 3.

"Two Chapters in Life of 'Dead' Indian." *St. Charles Herald,* (LA) June 12, 1920, 3.

62. Pierre the Prophet (Oklahoma)

"Hermit Awes Bridge Men." *The Gazette,* (Stevens Point, WI) March 3, 1909, 9.

"Wins Prophet Fame." *Osage County Chronicle,* (Burlingame, KS) May 13, 1909, 9.

63. The Mysterious Adolph Hauserhufen (Oklahoma)

"Romance was in Life of an Osage Hermit." *Independence Daily Reporter,* (KS) August 8, 1912, 5.

The Gazette Globe, (Kansas City, KS) August 7, 1912, 3.

64. A Sad Story of What Might Have Been (Oklahoma)

"Diary Reveals Recluse's Life." *New Oxford Item,* (PA) February 4, 1915, 8.

"His Diary Reveals Hermit's Romance." *Leavenworth Times,* (KS) October 24, 1914, 10.

"Recluse's Romance Shown by a Diary." *Western Sentinel,* (Winston-Salem, NC) November 6, 1914, 7.

65. The Tragic Fate of William Hamley (Idaho)

"Demented Hermit's Death." *Salt Lake Herald,* March 10, 1898, 7.

"Was a Crazy Hermit." *Idaho Statesman,* (Boise, ID) March 10, 1898, 3.

66. An Ogre's Ship Comes In (Idaho)

"Hermit of the Hills Finds Wealth." *Salt Lake Tribune,* February 12, 1905, 2.

"Hermit is Heir to Fortune." *The Inter Ocean,* (Chicago, IL) February 17, 1905, 6.

"Hermit Gets a Fortune." *Pullman Herald,* (WA) February 18, 1905, 4.

67. Anton Glasmann (Colorado)

"Cursed Treasure." *Fort Wayne News,* (IN) June 6, 1900, 3.

"Found the Bandit Gang's Gold but Died Before He Could Disclose its Location." *Cincinnati Enquirer,* June 2, 1900, 13.

"Found the Gold and Died." *Greensboro Telegram,* (NC) July 20, 1900, 5.

"He Found Gold and Then He Died." *Independence Daily Reporter*, (KS) June 30, 1900, 3.

Jameson, W. C. *Colorado Treasure Tales*. Caldwell, ID: Caxton Press, 2001.

"Riches of Bandit Gang." *The Inter Ocean*, (Chicago, IL) May 20, 1900, 40.

"Searched a Lifetime for a Hidden Treasure and Died When He Found It." *The Times*, (Philadelphia, PA) May 27, 1900, 21.

68. The Ballad of Beatrice and John (Colorado)

"Actress Marries Hermit." *Vancouver Daily World*, (Vancouver, B.C.) May 26, 1911, 1.

Albright, Horace M. and Marian Albright Schenck. *Creating the National Park Service: The Missing Years*. Norman, OK: University of Oklahoma Press, 1999.

"Granite Altar Hewn by Bride." *Ottawa Journal*, (ONT) June 24, 1911, 12.

"Hermit and Artist in Weird Wedding." *Charlevoix County Herald*, (MI) August 19, 1911, 2.

"Hermit Divorces Bride Who Chose Cave Life." *Scranton Republican*, (PA) February 4, 1914, 1.

"Hermit Husband Divorces Girl Who Chose Cave Life." *The Evening World*, (New York, NY) February 3, 1914, 2.

"John Otto: One Man's Vision," National Park Service website. http://www.nps.gov/colm/learn/historyculture/john-otto.htm.

"'Matrimonial Furlough' When Attempt at Perfect Life Fails." *The Inter Ocean*, (Chicago, IL) March 31, 1912, 10.

"Mrs. Beatrice Farnham Benson." *Harrisburg Telegraph*, (PA) April 2, 1915, 14.

Oregon Daily Journal, (Portland, OR) July 16, 1911, 43.

"Pair Are Wed High in the Air." *Harrisburg Daily Independent*, (PA) June 21, 1911, 1.

"Romance of Hermit Keeper at an End." *Scranton Truth*, (PA) April 12, 1912, 7.

"Silent Builder of Trails, All Alone, Makes Magnificent National Park." *South Bend News-Times*, (IN) September 30, 1913, 9.

"Topics of Interest in the Realm Feminine." *Oregon Daily Journal*, (Portland, OR) July 10, 1911, 7.

"Wed on Mountain Ledge." *Washington Post*, (Washington D.C) June 22, 1911, 7.

"Woman Carries a Wedding Altar." *Monroe News-Star*, (LA) June 23, 1911, 1.

69. Old Man Reavis (Arizona)

"A Ghastly Find." *Arizona Silver Belt*, (Globe, AZ) May 14, 1896, 3.

"A Horrible Death." *Mojave County Miner*, (Mineral Park, AZ) May 16, 1896, 6.

"A Simon-Pure Hermit." *Lafayette Advertiser*, (LA) April 28, 1894, 6.
"Lonely Old Man Dies." *Ironwood News-Record*, (MI) July 4, 1896, 3.
"Old Man Reavis Is Dead." *Arizona Sentinel*, (Yuma, AZ) May 16, 1896, 1.
"The Hermit of Superstition Mountain." *Iowa City Press-Citizen*, (IA) October 27, 1899, 3.

70. Lord Neville of the Garbage Dump (Arizona)
"Legacy for Hermit Baron." *The News-Palladium*, (Benton Harbor, MI) August 16, 1905, 8.
"Lord Melville Works on Dumps." *San Francisco Chronicle*, July 4, 1905, 1.
"Lord Neville of the Garbage Dump." *Spokane Press*, July 19, 1905, 4.
"Story of Philip E. Neville." *Arizona Republican*, (Phoenix, AZ) September 30, 1905, 3.

71. The Green River Hermit (Wyoming)
"An Erudite Hermit." *Lawrence Daily Journal*, (KS) January 11, 1888, 4.
"Why a Hermit? The Queer and Lonely Home of an Old Literary Scholar." *St. Paul Daily Globe*, December 23, 1887, 5.

72. Upside-Down Mullen (Wyoming)
"He Lived Upside Down." *Sedalia Weekly Democrat*, (MO) May 31, 1907, 5.
"Up-Side-Down Mullen." *York Daily*, (PA) July 1, 1907, 4.
"Wyoming's Hermit Freak." *Omaha Daily Bee*, June 1, 1907, 9.

73. The Skunk Whisperer (Washington)
"Skunks Guard Hermit When All Else Fails." *Tacoma Times*, August 22, 1917, 7.
Symons, W. Thomas, Lieut. *Report of an Examination of the Upper Columbia River and the Territory in Its Vicinity in September and October, 1881, to Determine Its Navigability and Adaptability to Steamboat Transportation: Made by Direction of the Commanding General of the Department of the Columbia*. Symons, 121.

74. Ike Powell (Oregon)
"Romance is Ended, Lone Hermit of Baker County is No More." *East Oregonian*, (Pendleton, OR) August 2, 1905, 3.

75. Sailor Jack Seeks a Bride (Oregon)
Dodge, Orville. Pioneer History of Coos and Curry Counties, Oregon. Salem: Capital Printing Company, 1898.
"'Sailor Jack,' Aged Hermit, Waits 40 Years in Little Hut for Woman Who'll Marry Him." *Bisbee Daily Review*, (AZ) September 3, 1922, 9.

76. The Frontier Pharmacist (Texas)

"A Mysterious Hermit Dead." *Alton Evening Telegraph*, (IL) December 15, 1890, 1.

Biesele, Rudolph Leopold. *The History of the German Settlements in Texas 1831-1861*. Austin: Von Boeckmann-Jones Company, 1930.

"Death of a Hermit." *Logansport Pharos-Tribune*, (LA) December 14, 1890, 1.

"Hermit Bayard's Will." *Pittsburgh Dispatch*, December 24, 1890, 1.

"Is He Secretary Bayard's Uncle?" *Atlanta Constitution*, October 12, 1888, 5.

"Life of a Hermit." *Indianapolis News*, October 9, 1888, 1.

77. The Hermit Priest of Old Baldy (New Mexico)

"Hermit Lived on Peak." *Las Vegas Daily Optic*, (East Las Vegas, NM) August 1, 1957, 6.

"Hermit's Peak Attracts All Ages of Climbers for Years." *Las Vegas Daily Optic*, (East Las Vegas, NM) August 4, 1960.

"Hermit's Peak Named for Italian Who Lived There." *Las Vegas Daily Optic*, (East Las Vegas, NM) August 5, 1965, 6

"Land of Romance and Tragedy." *Tensas Gazette*, (St. Joseph, LA) May 26, 1916, 8.

"Legend of a Hermit Still Lives Atop a Barren Mountain Peak." *Ames Daily Tribune*, (IA) November 3, 1965, 7.

"Mystery of Augustiniani is Unsolved." *Las Cruces Sun-News*, (NM) October 9, 1949, 67.

Nicols, Marvin J. "Augustiani, a Wanderer." *Houston Post*, August 3, 1919, 51.

"Saved by a Hermit Monk." *The Sun*, (New York, NY) May 31, 1896, 2.

"The Hermit Priest of the Old Santa Fe Trail." *Evening Star*, (Washington, D.C.) June 18, 1898, 16.

"The Hermit of Old Baldy in the Raton Mountains." *El Paso Herald*, July 15, 1908, 6.

"Will Hermit Monk's Miracle Come to Pass in N. Mexico?" *Redlands Daily Facts*, (CA) May 6, 1967, 2.

78. Billy Pester Goes Hollywood (California)

"Calls City-Dwellers 'Crazy.'" *Washington Herald*, (Washington, D.C.) August 4, 1919, 5.

"Desert Hermit Does Not Like Hustling and Bustling of City Life." *The Courier*, (Harrisburg, PA) June 22, 1919, 5.

"Desert Recluse Pays Visit to Movieland." *Atlanta Constitution*, February 1, 1920, 2.

"Desert Hermit Seeks Lonely Island—Travel Too Near Home Cabin." *Decatur Daily Review*, (IL) June 11, 1949, 1.

"Fruitarian Hermit, Shaveless 13 Years, Meets Soup Again." *New-York Tribune*, July 20, 1919, 6.

"Hermit Leaves Mountain and Sees His First Film." *Pittsburgh Post-Gazette*, February 8, 1920, 65.

"Hermit Guards Deadly Snakes." *Muskogee Times-Democrat*, (OK) October 18, 1920, 11.

"Hermit Has 'Code of Living' and Believes Others Are Crazy." *Santa Cruz Sentinel*, (CA) August 11, 1958, 2.

Kennedy, Gordon and Kody Ryan. "Hippie Roots & the Perennial Subculture." http://hippy.com/modules.php?name=News&file=article&sid=243.

"Lives Life of Hermit." *South Bend News-Times*, (IN) July 25, 1919, 12.

"Palm Canyon Hermit: 73-Years-Young Bill Pester Tells Life Views." *Independent Star-News*, (Pasadena, CA) August 3, 1958, 7.

Wild, Peter. *William Pester: The Hermit of Palm Springs*. The F.M. Shady Myrick Research Project, 2008.

79. The Hermitess of Santa Anita Canyon (California)

"A Courageous Widow Who Has Gone Alone to the Klondike." *Logansport Pharos-Tribune*, (IN) December 11, 1897, 23.

Carque, Otto. "Female Explorer in Alaska." *Los Angeles Herald*, June 19, 1910, 60.

"Dietrich Leads in Hill Climb." *Los Angeles Herald*, April 16, 1909, 5.

"Finds Riches in Frozen Alaska." *Los Angeles Herald*, May 8, 1906, 14.

"Fortune in Mines for Woman Hermit." *Daily Industrial News*, (Greensboro, NC) March 28, 1908, 9.

"Mrs. Riedeselle's Outfit." *Seattle Post-Intelligencer*, December 26, 1897, 8.

"Once a Belle; Now a Hermit." *Custer County Republican*, (Broken Bow, NE) December 5, 1907, 6.

"Strange Little Woman, at 45, Bests Trained Athletes in Grueling Race." *Tacoma Times*, May 13, 1909, 3.

"The Woman Klondiker." *Seattle Post-Intelligencer*, December 15, 1897, 2.

"Woman Hermit to Leave Santa Anita Canyon for Alaska." *Los Angeles Herald*, June 5, 1909, 8.

80. Roscoe Overhardt (Montana)

"Strange Life of Hermit Is Explained After Death." *New Castle Herald*, (PA) July 12, 1906, 7.